Accelerating Nonprofit Impact with Salesforce

Implement Nonprofit Cloud for efficient and cost-effective operations to drive your nonprofit mission

Melissa Hill Dees

BIRMINGHAM—MUMBAI

Accelerating Nonprofit Impact with Salesforce

Group Product Manager: Alok Dhuri

Publishing Product Manager: Harshal Gundetty

Senior Editor: Ruvika Rao

Content Development Editor: Urvi Shah

Technical Editor: Pradeep Sahu

Copy Editor: Safis Editing

Language Support Editor: Safis Editing

Project Coordinator: Deeksha Thakkar

Proofreader: Safis Editing

Indexer: Subalakshmi Govindhan

Production Designer: Joshua Misquitta

Marketing Coordinator: Deepak Kumar

First published: March 2022

Production reference: 1170322

Published by Packt Publishing Ltd.
Livery Place
35 Livery Street
Birmingham
B3 2PB, UK.

978-1-80107-091-1

www.packt.com

To my mother, Ruby Neisler Hill, who gifted me with the love of books. To my husband, Mitch; if he did not do the things he does, I could never do the things I do, including this book! To Sharif Shalaan and the countless Trailblazer Community members who encouraged, listened, and actively helped me present all the goodness of Nonprofit Cloud.

– Melissa Hill Dees

Contributors

About the author

Salesforce MVP **Melissa Hill Dees** has an MBA in digital entrepreneurship and is six times Salesforce certified. With 15 years of experience as a nonprofit executive and over 10 years leveraging Salesforce, her goal is to automate what can be automated so nonprofits have more time to do what can't be automated. She is a founding partner at HandsOn Connect Cloud Solutions, a nonprofit community group leader, a Dreamforce speaker, and an Open Source Commons Sprinter. Melissa serves on the board of directors of Amplify and ToolBank USA, and is a cofounder of Nonprofit Dreamin and Foodforce. In her free time, she advocates for equality for all, especially mentoring women in technology. Her favorite hobby is traveling!

I want to thank the people who have been close to me and supported me, especially my family and my colleagues.

About the reviewer

Libby Ziemelis has been working with and at nonprofits for over 20 years and since 2010 has been focused on Salesforce and the Nonprofit Success Pack. After working in the nonprofit world directly, she continued supporting nonprofits using Salesforce while employed at a Salesforce **Independent Software Vendor** (**ISV**) for over 5 years and currently works as a nonprofit customer success manager at DemandBlue where she continues to support nonprofit and educational institutions using Salesforce. Libby currently holds six Salesforce certifications as well as her **CNP**, or **Certified Nonprofit Professional**, credential. She lives in the greater Phoenix area with her husband, two amazing children, and one lazy dog.

Table of Contents

6
What Else Is Needed from Nonprofit Cloud?

Section 2: Get Set – Correlating Need with Nonprofit Cloud Tools

7
Is Change Difficult for an Organization?

8

What Is the Organization Trying to Achieve?

9

Installing Solutions from Nonprofit Cloud

10

Configuring Fundraising Features

11

Configuring Additional Nonprofit Cloud Features and Security

Section 3: Go! – Data for Impact

12
Declarative Tools and Modules

13
To Customize or Not to Customize?

14
Testing and Deployment Strategies

15
Implementing Analytics Tools for Impact

16
Ongoing Data Management and Best Practices

Preface

Salesforce Nonprofit Cloud enables a 360-degree view of people related to your nonprofit to connect fundraising, program management, and grantmaking.

This book starts by covering the tools and features that make up Nonprofit Cloud, helping you understand their standard functionalities and how **Nonprofit Success Pack** (**NPSP**)'s data architecture is critical to implementation. You'll learn how the Nonprofit Cloud Program Management Module can connect your programs, automate case management, and track client progress. After that, you'll explore the tools to create a change management process to increase user adoption. Moving ahead, you will understand how to configure necessary permissions for NPSP administration and will explore how declarative tools help better align the goals of a nonprofit organization. Toward the concluding chapters, you'll cover customizations, deployment, custom reports, and dashboards for fundraising analytics, as well as best practices for data management to maintain data integrity.

By the end of this book, you'll be able to build and configure Nonprofit Cloud for a variety of use cases to achieve maximum social impact with the least amount of technical debt.

Who this book is for

This book is for business analysts, consultants, architects, and other certified Salesforce administrators using Salesforce to automate and optimize processes for nonprofit organizations.

What this book covers

Chapter 1, Overview of Nonprofit Cloud, as Nonprofit Cloud has a lot of moving parts, looks at the big picture and a high-level overview of the smaller parts that make up that big picture. What does each component do? How does it fit into the larger whole? Do we need to use all of this?

Chapter 2, *What Is NPSP?*, looks at NPSP, the foundation of Nonprofit Cloud. Its data architecture and native functionality are critical to additional components and implementation. NPSP is the foundation of all of the Nonprofit Cloud fundraising features.

Chapter 3, *Tracking Impact with Program Management Module*, looks at the Nonprofit Cloud Program Management Module. Nonprofits are more than just fundraisers. Programs are what fundraisers fund. Let's dive into how the Nonprofit Cloud Program Management Module can connect your programs and the impact they are having on the funds you are raising. How do you track program engagement or delivery of the service your nonprofit provides? Are you managing a single program or multiple programs?

Chapter 4, *Automating Case Management for Better Human Services*, looks at Case Management. Case Management is to people what Program Management is to programs. Case Management streamlines workflows and tracks client progress for human services. Case Management is a paid extension of Program management Module.

Chapter 5, *Tracking Volunteer Impact*, looks at Volunteers for Salesforce, which helps nonprofits manage and engage their volunteers. Although not as commonly used as the fundraising features, managing volunteers is vital for some organizations.

Chapter 6, *What Else Is Needed from Nonprofit Cloud?*, looks at additional features of Nonprofit Cloud. Nonprofit Cloud offers a full suite of tools for nonprofits. In previous chapters, we cover a lot about how Nonprofit Cloud helps with fundraising, program management, and volunteers. But there is more! Grantmaking, grants management, marketing, engagement, and accepting donations and accounting for them are also included.

Chapter 7, *Is Change Difficult for Your Organization?*, as we know that the most difficult part of creating something new is often not the technology itself but creating an atmosphere that will welcome change, explores the tools you need to create a change management process to increase user adoption and decrease the time to realized value.

Chapter 8, *Requirements – User Stories – Business Processes – What Is Your Organization Trying to Achieve?*, now that you understand the components of Nonprofit Cloud, helps you understand which of these components is a solution for a client. First, you have to understand the client's needs, resources, and critical outcomes.

Chapter 9, *Installing Nonprofit Cloud Solutions*, covers the nitty-gritty of installing and implementing the solutions available with Nonprofit Cloud.

Chapter 10, *Configuring Fundraising Features*, as fundraising is the first and best use case for NPSP, shows you how to configure it appropriately to work with the larger solution that is being implemented by the nonprofit organization.

Chapter 11, Configuring Additional Features and Security, looks at additional features and security. Sometimes, a larger solution requires additional features to truly streamline the work a client is doing. It may be program management or an interface for volunteers. This is the icing on the cake. To protect this work, be sure your security is configured appropriately.

Chapter 12, Declarative Tools and Modules, looks at declarative tools, which are one way that Salesforce and Nonprofit Cloud can be better aligned with the goals of the nonprofit organization. You will explore the options for extending the standard functionality of Nonprofit Cloud and NPSP.

Chapter 13, To Customize or Not to Customize?, Sometimes what you really need is custom Apex code in order to make use of the biggest benefit of Nonprofit Cloud automation. Table-Driven Trigger Management is all about automation.

Chapter 14, Testing and Deployment Strategies, looks at testing and deployment strategies, which should be determined before the build starts. Let's explore the tools that Nonprofit Cloud offers for successful testing and deployment.

Chapter 15, Implementing Analytics Tools for Impact, looks at using the data that has been collected and tracked to show impact and help organizations make better decisions based on actual data.

Chapter 16, Ongoing Data Management and Best Practices, discusses how managing the vast amounts of data coming into your Salesforce instance will be an ongoing process. Keeping the data accurate and free of duplicates requires some maintenance and best practices.

To get the most out of this book

The Salesforce Administrator certification is highly recommended before beginning work on Salesforce Nonprofit Cloud.

Any errata related to this book can be found on the following link: `https://github.com/PacktPublishing/Accelerating-Nonprofit-Impact-with-Salesforce`.

Download the color images

We also provide a PDF file that has color images of the screenshots and diagrams used in this book. You can download it here: `https://static.packt-cdn.com/downloads/9781801070911_ColorImages.pdf`.

Conventions used

There are several text conventions used throughout this book.

Bold: Indicates a new term, an important word, or words that you see onscreen. For instance, words in menus or dialog boxes appear in **bold**. Here is an example: "**Funding Program** – The foundation of the Outbound Funds module, the program can be thematic or strategic and allows for a hierarchy of programs."

> **Tips or Important Notes**
> Appear like this.

Get in touch

Feedback from our readers is always welcome.

General feedback: If you have questions about any aspect of this book, email us at customercare@packtpub.com and mention the book title in the subject of your message.

Errata: Although we have taken every care to ensure the accuracy of our content, mistakes do happen. If you have found a mistake in this book, we would be grateful if you would report this to us. Please visit www.packtpub.com/support/errata and fill in the form.

Piracy: If you come across any illegal copies of our works in any form on the internet, we would be grateful if you would provide us with the location address or website name. Please contact us at copyright@packt.com with a link to the material.

If you are interested in becoming an author: If there is a topic that you have expertise in and you are interested in either writing or contributing to a book, please visit authors.packtpub.com.

Share your thoughts

Once you've read *Accelerating Nonprofit Impact with Salesforce*, we'd love to hear your thoughts! Scan the QR code below to go straight to the Amazon review page for this book and share your feedback.

https://packt.link/r/1-801-07091-1

Your review is important to us and the tech community and will help us make sure we're delivering excellent quality content.

Section 1: Get Ready – Learn the Basics of NPSP

Dive into the tools and features that make up Nonprofit Cloud to understand their standard functionality. This section contains the following chapters:

- *Chapter 1, Overview of Nonprofit Cloud*
- *Chapter 2, What Is NPSP?*
- *Chapter 3, Tracking Impact with the Program Management Module*
- *Chapter 4, Automating Case Management for Better Human Services*
- *Chapter 5, Tracking Volunteer Impact*
- *Chapter 6, What Else Is Needed from Nonprofit Cloud?*

1
Overview of Nonprofit Cloud

Nonprofit Cloud from Salesforce is a collection of applications designed specifically for nonprofit organizations to extend and adapt the power of Salesforce's **Customer Relationship Management (CRM)**. Each nonprofit and charity may have a different mission, specific goals, or even unique measures of success. Consequently, Nonprofit Cloud has a lot of moving parts. Let's start by taking some time to look at the big picture with a high-level overview of the moving parts that make up Nonprofit Cloud. What do these parts or components do? How do they fit into the larger bucket of Nonprofit Cloud and the Salesforce CRM itself? And how do I know which components to use and when? Which components are included as part of the Power of Us donation from Salesforce? And which are paid add-ons?

As a Salesforce administrator, you have already explored the foundation for what we are going to learn. Nonprofit Cloud utilizes all that learning but adds additional layers of flexibility, configuration, and complexity to meet the needs of nonprofits. Understanding Nonprofit Cloud will give you the tools to help nonprofits and charities increase their impact using Salesforce as well as assist in your study for the Nonprofit Cloud Consultant certification.

In this chapter, we're going to cover the following main topics:

- The making of Nonprofit Cloud
- Fundraising features
- Program management features
- Additional features
- The making of Nonprofit Cloud

Let's take a quick look at the origins of Nonprofit Cloud and the cornerstone it is built upon – **Nonprofit Success Pack**.

The making of Nonprofit Cloud

From the very beginning in 1999, Salesforce made a commitment to nonprofits and charities around the world. That commitment encompassed 10 free Salesforce licenses provided by the Salesforce Foundation. There are geographic limitations to the 100 Enterprise license donations; see the eligibility guidelines at `https://www.salesforce.org/power-of-us/eligibility-guidelines/`. Although nonprofits had similar requirements around what a customer relationship management platform should do, those requirements were not always easily met within the standard Salesforce architecture that was focused on corporate use cases.

As more nonprofits began to embrace Salesforce to automate processes, implementations varied wildly and became more and more expensive to maintain. As I have worked with nonprofits, I have seen the standard **Salesforce Account** functionality used. However, I've also seen other iterations designed to adapt the data structure to be more useful to donors and members rather than customers. For example, the *bucket model* was used to accommodate individuals at one point. This was before Person Accounts were introduced by Salesforce. There was one account named *Individual* and, you guessed it, individual contacts were assigned to that account. As with all things Salesforce, there are limits. As a Salesforce administrator, you know that best practices recommend a maximum of 10,000 child records. Hundreds of thousands of donor or volunteer contact records, all associated with the Individual account record, can cause challenges. This was just one area that needed a solution.

Other nonprofits, with more resources, began to customize Salesforce to meet their needs. New York Cares – an early nonprofit adopter of Salesforce – hired Avviato, Inc. to help design, build, and implement a data structure very similar to what would become Nonprofit Starter Pack. In 2009, Contributor Development Partnership and roundCorner partnered to build the NGO Connect app on Salesforce. The fundraising software was used by dozens of public broadcasting stations and other nonprofits. Once again, the data structure and functionality hinted at what was to come in Nonprofit Starter Pack's initial offering. However, these early implementations make it very time-consuming and complex to migrate customers to Nonprofit Success Pack because there are so many conflicting triggers that must be resolved.

What we know today as Salesforce.org started out as the Salesforce Foundation, and, as already mentioned, they handled the donation of 10 Salesforce Enterprise licenses for any qualifying nonprofit organization as part of Salesforce's original Pledge 1% model. In 2019, Salesforce.org was acquired by Salesforce.com; so, when we refer to Salesforce.org, it is in reality a team within the larger Salesforce ecosystem.

It didn't take long to realize that nonprofits needed more than just a Salesforce instance; they needed it configured to better meet their needs. What was then known as Nonprofit Starter Pack was conceived and created as an open source application on Salesforce. It was created by volunteers and community members who were anxious to help nonprofits succeed with Salesforce. It went through a couple of iterations before it became Nonprofit Success Pack, now maintained by Salesforce.org, with minor bug-fix releases every other week as well as the three major releases per year – not bad for a free product! The following is a brief history of NPSP:

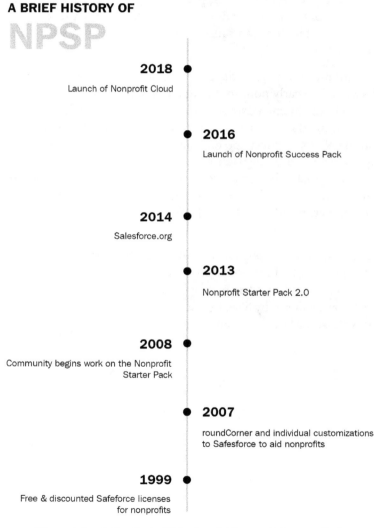

Figure 1.1 – A timeline of Salesforce's Nonprofit Success Pack

Nonprofit Starter Pack (**NPSP**) consisted of five separate apps – all free and open source. NPSP is important to understand because it sets the data architecture as well as the core functionality for today's Nonprofit Cloud. NPSP focuses primarily on fundraising and donor management, and includes basic reporting and analytics. Improvements to NPSP with core donation management, donor engagement, and basic reporting and analytics prompted a rebranding, and NPSP 2.0 was born and launched. The following is the way the NPSP apps originally looked in the installed packages section of the Salesforce setup:

	Contacts & Organizations	salesforce.com Foundation	2.1.4	npe01
	Households	Salesforce.com Foundation	2.4.8	npo02
	Affiliations	Salesforce.org	1.55	npe5
	Relationships	Salesforce.com Foundation	2.0.2	npe4

Figure 1.2 – Original objects for NPSP

Nonprofit Success Pack (**3.0**) is now on AppExchange as a complete integrated suite that includes Lightning Experience as well as a robust partner ecosystem, with a great number of ways to extend the functionality of NPSP. It is the core of Nonprofit Cloud, but Nonprofit Cloud comprises so much more. Originally announced in 2018, Nonprofit Cloud is advertised as the one place to work with all nonprofit relationships (see `https://www.salesforce.org/nonprofit/`), using tools for fundraising, program management, and marketing and engagement:

Figure 1.3 – The three pillars of NPSP

Throughout the course of this book, we will explore, in depth, the following areas of Nonprofit Cloud:

- Nonprofit Success Pack
- Fundraising

- Program management
- Volunteer management

You will be able to ascertain when to use these tools, how to implement them, and how to configure them for the organization.

Subsequent chapters will also include learning around additional functionalities:

- Grantmaking and grants management
- Insights
- Elevate
- Accounting subledger
- Marketing and engagement

> **Important Note**
> These add-on modules may be free or paid. Some are part of the Open Source Community Sprints and others Salesforce donates to nonprofit organizations.

The other important part of Nonprofit Cloud – beyond the core architecture, packaged functionality, and configuration – is the ability to customize the functionality. **Trigger Driven Management Tables (TDTM)** plays an important role in Nonprofit Cloud and may be a new concept to Salesforce administrators.

We've got a lot to cover, so let's get started!

Fundraising features

Fundraising was the initial use case when the community started work on Nonprofit Success Pack in 2008. Understanding donor behavior seemed to be a great fit for a customer relationship management system, that is, Salesforce. However, donors donate individually rather than in conjunction with their employer. There are some notable exceptions, such as United Way's use case for corporate-driven pledges and employer-matching gifts, which we will explore in *Chapter 10, Configuring Fundraising Features*.

The pain point was that the standard Salesforce data structure is focused on accounts. Accounts equate to businesses. And, as mentioned, donors generally give individually. Sometimes donors give as a family. And donor campaigns often target those individuals living at the same physical address. Donors may also give at work or be instrumental in influencing corporate entities to donate. In today's environment, donors want an easy way to donate online but there are those donors who are still more comfortable mailing a check.

Fundraisers employ many strategies to meet their revenue goals; each strategy may require different data and tracking. You begin to see how quickly the situation can become complicated.

Nonprofit Success Pack starts with these considerations in mind and uses many standard Salesforce objects you already know and love as the base for fundraising features:

- **Account**: An object that holds information about companies

- **Contact**: An object that holds information about individuals

- **Opportunity**: An object that holds information about sales

- **Campaign**: An object that holds information about marketing initiatives, responses, and metrics

The following figure shows the relationships and fields for the four standard Salesforce objects just discussed:

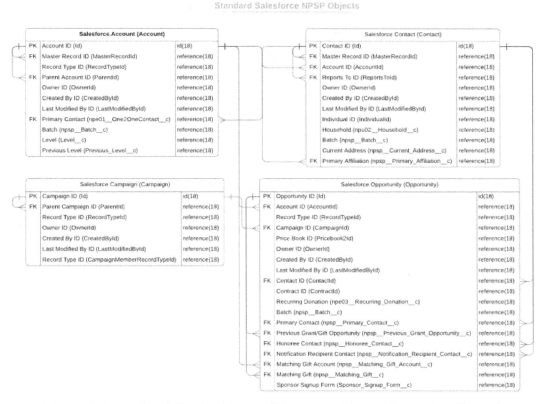

Figure 1.4 – An entity-relationship diagram of standard Salesforce objects used in Nonprofit Success Pack

Configuring the NPSP settings appropriately to handle your organization's use cases requires understanding the use case requirements as well as the settings themselves. We'll get into great detail on the ways to determine what the settings should look like when we install and configure NPSP in *Chapter 9, Install Nonprofit Cloud Solutions.*

Here is an outline of the various settings we will learn to appropriately configure the Nonprofit Success Pack fundraising features:

- **Account Model**: This will provide the basis of the rest of the data architecture.
- **Households**: This is the most common and currently recommended account model used with NPSP and allows the following settings.
- **Addresses**: This is a custom object in NPSP to allow more than one address.
- **Lead Settings**: These provide the basis of potential donor information.
- **Relationships**: This object provides context for how people are connected to people.
- **Donations**: This is the standard opportunity object renamed.
- **Recurring Donations**: This is a custom object in NPSP to track recurring donations.
- **Bulk Data Processes**: These settings establish various automated processes throughout NPSP.

All these settings are found on the **NPSP Settings** page in the Nonprofit Salesforce instance:

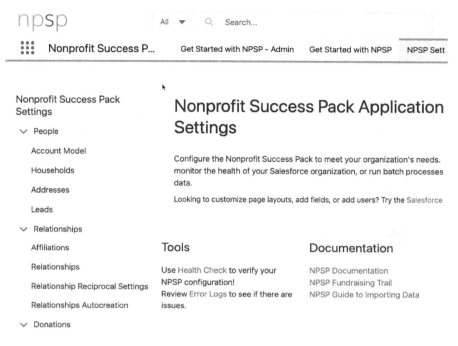

Figure 1.5 – the NPSP Settings page as seen in an actual Salesforce instance

All of these are included in the fundraising features for Nonprofit Success Pack as configurable settings. How the settings are configured will be predicated by the business use cases for the nonprofit customer. We will get into detailed use cases in the chapter on setting up NPSP.

Program management features

The **program management features** are much more recent in the Salesforce.org timeline. Program management features include both open source and paid modules.

The open source programs include the following:

- Program Management Module
- Volunteers for Salesforce
- NPSP Reports and Dashboards

The paid programs include the following:

- Nonprofit Cloud Case Management with Service Cloud
- Tableau

Program Management Module

Program Management Module (PMM) encompasses a wide range of programs and/or services and provides a framework to track and automate what your team may currently be recording in a spreadsheet. The module is easily installed from AppExchange and comes with a pre-created profile and unmanaged reports to get you started quickly.

PMM only consists of five custom objects, so it is highly customizable. It starts with a baseline and accurate reporting to get your programs up and running in the Salesforce environment. It's a 1, 2, 3 process (once it's been configured) to define the nonprofit's programs and services, add clients to those areas, and report on the metrics with the handy prebuilt reports included in PMM:

Figure 1.6 – A sample Program Management home page in Salesforce

Volunteers for Salesforce

Volunteers for Salesforce is also a free, open source application available on AppExchange. You may also see it abbreviated as **V4S**. It is also considered a part of PMM, although it is installed separately, and is designed to help nonprofits manage volunteers and track their volunteer hours, shifts, and jobs. The functionality to host volunteer signup for a specific job and/or shift on a nonprofit website is also an available feature. V4S has been around since Groundwire originally created it in 2012 and became a part of the NPSP offering in 2016. We will explore the use cases for V4S and best practices for implementing it in *Chapter 11, Configuring Additional Features and Security:*

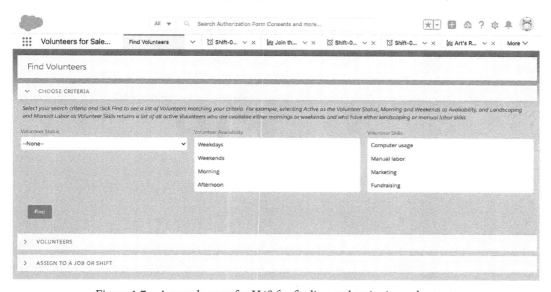

Figure 1.7 – A sample page for V4S for finding and assigning volunteers

NPSP Reports and Dashboards

NPSP Reports and Dashboards provides a set of pre-configured reports and dashboards commonly used by nonprofits. We'll look at and learn about the following reports as well as other reports associated with the various modules:

- **NPSP Campaign Household Mailing List**: This is a basic family name and address listing.

- **SYBUNT Report**: This is a prospecting report of lapsed donors that shows donors who gave during some years but not this year.

- **LYBUNT Report**: This is a prospecting report of donors who gave last year but not this year.

- **Households and Donations Report**: This is a composite report showing combined donations per household.

Dashboards can be extremely helpful to visualize, at a glance, an overall picture of data collected:

Figure 1.8 – A sample volunteer data dashboard based on reports in Salesforce

Nonprofit Cloud Case Management with Service Cloud

Although they are paid products, Nonprofit Cloud Case Management with Service Cloud and Tableau for Nonprofits are both considered part of the program management features in Nonprofit Cloud. Nonprofit Cloud Case Management is designed for organizations that are offering direct programs and services to clients; it helps manage caseloads with personalized care plans and accountability. Nonprofit Cloud Case Management simplifies intakes and referrals, and helps service providers keep clients on track with built-in assessment functionality.

Tableau

Tableau for Nonprofits makes available starter dashboards for program management to visualize program data and easily identify trends. We will look at how these paid features could be necessary to enhance and extend program functionality.

Additional features

Beyond the scope of fundraising and program management, nonprofits vary vastly in what they track and hope to automate. Each of the additional features covers a more specific area in Nonprofit Cloud. Use cases and implementation for these are covered in *Chapter 12*, *Declarative Tools and Modules*. The following is a general overview of these features.

Grantmaking and grants management

As more and more nonprofits use Salesforce and Nonprofit Cloud, there are more common use cases. Foundations have always been a large part of the Nonprofit Cloud customer base. **Grantmaking** and **grants management** are two sides of the same coin that we will explore and understand when we get to *Chapter 12*, *Declarative Tools and Modules*.

The **Outbound Funds Module** serves as the foundation for grantmaking. It was built by the Salesforce.org Open Source Community and led by volunteers from nonprofits, grantmakers, partners, and staff under the Open Source Commons program. It is free and available through AppExchange. The Outbound Funds Module was designed to track funding programs and requests, gain insight on financial commitments, and manage disbursements. The Outbound Funds Module extends the capabilities of Nonprofit Success Pack; the following diagram shows the standard Salesforce objects in blue, standard NPSP fundraising objects in yellow, and the core package of outbound funds in pink:

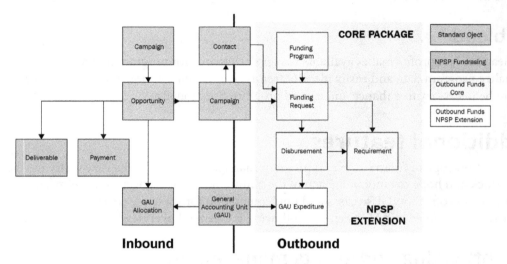

Figure 1.9 – The entity-relationship diagram for Outbound Funds Module from the Open Source Community

Grants management is a paid offering from Salesforce.org to improve grantee experience with a branded grantee portal built on Experience Cloud.

Accounting Subledger and Elevate

Accounting Subledger helps prepare fundraising data and information for the accounting system of your choice. It is a paid product from Salesforce.org that cuts down on time spent on reconciliation tasks while providing a single source of truth for donor data.

And, speaking of donors, Nonprofit Cloud has come full circle with **Elevate**. Elevate is a paid offering from Salesforce.org and is a comprehensive suite of tools to integrate fundraising operations and streamline the donor journey. Elevate provides payment services, giving pages, and an administrative interface in conjunction with Philanthropy Cloud. Elevate works with both Nonprofit Cloud and Education Cloud and is currently only available to US-based organizations.

Marketing and engagement

Marketing and engagement have many options in Nonprofit Cloud, from the built-in engagement tool in NPSP to the sophisticated paid tools. These tools are designed to complete the circle that gives nonprofits a 360-degree view of their constituents, engage with those constituents by creating personalized journeys, and analyze the impact of the nonprofit. The Nonprofit Cloud marketing and engagement options offer a variety of tools:

- **Journey Builder**: Build customer interactions based on customer behavior.
- **Email Studio**: Build smarter emails using data.
- **Mobile Studio**: SMS, push, and chat app messaging.
- **Social Studio**: Creates advocates via social media interaction powered by AI.
- **Advertising Studio**: Secure 1:1 advertising across platforms.
- **Customer 360 Audiences**: Unify customer data.
- **Datorama**: Measure marketing performance and impact.
- **Interaction Studio or Pardot**: Connected customer journeys across email, SMS, and social media.

All of the aforementioned features are available through Salesforce's Nonprofit Cloud. Already, you can see some of the breadth and depth of what can be done.

Summary

After reading this first chapter, you can see how robust Nonprofit Cloud truly is and how it can provide what is necessary for tens of thousands of different nonprofit organizations across the world. The incredible variety of tools available in Nonprofit Cloud may seem a little overwhelming at first glance, but don't worry!

In the upcoming chapters, we will dive more deeply into the core products of Nonprofit Cloud to understand when to use specific features, how to implement and configure those features, and how to work with nonprofit organizations to understand their needs to fully utilize Nonprofit Cloud.

Let's get started with a deeper dive into NPSP in the next chapter.

2
What Is NPSP?

Nonprofit Success Pack, also known as **NPSP**, is the foundation of Nonprofit Cloud.
Its data architecture and native functionality are critical to additional components and
implementation. NPSP is the foundation of all of the Nonprofit Cloud fundraising features.

In this chapter, we're going to cover the following main topics:

- Basic premises and use cases for NPSP
- NPSP data architecture
- Fundraising in NPSP

The goal of this chapter will be to understand how NPSP originated and how its original
use cases continue to utilize NPSP. Understanding the architecture of NPSP and the
similarities and differences between the Nonprofit Cloud architecture and the standard
Salesforce architecture is critical to understanding how a nonprofit's business processes fit
into the architecture, along with the fundraising features built into NPSP.

Technical requirements

For this chapter, you will need the Salesforce Foundation/NPSP GitHub repository: `https://github.com/SalesforceFoundation/NPSP`, which contains the current version of NPSP. NPSP is an open source package that's licensed by Salesforce.org (SFDO) under the BSD-3 Clause License, which can be found at the following link:

`https://opensource.org/licenses/BSD-3-Clause`.

You will also need the NPSP Public Data Dictionary: `https://quip.com/yD1wAsdz1m1Q#bTIACArbZT9`.

Basic premises and use cases for NPSP

As we learned in *Chapter 1, Overview of Nonprofit Cloud*, Salesforce was founded on the principle of giving back. One of the simplest and easiest ways to give back was to donate the Salesforce product licenses to registered nonprofits to use. The challenge is that Salesforce was created to help corporations and their sales leaders track leads and opportunities and business relationships. Salesforce is defined as a customer relationship management tool. Nonprofits don't have customers.

Let's explore the pain points nonprofits came across in trying to use Salesforce by comparing corporate versus nonprofit. By looking at the differences in what Salesforce offers businesses and what nonprofits need, we can see the gaps that existed before NPSP. The following table outlines some of these considerations:

Business	Nonprofit	Bridge
Customers.	Constituents, donors, volunteers, and advocates.	The Contact object holds information on people, regardless of the classification of those people.
Customers are associated with Accounts in a business-to-business sales model.	These individuals are most likely associated with no business at all. However, there may be a reason to associate an individual with the business where they work. So, maybe nonprofits need business-to-business and business-to-individual relationships. Plus, it would be very helpful to associate individuals with their households/families at a personal level.	Not available.

Business	Nonprofit	Bridge
Leads are people who might be potential buyers of your product.	There is nothing to "buy" from a nonprofit. However, donors are people who should be cultivated and developed to contribute to the nonprofit.	Not available. Standard lead processes are not helpful.
Business deals involve selling a lead your product, packaging, discounting, quantities, and invoicing the sale.	Again, there's nothing to buy, and the Internal Revenue Service is very strict about what constitutes a donation to a nonprofit. Many donations are made by individuals. Sometimes, companies make donations as well, and sometimes, one or the other influences a donation. What if the donation is not monetary but in kind or pro bono time? How does that fit into the Salesforce model?	Not available. Although opportunities show monetary information, the standard sales processes do not align with donation processes.
Managers receive reports and dashboards on sales' key performance indicators (KPIs). Forecasting and pipelines tell the story of how well marketers, lead generators, and salespeople are doing.	Although seeing how many donations are coming into a nonprofit is important, the real measure of a nonprofit is the impact they are having via their mission.	Not available.
Customer satisfaction is the key to success.	Impact is the key to success.	Not available.

Table 2.1 – Comparison of standard Salesforce business use cases versus Salesforce nonprofit use cases without NPSP

The gaps between standard Salesforce business use cases and what nonprofits need are considerable. NPSP was designed to extend the functionality of Salesforce via a series of managed packages. The data architecture and the fundraising features in this open source, BSD-licensed package will be the focus of the remainder of this chapter.

Before any customizations or additional features could be conceived for nonprofits, the standard Salesforce data architecture needed to be addressed. The entire Salesforce architecture is built on the Account object. 90% of nonprofits do not need to associate an individual with an Account. So, where do we start? What does the standard Salesforce Account model look like? Let's take a look:

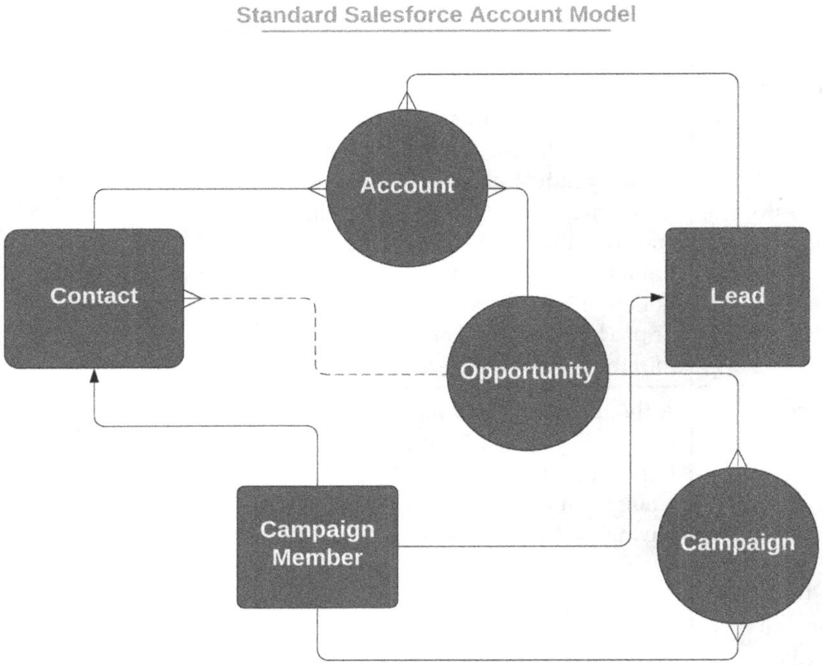

Standard Salesforce Account Model

Figure 2.1 – Standard Salesforce Account model

Based on the standard Salesforce Account model, there are discrepancies in what a nonprofit organization would need.

Introducing Account models

Three basic Account models are supported in the Nonprofit Cloud data architecture with NPSP. Each of these models meets a different need and should be implemented based on the differentiators for that model; two of the Account models are now considered legacy models. Nonprofit Success Pack does not currently support the Person Account model; however, they can co-exist.

Household model

The Household model is the default Account model for NPSP and unless there are express reasons to use a different Account model, the Household Account model is highly recommended. Most of the improvements and features are built around the Household model. The Household Account model leverages the Account object slightly differently than the standard model. It creates a Household for each Contact.

The Household model uses Salesforce's standard objects:

- **Account**: Households, companies, foundations, sponsors, and partner organizations.

- **Contact**: Individuals of all kinds. Each Contact is related to an Account record of some type.

- **Opportunity**: Donations, grants, membership amounts, and stages for individuals and/or organizations.

- **Campaign**: Tracks outreach via email or other forms of communication.

The following diagram shows how these standard objects work together:

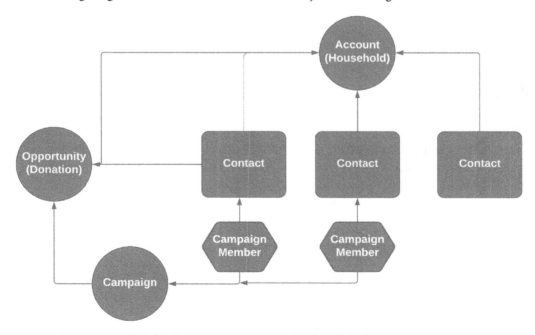

Figure 2.2 – High-level overview of the Household model's data structure in NPSP

1-to-1 Account model

The 1-to-1 Account model is considered a legacy model for NPSP. It is still supported; however, it is not recommended if you are setting up a new instance of Nonprofit Cloud. The 1-to-1 Account model behaves very similarly to the Salesforce standard **Person Account** model because it creates a new Account for each Contact automatically and names the Account the same name as the Contact. Using the separate Household object in NPSP, households can be created by manually joining Contacts. This data flow is represented in the following diagram:

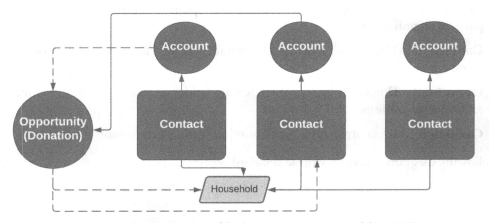

Figure 2.3 – Representation of the legacy 1:1 Account model in NPSP

Individual (Bucket) Account model

The Individual or Bucket Account model only has one Account named Individual, where all Contact records are associated. Households must be created manually. Once there are 10,000 Contact records associated with the Individual Account record, the system may not perform as expected. This can particularly be a hindrance to any DML transactions or record retrievals; for specific information, visit `https://developer.salesforce.com/`. This is considered a legacy Account model and is not recommended for new implementations of NPSP. This is what the model looks like:

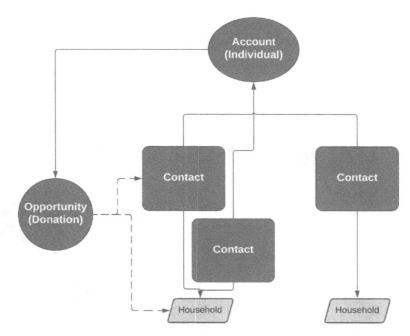

Figure 2.4 – Representation of the legacy Individual (Bucket) Account model in NPSP

The rest of the data architecture

With the standard objects and the Household model as the foundation, NPSP adds custom objects to address the additional gaps between standard Salesforce and what nonprofits need:

Object	Use case
Address	In standard Salesforce, a shipping address and a billing address are available on the Account record. The custom Address object provides a place for additional addresses for Households that might include a seasonal or other address.
Affiliation	The Affiliation custom object offers a way to connect an individual to another organization other than the individual's default Household. For example, you can affiliate an individual with their employer, as well as affiliate an individual with a nonprofit organization where they serve as a board member. Affiliations are Contact to Account (Organization) junction object records.
Relationship	The Relationship custom object connects Contacts to Contacts, even if they're outside the same Household Account. Relationships can be reciprocal or not. Examples include spouse, child, parent, friend, and colleague.

Table 2.2 – The most commonly used custom objects in the Household model in NPSP

The following is a rendering of the Household model entity-relationship diagram, showing the standard Salesforce objects and the most commonly used custom objects that are included in NPSP:

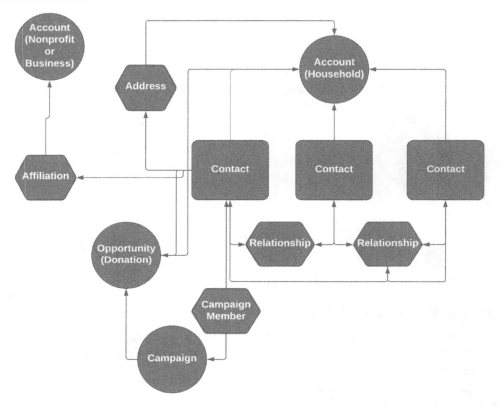

Figure 2.5 – A high-level overview of the Household model with
the most commonly used custom objects in NPSP

Additional custom objects in NPSP for fundraising include the following:

Object Label	Object Description
Account Soft Credit	A junction object to associate donations and Accounts.
AutoNumber	Contains information related to custom autonumbers.
Batch	A holding object for batch entry.
Deliverable	A custom object that's used to track deliverables related to grants or donation seeking.

Object Label	Object Description
Engagement Plan	Holds a set of tasks that are used to engage constituents.
Engagement Plan Task	Details of each engagement task.
Engagement Plan Template	Tracks the processes and related set of tasks needed for an Engagement Plan.
Error	NPSP errors generated during normal operations.
Form Template	Default fields and values for donation entry.
GAU Allocation	A junction object that's used to link General Accounting Units and a donation, campaign, payment, or Recurring Donation.
General Accounting Unit	Accounting units used for assigning donations.
Get Started Completion Checklist State	NPSP Get Started Checklist.
Household (Address)	A physical mailing address for grouping Contacts.
Level	Defines Levels for any object.
Recurring Donation	An object for donations that are made on a regular, recurring basis.
Recurring Donation Schedule	Contains the current and past schedule(s) for each Recurring Donation. Records in this object are system maintained and should never be edited directly.
Soft Credit	A Junction object to relate a donation to the influencer.
Trigger Handler	Stores which classes to run in response to a DML being performed on an object.

Table 2.3 – Additional custom objects in NPSP to accommodate fundraising

Here is the overall schema for the various NPSP objects:

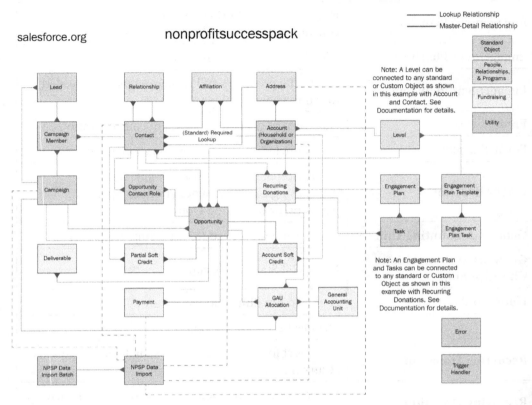

Figure 2.6 – NPSP entity-relationship diagram from https://github.com/SalesforceFoundation/NPSP

Now that you have an understanding of the Household Account model and the additional custom objects in NPSP, we can start exploring the fundraising features in Nonprofit Cloud.

Fundraising with NPSP

Now that you have a basic understanding of how the data architecture of NPSP is different than the standard Salesforce data architecture, we can explore the next layer of NPSP and one of the driving motivators behind the creation of NPSP: **fundraising**. Building on Accounts, Contacts, and opportunities – or as you will often see in a Salesforce nonprofit instance, organizations or households, donors, and donations – let's look at use cases and the solutions that the fundraising features in NPSP offer.

Donation features in NPSP

The most common goal of tracking information for nonprofits is to track donations and the donors who provide those donations. NPSP uses the standard Opportunity object in Salesforce to track donations of all kinds. Any revenue that comes into a nonprofit can be tracked in donations; each donation can be designated as a specific type of revenue. Let's look at a sample case:

1. Suppose Diana, a board member for the nonprofit, makes a financial donation.

2. Then, Diana makes that same donation every month.

3. Afterward, Diana convinces her employer to donate office space for the nonprofit to use.

4. Additionally, Diana's employer provides matching donations for organizations based on what the employee gives.

Are there features in NPSP to track all of that information? The short answer is *yes*. Donation record types cover all of those possibilities, as shown in the following screenshot:

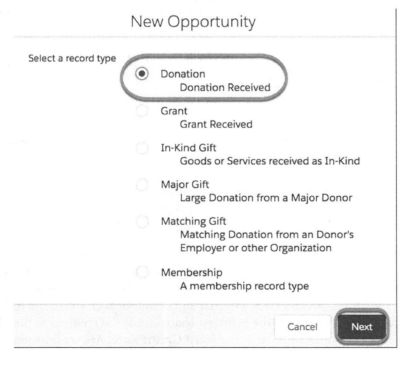

Figure 2.7 – The standard donation types for NPSP opportunities include Donation, Grant, In-Kind Gift, Major Gift, Matching Gift, and Membership

Here, you can see that Diana has donated or influenced four different types of donations:

- Donation
- Recurring Donation
- In-Kind Gift
- Matching Gift

For the initial donation, Diana receives credit for that donation. The donation itself will automatically be added to all her other donations to provide dated totals for giving. If the donation has been designated for a specific purpose, the appropriate allocations can be applied to track that funding stream.

Recurring Donations are donations that are given regularly over time – every fundraiser's dream! Some Recurring Donations, like Diana's, are a specific amount of money that's given at regular intervals with no specific end date. **Pledges** may seem like Recurring Donations; however, in fundraising, there is a difference. Generally, pledges are handled in NPSP using the *Payment* object. Interrogate the nonprofit's policy on pledges versus Recurring Donations. Other Recurring Donations may be more like installment payments. Perhaps a corporate donor pledges $1,000 but wants to break it up into two equal payments of $500 each. This is also tracked using Recurring Donations.

But what about the other two donations – the **In-Kind Gift** and the **Matching Gift**? Shouldn't Diana get some recognition for those as well? How is that done in NPSP?

Soft credits in NPSP

Soft credits are designed to help track a donor's influence on donations that are made to the nonprofit. In the case of Diana, both the in-kind donation of office space and the matching donation from her employer should be soft credits related to Diana's giving history. Often, board members are asked to raise a certain amount of money each year; however, the board member does not necessarily have to write the check themselves. Soft credits allow organizations to track additional funding a board member influences.

When Diana influences her employer to donate space for the nonprofit's use, it is considered an *in-kind donation*; the opportunity itself is associated with Diana's employer as the primary donor. Diana receives the soft credit because her **Contact Role** has been designated as a solicitor. Diana receives a similar soft credit for scenario 3, the In-Kind Gift of office space. Her employer is the primary donor and she is credited as the **Matched Donor**. The primary donor is, by default, the **Hard Credit Role**. Are we finished with soft credits for Diana? Almost. If Diana has a partner or other **Household Member**, the Household Member would receive soft credit for Diana's contributions.

There are nine opportunity Contact roles that are standard with NPSP. You can add to or edit these roles based on specific use cases for the nonprofit. The following is a brief overview of the Contact roles and their use cases:

Decision Maker	Generally related to a corporate donor, this is the Contact that has signatory power.
Donor	By default, this is a Hard Credit Role and is the actual giver.
Honoree	When a donor gives "in honor," the Honoree receives a soft credit.
Household Member	Household members receive soft credits for each others' donations.
Influencer	Diana was the "Influencer" for the in-kind donation of office space by her employer.
Notification Recipient	When a donation is made "in memory," the Notification Recipient is who should receive this information.
Soft Credit	Soft credit is used when a more defined role is not available.
Solicitor	This role may be more closely aligned with peer-to-peer fundraising or fundraising quotas.
Matched Donor	When a matching donation is made, the Matched Donor is the original giver who prompted the matching.

Table 2.4 – NPSP standard Contact roles for donations

NPSP is also designed to track more complex calculations and information on donations and soft credits. For example, a single check from Diana's employer arrives in the amount of $1,000; Diana is to be credited for having raised $500 of that sum with the remaining funds split between Alfred and Clark. NPSP uses a special related object called Partial Soft Credits to track this information.

NPSP provides ways to collect all of this data, relate it to donors and their households, and even their employers or other affiliations. Collecting the data is not where NPSP's fundraising features end. Leveraging that data is another important feature.

Getting donors and funders to the next level

Up to this point, donations come in and NPSP tracks them. Great work so far! Fundraisers and nonprofit development teams all know that growing the fundraising base not only means more donors but donors who are more deeply engaged with the nonprofit. Similar to what salespeople do in standard Salesforce, fundraisers can use NPSP **Levels** to identify, score, and segment donors. Once a donor is designated at a specific level, the development team can work to engage them at the next level. Sometimes, this is called **Moves Management**.

Although some organizations start with the donor level, there is statistical evidence that Volunteering is often the entry level for engaging with an organization. Using **engagement plans** in NPSP, a volunteer or donor can be encouraged to rise to the next level of engagement. The following is a sample chart:

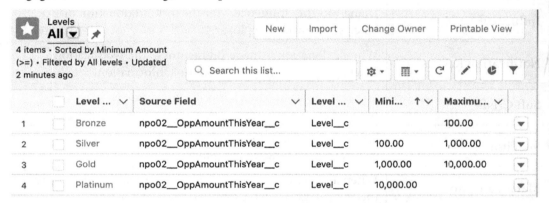

Figure 2.8 – Sample levels in NPSP

Engagement plans leverage native Salesforce capabilities to help fundraisers plan, implement, and track activities that lead constituents to the next level. This includes tasks, emails, calls, notes, meetings, and more. Visualizing the success of these moves is simple with other native Salesforce tools such as **Path**, **Kanban**, and inline editing with **list views**.

These are great tools for managing individual donors. However, most fundraisers are working with large numbers of donors, segmented into different groups, some of whom overlap and some who are brand new. Each donor has different interests and possibly different starting points to engage with the nonprofit. Does NPSP have a feature to facilitate communicating with all these different donors?

Campaign management coordinates communication

Campaigns are standard Salesforce objects that help us plan communications and track movement toward a specific goal. In conjunction with related data already in NPSP, campaigns can be used in every facet of fundraising. Nonprofits use campaigns to help manage a variety of campaigns: *email, direct mail, social media, and events*. Donors want to know that their funding is making a difference; campaigns not only allow fundraisers to ask for donations but also report to donors based on their past giving.

Although we are specifically looking at the fundraising features in NPSP in this chapter, campaigns can also be used for volunteer engagement, advocacy, and other areas of focus. Campaigns can be created with a hierarchy that is unique to the nonprofit organization using NPSP. The following is an example of a hierarchy that can assist each team at a nonprofit with their unique communications:

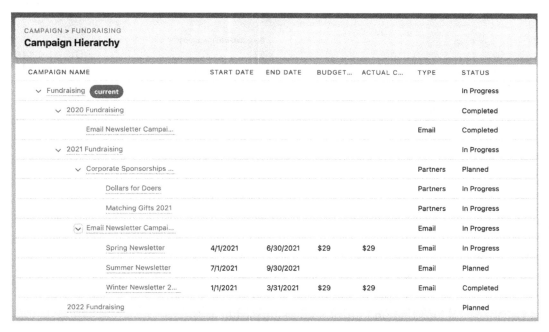

CAMPAIGN > FUNDRAISING
Campaign Hierarchy

CAMPAIGN NAME	START DATE	END DATE	BUDGET...	ACTUAL C...	TYPE	STATUS
⌄ Fundraising `current`						In Progress
⌄ 2020 Fundraising						Completed
Email Newsletter Campai...					Email	Completed
⌄ 2021 Fundraising						In Progress
⌄ Corporate Sponsorships ...					Partners	Planned
Dollars for Doers					Partners	In Progress
Matching Gifts 2021					Partners	In Progress
⌄ Email Newsletter Campai...					Email	In Progress
Spring Newsletter	4/1/2021	6/30/2021	$29	$29	Email	In Progress
Summer Newsletter	7/1/2021	9/30/2021			Email	Planned
Winter Newsletter 2...	1/1/2021	3/31/2021	$29	$29	Email	Completed
2022 Fundraising						Planned

Figure 2.9 – Campaign hierarchy example based on recurrent annual fundraisers, along with other advocacy and donor campaigns

Once the campaign hierarchy has been created, **Campaign Members** can be assigned to a campaign individually. Assigning Campaign Members can be done manually as a group, automatically based on certain criteria, or manually by individual Contact records. The possibilities are endless. A Campaign Member record is related to the Contact record (or a Lead record). The status of the Campaign Member is tracked based on the response.

In the preceding campaign hierarchy example, you may have noticed that the Storybook Gala in *Figure 2.9* is an annual event. Many donors return year after year to attend the gala. Additionally, new potential attendees are added. Unless someone asked to be removed from the email list, fundraisers want to invite everyone again next year. Campaigns and Campaign Members are designed with that in mind. This year's status may have been *Declined* in terms of attending, but that doesn't mean that is next year's answer. Tracking the responses to any campaign is critical to measuring constituent engagement.

NPSP's automatic Campaign Member management automates tracking campaign responses concerning donations that are received. All of the related data comes together to help fundraisers analyze what is working. At its most elemental level, the Campaign record shows the total Contacts in a campaign, responses, and donation information, as shown in the following screenshot:

∨ Campaign Member Information

Contacts in Campaign	Responses in Campaign
105	57
Expected Response (%)	Num Sent in Campaign
0.00%	0

∨ Donation Information

Won Opportunities in Campaign	Amount to Goal ⓘ
47	$20.00
Value Won Opportunities in Campaign	Expected Revenue in Campaign
$4,980	$5,000
Opportunities in Campaign	Budgeted Cost in Campaign
47	
Value Opportunities in Campaign	Actual Cost in Campaign
$4,980	$500

Figure 2.10 – The Campaign record fields showing Contacts, responses, and donation information

By using the Campaign, Campaign Member, and Opportunity report types, fundraisers can visualize vital information immediately using dashboards:

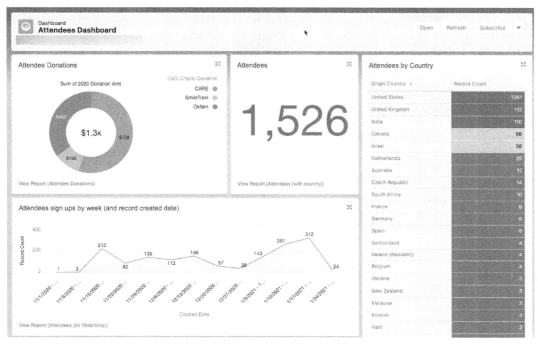

Figure 2.11 – Sample dashboard showing the sum of donations, attendee number, attendees by country, and attendees' responses by week

When it is time for the same campaign next year, it is a simple matter of cloning the campaign with its related records to begin anew.

Summary

Nonprofit Success Pack is an open source, managed package provided by Salesforce to facilitate the use of Salesforce CRM by nonprofits. The data architecture is the basis of the fundraising features, program management, and all the additional tools and features available for the Salesforce Nonprofit Cloud.

Understanding the NPSP data model is the first step. NPSP is what nonprofits use to incorporate the nonprofit-to-constituent model into Salesforce alongside the nonprofit-to-business model that is native to Salesforce. This encompasses everything from households to a separate address object to expanded uses of campaigns and opportunities.

Once the NPSP data architecture is in place, incorporating the appropriate fundraising features for the nonprofit's use case is critical to meeting the needs adequately while maintaining as much simplicity and ease of use as possible. The more familiar the feature, the easier it is to stave off complexity.

To recap on the vast amount of information that was provided in this chapter, let's look at the larger picture of business and nonprofit needs in Salesforce and how all those needs are addressed when the data architecture from NPSP is added to the standard Salesforce functionality:

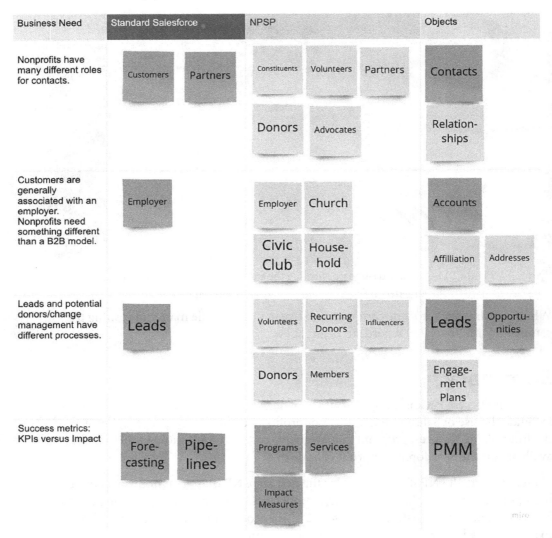

Figure 2.12 – Recap of nonprofit business needs using standard Salesforce and NPSP, as well as the Program Management module

Fundraising was the initial focus of NPSP; however, it has grown exponentially since its inception to assist nonprofits with other key areas as well. If fundraising is the vehicle for everything in the nonprofit ecosystem, programs and services are what fundraising drives. A critical area of fundraising is being able to share with donors and potential donors how the nonprofit is using funds to fulfill its missions.

In the next chapter, we will dig into what NPSP offers for Program Management and measure the impact that nonprofit programs and services have when it comes to meeting their mission goals.

3
Tracking Impact with Program Management Module

Nonprofits are more than just fundraisers. Programs are what fundraisers fund. Let's dive into how the Nonprofit Cloud **Program Management Module (PMM)** can connect your programs, and the **impact** it has on the funds you are raising. How do you track program engagement or the delivery of the service that your nonprofit provides? Are you managing a single program or multiple programs? Learning the basics of PMM and understanding how to leverage PMM for service delivery, as well as expanding upon the module to meet other needs, will be the focus of this chapter.

In this chapter, we're going to cover the following main topics:

- Building blocks and architecture to use PMM for service delivery
- Basic premises and use cases for PMM
- Extending the functionality of PMM

Donations solicited, grants received, and funds raised are all done to further the mission of the nonprofit. Programs are the actions that normally translate funds into impact. Impact is at the heart of what every nonprofit does. An impact is what donors want to see their dollars achieving.

Program management can be leveraged to go beyond tracking individual quantifiable data. Recording data, such as how many pounds of food have been distributed by a food bank, is only one use case. And does that truly show the impact of the program itself? What do you do when the programs are more complex, or when you need to scale and are growing quickly? Program managers need to evaluate the effectiveness and make iterations to improve. The goal of this chapter is to learn the basics of PMM and understand when and how to utilize PMM as the foundation of an organization's needs.

Building blocks for PMM

PMM is designed to help nonprofits optimize their services, as well as track the services themselves. Understanding how PMM works is essential to being able to analyze the data collected on programs and services of the nonprofit to show their impact (more about the analysis in *Chapter 15, Implementing Analytics Tools for Impact*). Think of all the different nonprofits. Programs and services vary significantly based on the organization. PMM is very flexible and offers a unique set of building blocks to adapt to any organization's needs. Let's start by learning about the objects and framework that make up PMM and serve as an extension of the NPSP.

PMM objects

PMM adds eight specific custom Salesforce objects to accommodate program management. The objects are designed to work in conjunction with the standard Salesforce accounts and contacts and, of course, within the Household account model of the NPSP. These objects help define the programs that the nonprofit provides, track engagement with those programs, correlate services, and track who, what, when, where, and how many. The following objects are listed in the subsections with a brief explanation of each object.

Programs

Programs are the areas of work that make up a nonprofit's mission, for example, meal distribution or mentoring. The program object is what connects everything in PMM together. Programs also provide the foundation for extending PMM's capabilities, such as the paid Nonprofit Cloud Case Management tool. The following is a screenshot of the program object in Salesforce:

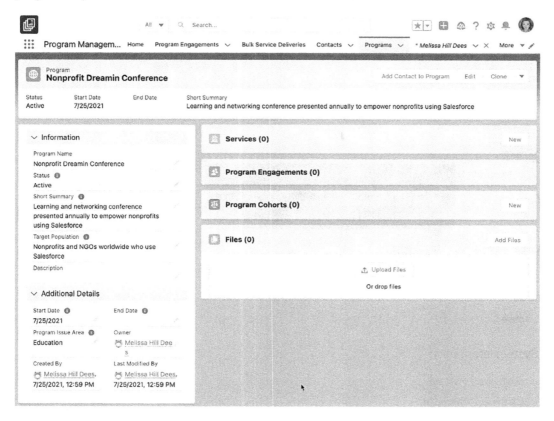

Figure 3.1 – Screenshot of the Program record page for a virtual conference

Additionally, programs is where you set the program issue area, status, and target population of the program.

Services

Services are the second tier in PMM. These are the actual activities that happen within programs and where metrics are recorded. Each service has a unit of measurement.

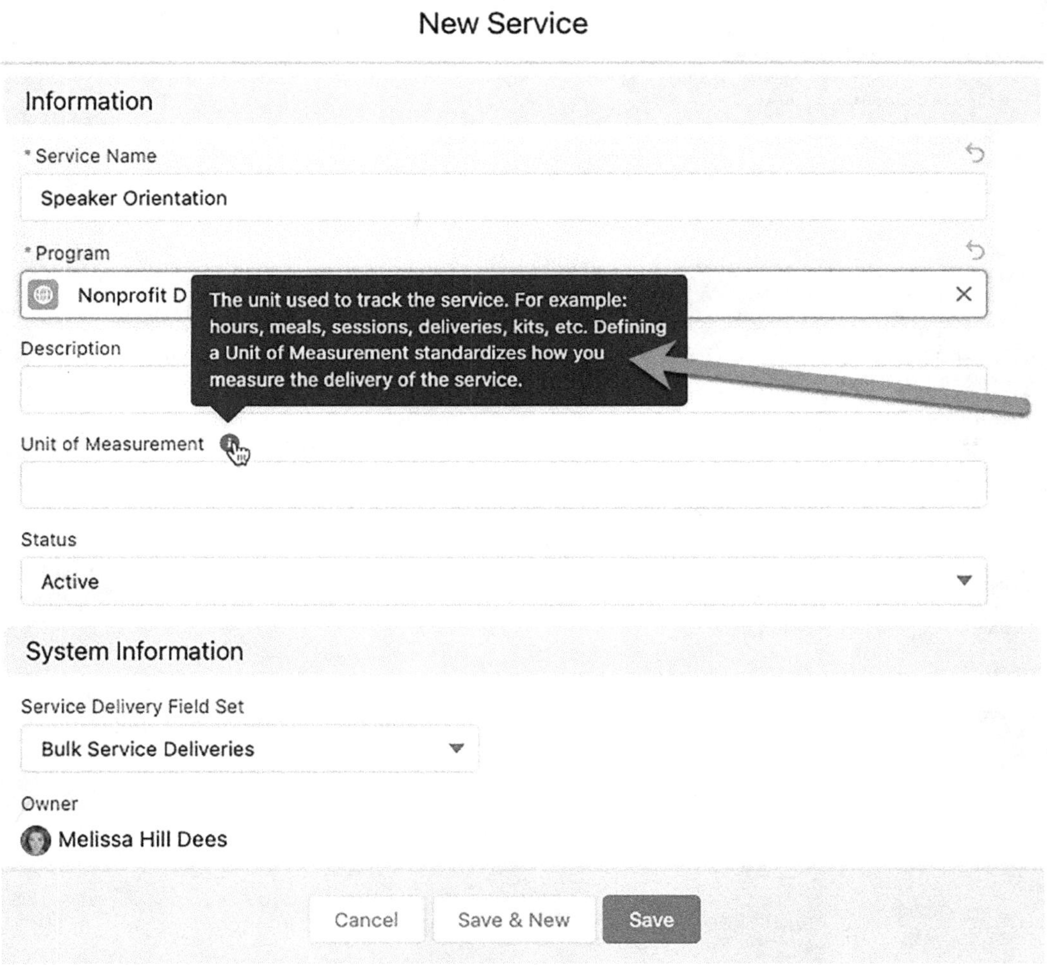

New Service

Information

* Service Name

Speaker Orientation

* Program

Nonprofit D

×

Description

The unit used to track the service. For example: hours, meals, sessions, deliveries, kits, etc. Defining a Unit of Measurement standardizes how you measure the delivery of the service.

Unit of Measurement

Status

Active

System Information

Service Delivery Field Set

Bulk Service Deliveries

Owner

Melissa Hill Dees

Cancel   Save & New   Save

Figure 3.2 – Creating a new service record

The unit of measurement could be the number of gift cards distributed for emergency needs, the pounds of food shared with a family, or the hours of mentoring invested.

Program Engagements

Program Engagements connect programs and clients.

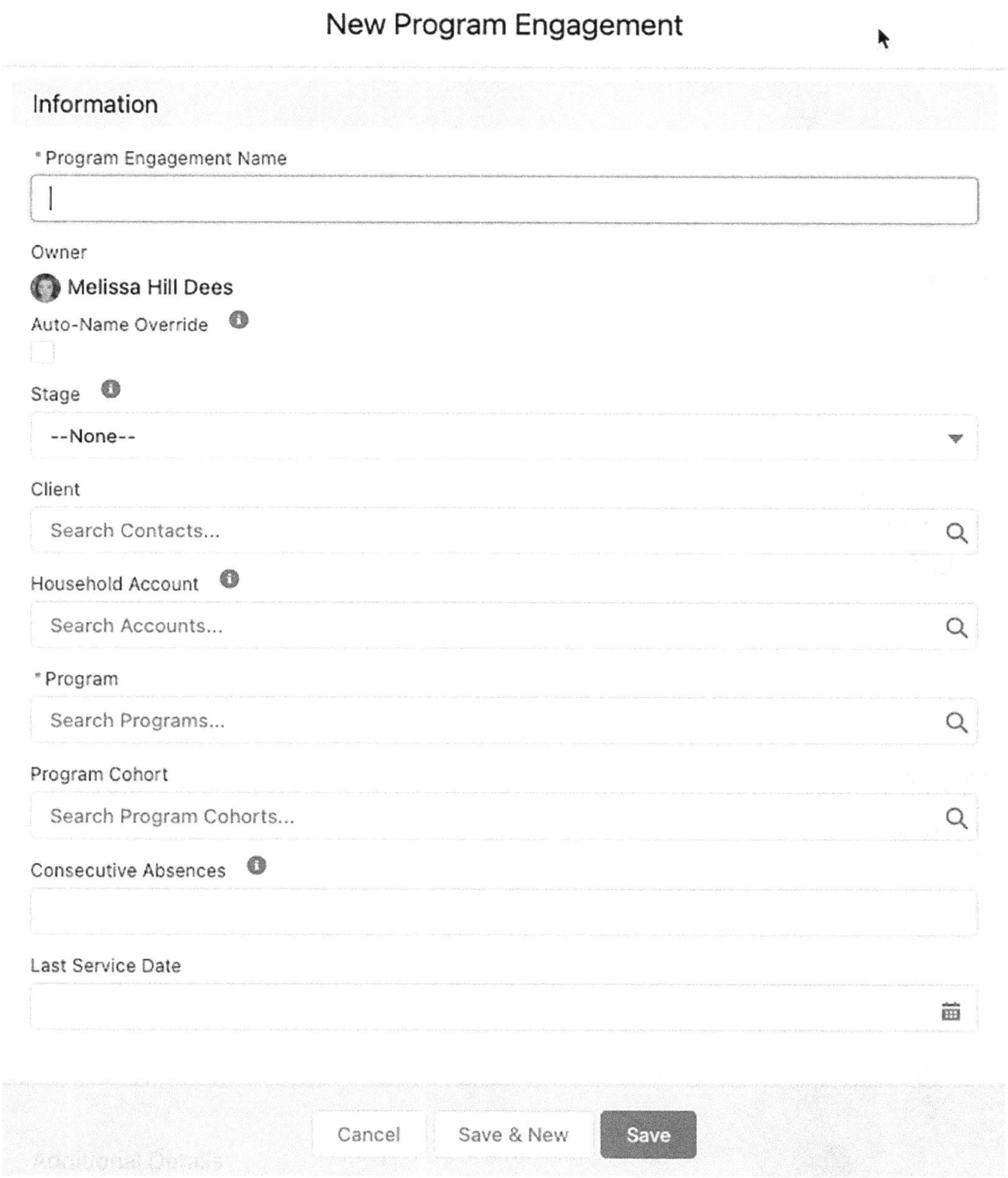

Figure 3.3 – Creating a new Program Engagement

Clients can refer to contacts, organizations, households, and/or custom objects with the use of program engagement.

Program Cohorts

Program Cohorts in PMM are comparable to Campaigns in standard Salesforce. Program Cohorts group program engagements and provide reporting capabilities on grouped engagements.

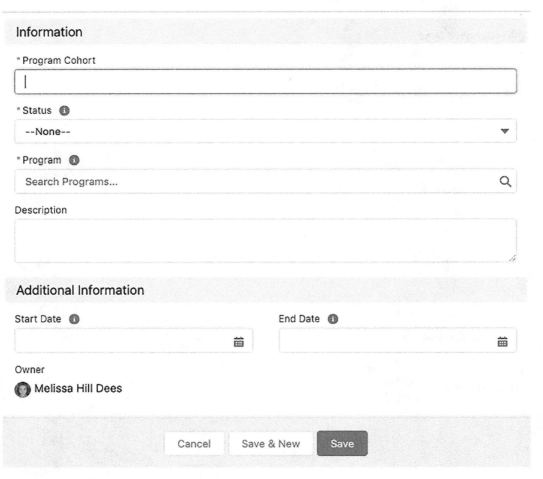

Figure 3.4 – New Program Cohort creation

Program Cohorts also allow for client and/or participant segmentation.

Service Deliveries

Service Deliveries are individual instances of a service. They also record timings and the quantity of the service. Service Deliveries connect the client and the service and can also connect the Service Session, Program Engagement, and Household Account.

You can see this in the following screenshot:

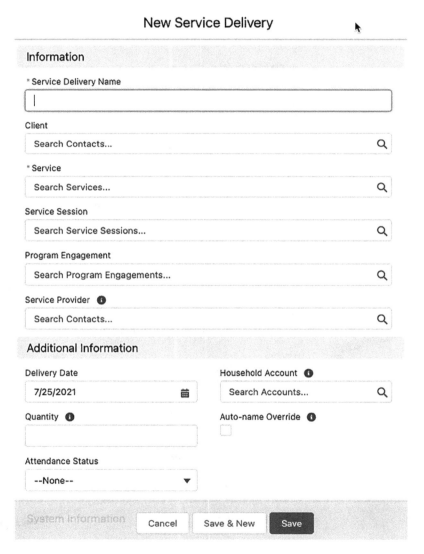

Figure 3.5 – New Service Delivery fields available

Now, let's understand **Service Schedules**.

Service Schedules

Service Schedules can be single sessions; however, the real value in Service Schedules is the ability to quickly and easily recreate sessions with a start and end date and time, and a recurring frequency. For example, mentoring sessions may happen for an hour each week for 13 weeks.

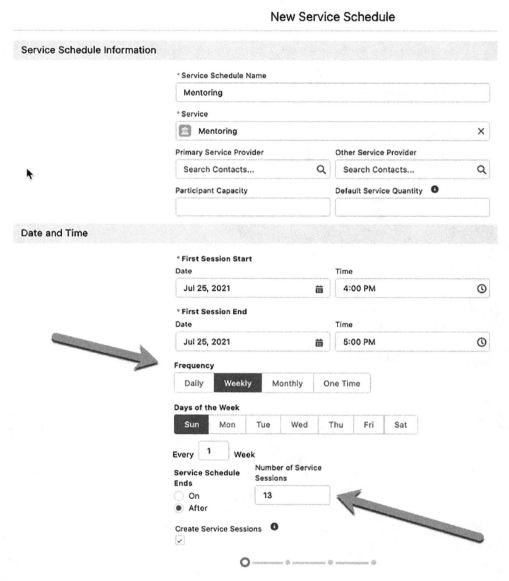

Figure 3.6 – Creating recurring sessions for a Service Schedule

Now, let's understand **Service Sessions**.

Service Sessions

A **Service Session** is a single instance of delivery of a service within a program. In the previous example of a Service Schedule, where mentoring takes place for an hour each week for 13 weeks, each hour would be a Service Session. Service Sessions are also where attendance is tracked for **Service Participants**:

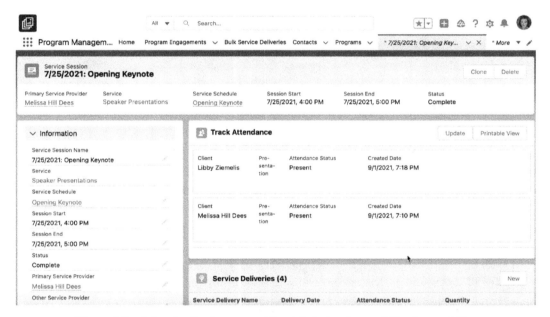

Figure 3.7 – A Service Session page with related attendance, deliveries, and files

Now, let's understand service participants.

Service Participants

The **Service Participants** object connects Service Schedules and clients in PMM. Attendance and hours, plus additional metrics, are tracked in the Service Participants record:

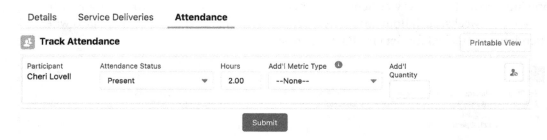

Figure 3.8 – Tracking attendance for Service Sessions for Service Participants

Now, let's understand the PMM schema.

The entire PMM schema

The following is a rendering of the PMM **Entity Relationship Diagram** (**ERD**), which pulls together the standard Salesforce Account and Contact objects along with the custom objects that make up PMM.

> **Note**
> The PMM custom objects can be divided into the primary PMM objects and the optional session-based objects.

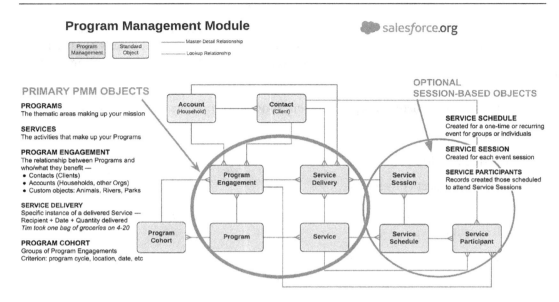

Figure 3.9 – PMM ERD

Now, let's understand how the PMM functionality works.

How the PMM functionality works

The use cases for program management are as varied and different as the nonprofits and their programs themselves. Let's consider a fictional organization called **The Neighbors**. Their mission is as follows:

"To help people in our zip code build economically sustainable lives
by meeting an immediate need to prevent hunger and homelessness,
connecting neighbors to wider community support services, and offering
training to help neighbors build skills for better employment prospects and
personal/family management."

As a first step, The Neighbors nonprofit went through a discovery process to better understand their business processes, their metrics for success, and what data is required to be collected and measured. The Neighbors concluded that they are implementing PMM for two specific reasons:

1. They want to consistently report to their donors and funders on the following:

    - Program impact

    - Meeting mission goals

    - Dollar to impact conversion

2. Additionally, they want to be able to iterate and improve programs based on the following:

    - Which programs are most in-demand and by whom

    - How/if/when people move into more sustainable futures after receiving help

    - What needs are not being well met in the community

Ascertaining these important business decisions first is the key to implementing PMM in a way that will provide the metrics and trends The Neighbors need to share with stakeholders, as well as iterate internally. With all of this in mind, The Neighbors can begin to lay out their programs and services and map them with the PMM objects. Let's look at three use cases The Neighbors might consider.

Managing more than one program

The Neighbors realize they really run three individual programs to meet their mission. Within those programs are specific services they provide as well. How can The Neighbors manage all these different moving parts? Let's begin by laying out the framework. The following is a sampling of what one program would look like with several services. Additional programs would be similar. The level of complexity makes it difficult to visualize here.

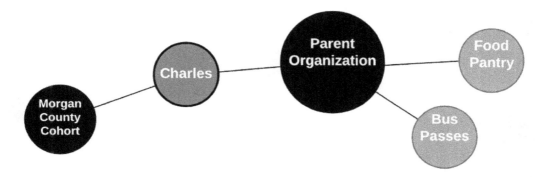

Figure 3.10 – Simple visual showing how a Contact is connected to more than one program and service

In this use case, Charles completes a program assessment and is assigned to the Morgan County Cohort. Once the assessment has been evaluated, Charles is identified as being a participant in a program currently handled by PMM: Parent Organization Immediate Needs. The program has two services that Charles needs, Food Pantry and Bus Passes. Engagement and participation records are created as Charles participates. From Charles' contact record, you can see his participation in the related records.

Providing services to organizations rather than contacts

The Neighbors also work with partner churches to extend their Financial Literacy classes. They can use PMM to track those partnerships by using Organization Accounts instead of Contacts. The framework would look something like this:

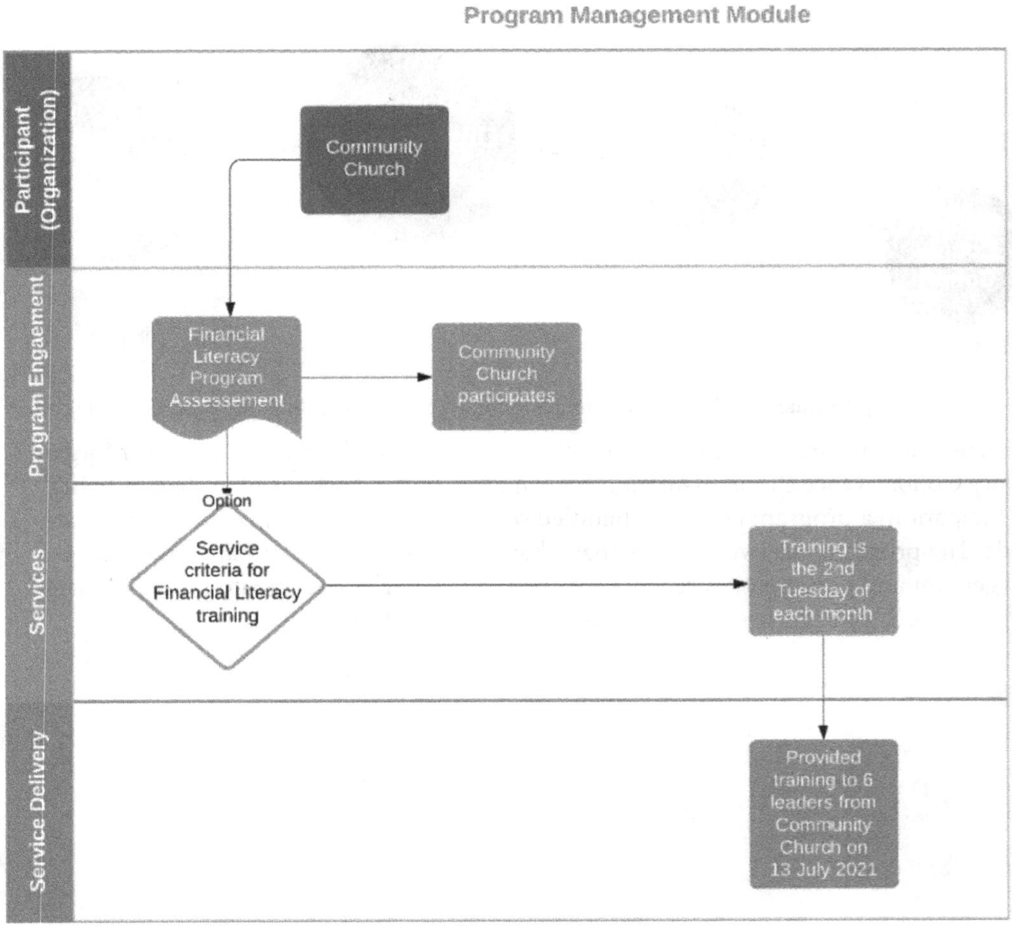

Figure 3.11 – Sample of PMM for Accounts rather than Contacts

> **Note**
> Not every custom PMM object is required for each program.

The relationship between the participating organizations and Engagements, Services, and Delivery also helps in tracking impact across all participation.

Providing services to those who are not Contacts or Organizations

The Neighbors realize there is one area they have not covered. They realize the support that a pet can provide to clients in need, so they offer services for animals as well. In order to be good stewards of donated funds, The Neighbors want to accurately report services benefiting animals. The following figure shows a way to use PMM to track those services using a custom object, related to the Contact object, to hold the animal's information:

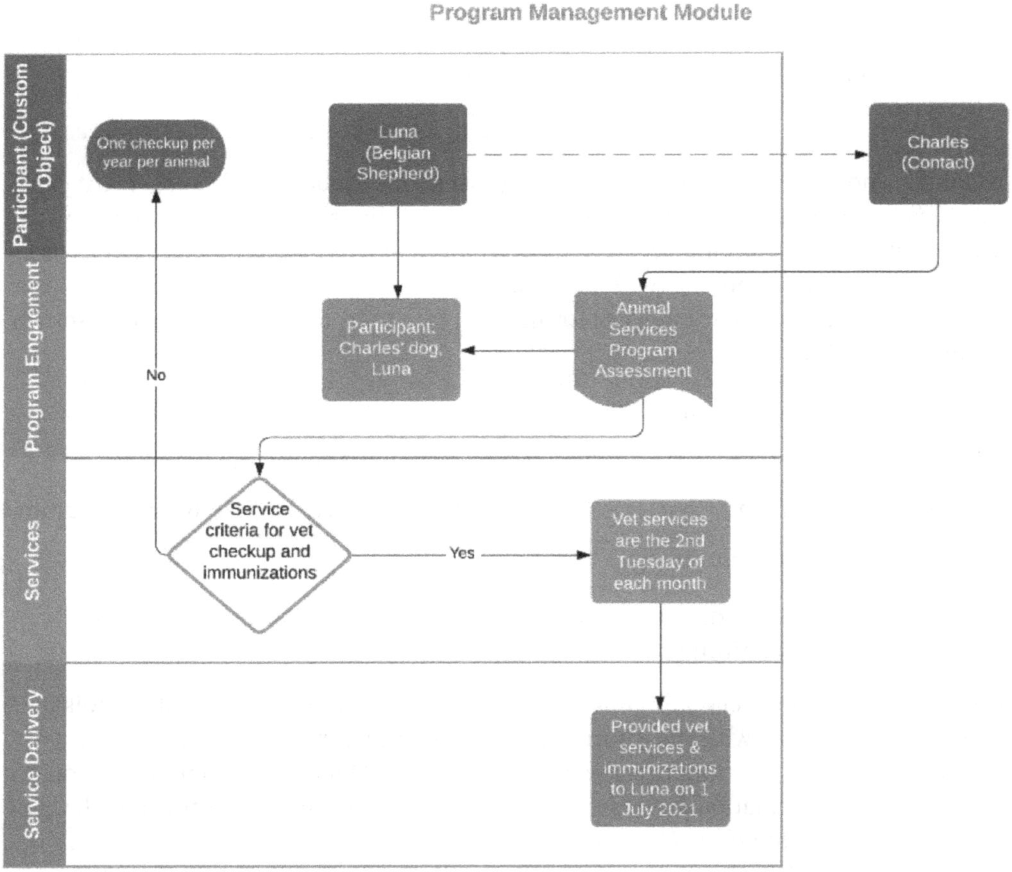

Figure 3.12 – Example of where a custom object fits into the PMM architecture

PMM was specifically built to handle a wide variety of use cases. Sometimes PMM may need an additional custom object, such as the Animal Services program. These three use cases are representative of standard situations. There are more long-term, complex use cases that need additional considerations; that is where **Nonprofit Cloud Case Management** is recommended.

Extending the use of PMM

Nonprofit Cloud Case Management is a paid product from Salesforce designed for better long-term client engagement and management. Case Management includes a new set of custom objects and processes to track intakes, referrals, clients, client notes, case plans, and assessments specifically designed for human services organizations.

> **Note**
>
> Don't confuse Nonprofit Cloud Case Management with Salesforce's standard Service Cloud Case object.

The Neighbors nonprofit has decided that using Nonprofit Cloud Case Management can automate and streamline the workload for their case managers so they can help more clients. They particularly want to apply it to their Training to Build Skills program in order to work more closely, one on one, with their clients and track their progress to achieving financial independence. The framework for the program does not change much, as shown in the following outline:

- Program: Training to Build Skills.

- Program Cohort: Clients are grouped by the year they entered the program.

- Program Engagement: Charles is enrolled in the long-term skills-building program.

- Service: Individual counseling.

Case managers work with individuals using Case Management; they track goals and progress made toward obtaining sustainable employment for Charles.

The framework may look very similar to our earlier use case, but the way that the folks at The Neighbors interact with the information is vastly different. Rather than a report at the end of each month, case managers work with the Case Management application on a daily basis. All the information for a client is in one place. We will look at this next level of PMM in *Chapter 4, Automating Case Management for Better Human Services.*

Summary

PMM is critical to tracking programs and the impact those programs are making to meet the mission of a nonprofit organization. Eight custom objects make up the bulk of PMM; they are highly flexible and can be configured for most use cases nonprofits have around programs and services and their delivery, as we saw in the examples of multiple programs and services for Charles, working with churches, and providing animal services. For complex and long-term human services program management, Nonprofit Cloud offers a paid Case Management application. All the data collected can be analyzed and reported on in order to share information with stakeholders and use it internally to iterate and improve programs and services. We'll go into more detail on analytics and reporting in *Chapter 15, Implementing Analytics Tools for Impact*.

In the next chapter, we'll look more closely at how Nonprofit Cloud Case Management provides additional tools, layered on top of NPSP and PMM, to track outcomes and impact for nonprofits working in human services.

Further learning

- *Salesforce Foundation/PMM*:

- `https://github.com/SalesforceFoundation/PMM`

- This is the GitHub repository for the current version of PMM. PMM is an open source package licensed by Salesforce.org (SFDO) under the BSD-3 Clause License, found at `https://opensource.org/licenses/BSD-3-Clause`.

- Public data dictionary for PMM: `https://salesforce.quip.com/TE3DASrEJ17t#ASCACAYi2na`.

4
Automating Case Management for Better Human Services

Case management is to people what program management is to programs. Case management streamlines workflows and tracks client progress for human services. It is a paid tool that leverages standard Salesforce Account, Case, and Contact objects, custom objects from the **Nonprofit Success Pack** (**NPSP**) and the **Program Management Module** (**PMM**), and new custom objects for case management.

In this chapter, we're going to cover the following main topics:

- What is the use case for case management?
- Key objects and features of case management
- Tracking and reporting for case management

For nonprofits that provide human services, their outcomes and impact can be even more difficult to understand. Case management, along with PMM, provides an application that works from client intake through to client assessments in a streamlined, 360 view of the client. When configured appropriately, case managers spend their time with the clients rather than trying to remember where a client is in the process or what was discussed with the client last week. For nonprofit directors and CEOs, case management can provide an aggregate overview of the impact programs and services are making.

So, let's explore how to use case management for these use cases.

What is the use case for case management?

Humans are incredibly complex, so no one is surprised that caring for them can be complex as well. Case management provides tools that can streamline and connect all the bits and pieces of client care to help caregivers and their clients achieve their goals. At times, this process may be predicated by a certain date that's required for completion. Other caregiving activities may go on until the client reaches a specific milestone or individual goal. The variety of service organizations and the uniqueness of each individual makes thinking of a common case management tool impossible. How can one system cover all the nuances, plans, and successes?

The following sections outline a few scenarios where case management can be helpful.

Making sure children get one good meal a day

According to nokidhungry.org, as many as 13 million children in the United States live in *food-insecure* homes. The challenge for nonprofits who want to help eradicate hunger among children is that the child is not necessarily the client; the parent or the caregiver is. The organization is probably advocating for free school lunch programs and working with churches and civic groups to pack weekend food backpacks. Although the program's impact, as shown in *Chapter 3*, *Tracking Impact with the Program Management Module*, may be targeted toward children, the parents are the clients in a case management scenario.

So, how can technology help fulfill the immediate needs of these children while helping their parents learn to cook nutritious meals, effectively use the funds they have, and offer skills they need to distance themselves from poverty, which is the largest cause of childhood hunger? When there is more than one group that a nonprofit needs to track for impacts, such as children and their parents, case management can provide that framework.

Meeting immediate needs versus ongoing recovery, training, and empowerment

Every client interaction is important. Every client is different. Each client needs different help at different points in a well-thought-out organizational process that provides wonderful outcomes. How does a case manager keep all this information organized so that the appropriate information is available at the best time so that the client can progress? The parents and/or caregivers of the potentially hungry children are identified and in the Nonprofit Cloud system. Next, we need to quickly understand where each client is and help them achieve the next or the best milestone for their case.

Is the parent enrolled in a nutrition class or have they signed up to visit the free store? Are their immediate food needs being met? Maybe they are beyond those points and are moving into an economic empowerment program with training and learning skills for better employment opportunities. Each family moves at a different speed and the trajectory is not always linear. Clients may sign up for services provided by the organization outside of the **case management tool**. Salesforce's relational architecture provides the case manager with information on those outside activities as well, as shown in the following example.

Case management is specifically designed to track each touchpoint. With Salesforce Nonprofit Cloud and PMM as the foundation, everything is related so that case managers and organization executives can get a 360-degree view of a constituent. Plus, there may be **personally identifiable information (PII)** or other confidential information that needs to be protected:

Shop the Free Store!

Click the time on the specific day you want to reserve your time slot to shop the Free Store.

You will be asked to supply your name, email, and (optionally) cell number so we can remind you of your time slot.

Aug 15 – 21, 2021   month week day   < > today

1:00 PM	Mon 8/16	Tue 8/17	Wed 8/18	Thu 8/19	Fri 8/20	Sat 8/21
Start Date & Time: 8/16/2021 1:00 PM Slots available: 3	1:00 PM 9:00 AM	1:00 PM 9:00 AM	1:00 PM 9:00 AM	1:00 PM 9:00 AM	1:00 PM 9:00 AM	

Figure 4.1 – Example of outside activities where a client may participate. Efficiency and accountability spur the impact

The recent pandemic has increased the number of children who are in danger of being hungry. New clients are added every day to the already overloaded case managers. Being able to have streamlined processes and data inputs creates more accurate information and more helpful access to client information. If processes can be automated, it gives staff the time to do the things that can't be automated, such as having a one-on-one conversation with a client. Think of all the things that a case manager might do in a day:

- Make client appointments and follow up on expectations
- Put together a plan for a client's success
- Enroll a client in the next best step
- Report on a client's wellbeing to the organization team
- Connect a client with government or education services

And that doesn't include meeting with the clients themselves and noting the conversations, pain points, and concerns of the client. Working with clients can be a team effort and knowing who the last touchpoint for a client was or who on the team is responsible for the next step saves time and energy. Case management can meet these logistical challenges.

Tracking the impact of the organization on their mission

Everyone, and their specific case, is vitally important; how an organization is doing overall is also critical. Capturing and leveraging all the data associated with case management is a perfect use case for Salesforce. Making it possible for nonprofit organization clients to succeed is what case management is designed to do. For the organization, aggregating the data and reporting it to stakeholders is the penultimate step in the process.

Is the number of children in danger of going to bed hungry tonight dropping? Is the work the organization is doing decreasing the likelihood that any of those children are not being fed appropriately? Accurate data that's been analyzed accurately will present a holistic picture of successful outcomes, both individually and corporately. Successful outcomes will encourage new and more supporters and donors.

The addition of new stakeholders can increase impact. Case management provides standard reports, custom reports, and connects with Tableau for advanced reporting.

Key objects and features of case management

Case management use cases have many moving parts. Let's look at how the key objects and features in the Nonprofit Cloud case management product handle a variety of use cases. Don't forget that case management extends what is already in Salesforce. Standard objects include Accounts, Contacts, and Cases. Custom objects from NPSP and PMM are also there, as outlined in *Chapter 3, Tracking Impact with the Program Management Module*; the architecture even adds a bit of **Financial Service Cloud** into the mix with Action Plans. The full schema can be seen in the following diagram:

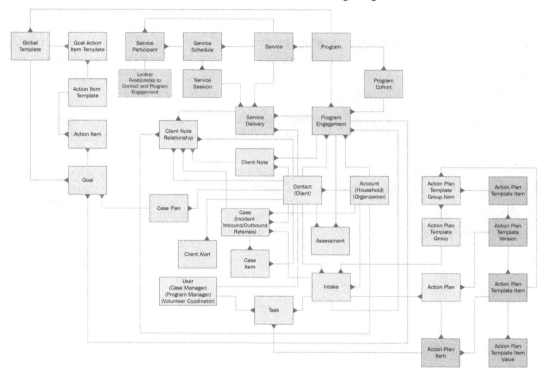

Figure 4.2 – Case management/PMM data architecture

The key objects in the case management/PMM data architecture provide the key features that are critical to streamlining the work of human services. Let's look at some specific features and the objects that are used.

Client intake and referrals

Depending on the organization's use case, clients come from two different sources:

- A person comes directly to the organization to request assistance
- A potential client is referred by another organization

Case management is configured to collect data either way. Often, a worker at the organization will create an **intake** record and fill that record in on the potential client:

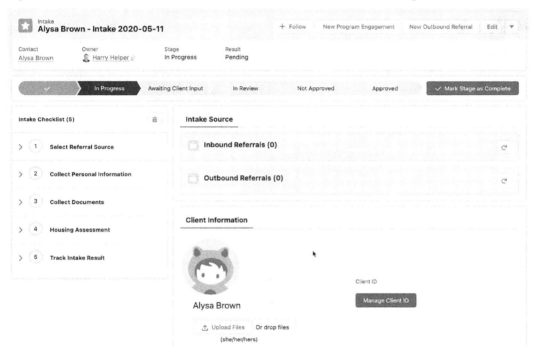

Figure 4.3 – A sample intake record showing the path and checklist functionality

Depending on the type of intake record that's created, a checklist is also created for the intake record. The progress of the intake record can be seen in the path, as shown in the preceding screenshot. The following screenshot shows an example of a case record:

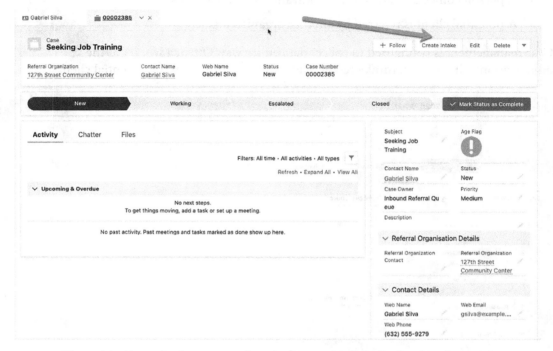

Figure 4.4 – Example of a case record used to create an inbound referral intake record

Inbound Referrals are initiated in a **case**. The **Create Intake** button, as shown in the preceding screenshot, is located on the case record and fills in the information on the newly created Intake record.

The Case Manager home page

Once the client's review of their intake record has been approved, they are assigned to case managers. The **Case Manager** home page, as shown in the following screenshot, is the one-stop shop for case managers. From this home page, the case manager can see or quickly navigate to the most frequently used tools in the case management application:

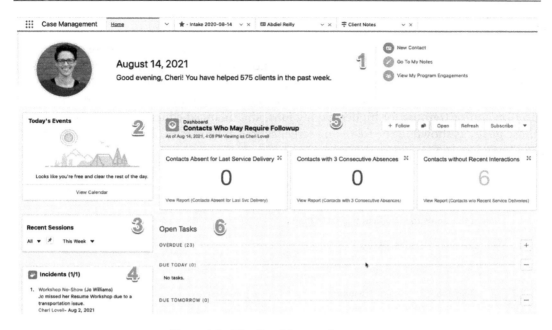

Figure 4.5 – The Case Manager home page

Let us see each of the components of the Case Manager home page:

1. In the top right-hand corner, there are links to create new **Contacts** and **Client Notes**, as well as view program engagements (from the PMM) for the case manager's clients.

2. **Today's Events** contains the case manager's calendar, including any client meetings.

3. Also from the PMM, **Recent Sessions** lets case managers easily track attendance.

4. **Incidents** tracks any unexpected or unplanned events in a client's timeline, such as injuries, behavioral issues, or emotional upsets.

5. The **Dashboard** area, which can be found on the right-hand side of the home page, shows how many clients have missed their last service delivery, had three consecutive absences, or do not have any recent interactions. Clicking **View Report** allows the case manager to drill into the specifics of each of these areas.

6. The **Open Tasks** portion of the home page is the case manager's checklist concerning client and program data. It can be broken into three areas based on the due date.

Now, let's understand what case plans are.

Case plans

An important part of a case manager's work is creating and updating client **case plans**. These comprehensive plans help case managers and clients work together to achieve goals. In the use case example of parents whose children lack adequate nutrition, the long-term care plan involves several goals: learning more about serving nutritious meals on a budget, education and/or training for higher-paying jobs, and financial education services. Each of those goals, as shown in the following screenshot, can be reached by choosing specific action items:

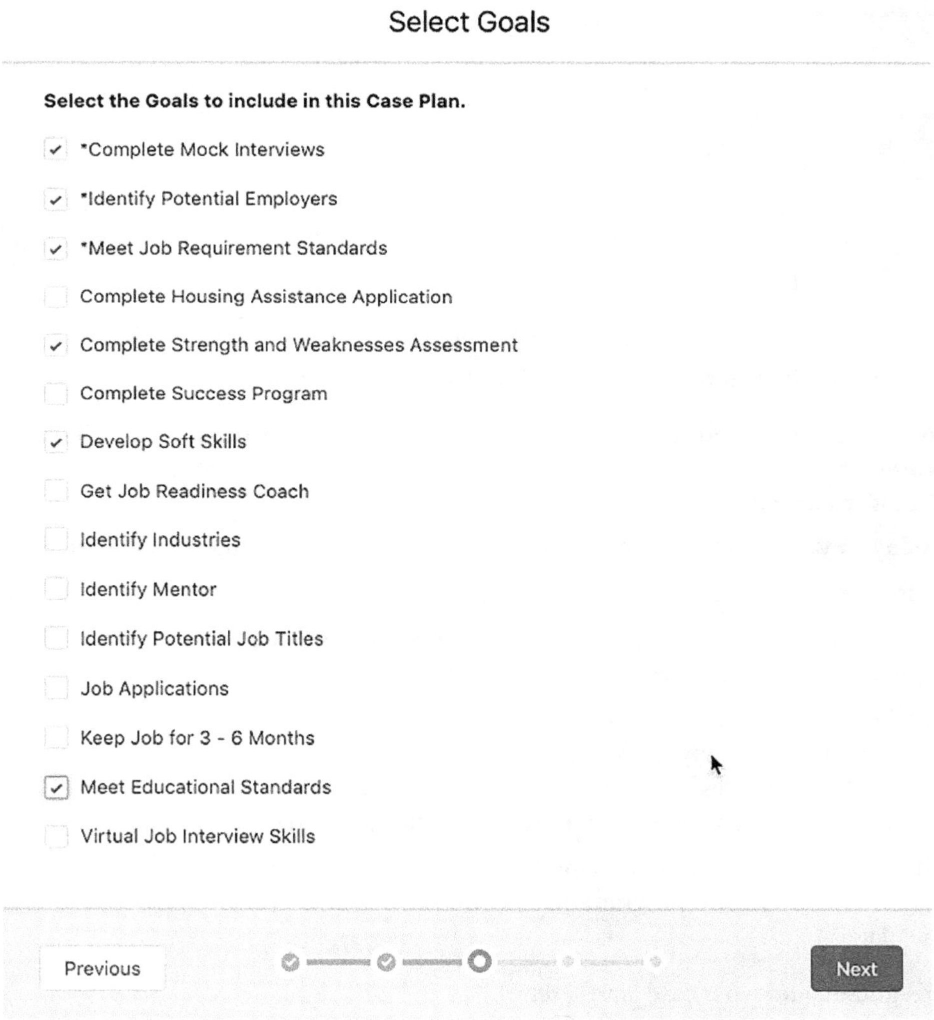

Select Goals

Select the Goals to include in this Case Plan.

- ✔ *Complete Mock Interviews
- ✔ *Identify Potential Employers
- ✔ *Meet Job Requirement Standards
- ☐ Complete Housing Assistance Application
- ✔ Complete Strength and Weaknesses Assessment
- ☐ Complete Success Program
- ✔ Develop Soft Skills
- ☐ Get Job Readiness Coach
- ☐ Identify Industries
- ☐ Identify Mentor
- ☐ Identify Potential Job Titles
- ☐ Job Applications
- ☐ Keep Job for 3 - 6 Months
- ✔ Meet Educational Standards
- ☐ Virtual Job Interview Skills

Previous   Next

Figure 4.6 – Creating a case plan from a template with choices for goals

There may be other items on a client's plan, but these are the three that are common to all clients. When the nonprofit uses **case plan templates**, as shown in the following screenshot, to create these goals and action items, the case managers can quickly create a new **case plan** for a client and then add additional goals and action items as needed:

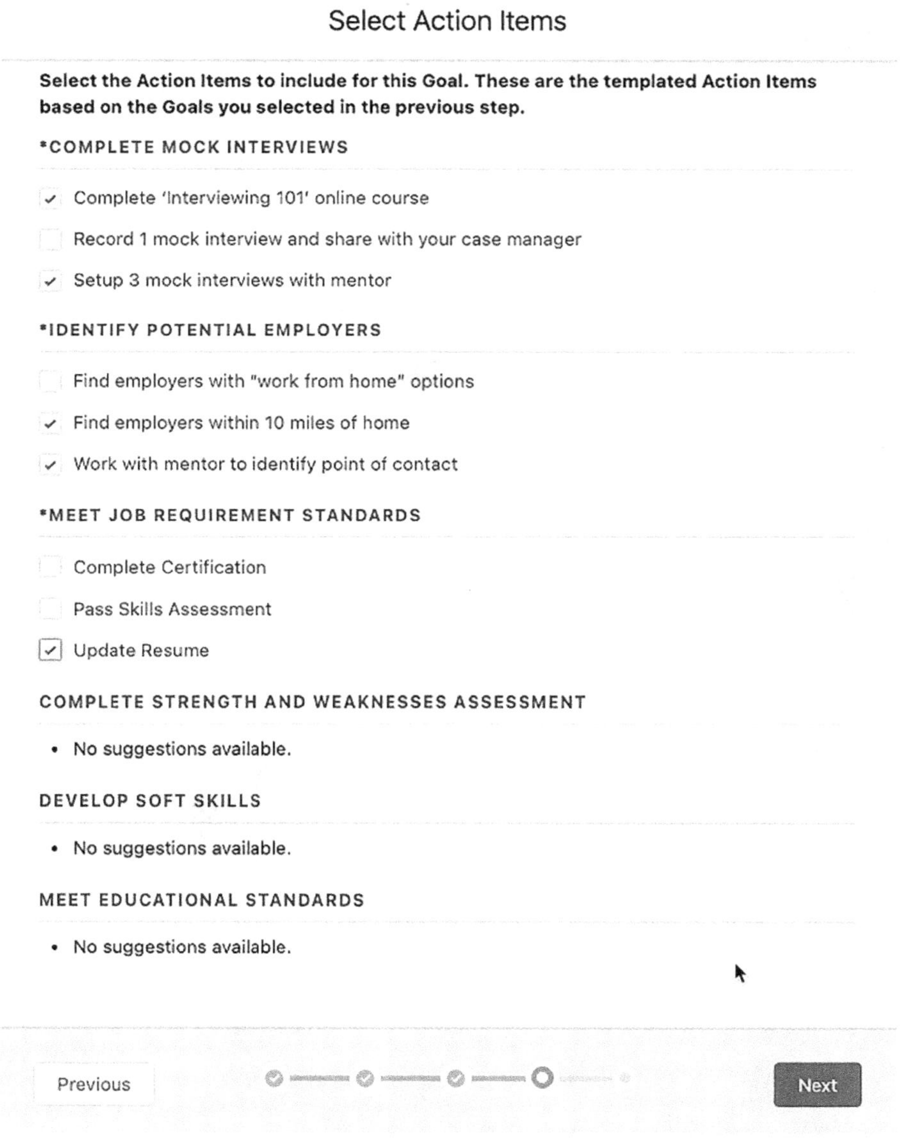

Select Action Items

Select the Action Items to include for this Goal. These are the templated Action Items based on the Goals you selected in the previous step.

*COMPLETE MOCK INTERVIEWS

- ✓ Complete 'Interviewing 101' online course
- ☐ Record 1 mock interview and share with your case manager
- ✓ Setup 3 mock interviews with mentor

*IDENTIFY POTENTIAL EMPLOYERS

- ☐ Find employers with "work from home" options
- ✓ Find employers within 10 miles of home
- ✓ Work with mentor to identify point of contact

*MEET JOB REQUIREMENT STANDARDS

- ☐ Complete Certification
- ☐ Pass Skills Assessment
- ✓ Update Resume

COMPLETE STRENGTH AND WEAKNESSES ASSESSMENT

- No suggestions available.

DEVELOP SOFT SKILLS

- No suggestions available.

MEET EDUCATIONAL STANDARDS

- No suggestions available.

Previous   Next

Figure 4.7 – Creating a case plan from a template with goal-dependent action items

Once the case plan has been created, each step is laid out so that it can be checked off as the steps are accomplished:

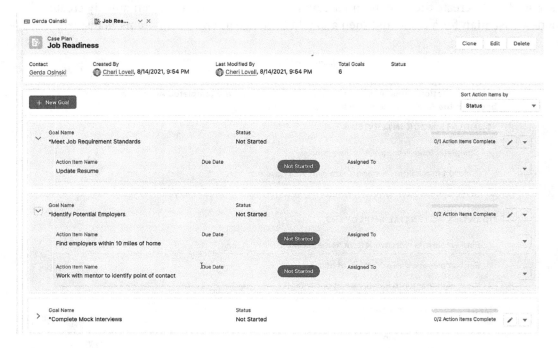

Figure 4.8 – A case plan built from a case plan template showing the goals and action items, as well as their level of completion

> **Note**
> New goals can be added as needed; see the + **New Goal** button in the preceding screenshot.

Case notes

Note-taking may be the most underappreciated skill of a case manager. While checking in each week with a client, the case manager takes notes of pertinent information during the conversation. Rather than interrupt the flow of the client by looking for specific fields, **case notes** are open text boxes that can be created in draft mode for later review. A sample case note is shown in the following screenshot:

Figure 4.9 – A case notes record for a meeting with the client regarding interview skills

Once the case note has been reviewed and the appropriate tasks have been created or updates have been made based on that interaction, the case manager can publish the case note as part of the client's record.

Assessments

Assessments are the quantifiable pieces of the case management puzzle. Using the built-in assessment tool, case managers can assign a score to record the client's progress. The assessment tool was built to be flexible enough to use in different ways based on the nonprofit's specific use case:

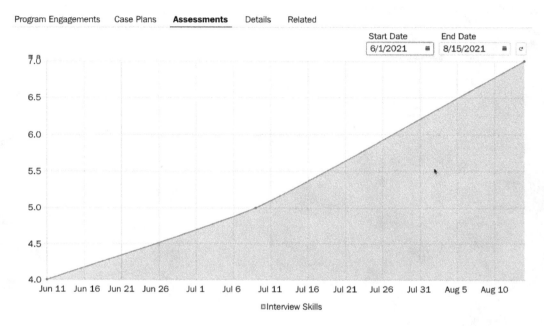

Figure 4.10 – A trendline and individual assessment-related list on the Contact record

For example, the score can be calculated by using the information that was collected during conversations with the client. Alternatively, the score could be a cumulative total based on a written assessment, with individually weighted scores for nutrition comprehension, budget food buying, and mathematics for cooking.

Assessments provide the foundation for impact measurement by tracking client progress over time.

Additional tools

Client alerts, **incidents**, and **watchlists** are shared tools and convey specific information on a client that is important for the team to know. For example, a client alert may signal a severe food allergy, or it may indicate that a client is currently on probation. Client alerts appear on the Contact record.

Incidents are generally not as time-sensitive as client alerts, but it is a way to record a potential challenge. An example of an incident may be a report stating that this client saw a spider in the interview room and almost fainted due to their fear of spiders. Documenting this information helps other workers at the nonprofit be better prepared. A watchlist can be used by a case manager to let the nonprofit staff know that the case manager is concerned for this client and that the client may need some special attention, particularly if the client has stopped interacting with the case manager or does not reply to outreach. Incidents and watchlists are generally surfaced on the **Case Manager** home page.

Tracking and reporting for case management

The **Case Manager** home page is a great example of visual tracking and reporting in the case management application. Case management comes with 23 pre-configured reports and four out-of-the-box dashboards that use those reports. Additionally, custom lightning components, such as the assessment trend chart shown in *Figure 4.10*, are included.

For advanced reporting, case management connects with Tableau. With a Tableau subscription, you can download Tableau's Dashboard Starters for ready-made dashboards that you can use to the organization's Salesforce instance. For case management, there are five different starters:

- Intake
- Clients
- Service Delivery
- Assessments
- Staff Capacity

Each Tableau dashboard compiles several datasets and can be filtered by specific fields and/or dates:

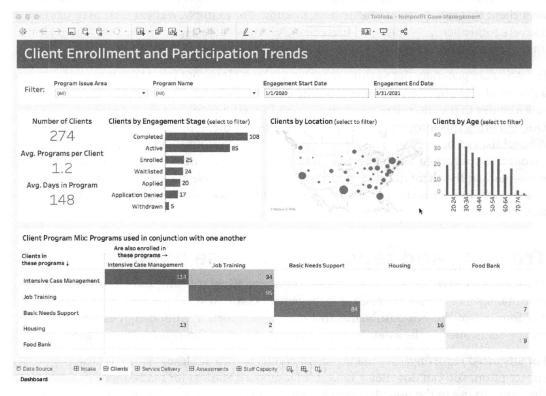

Figure 4.11 – Example of the Clients dashboard from Tableau's Dashboard Starters

Salesforce acquired Tableau in August 2019. Although Tableau is a paid product, there is the option for small nonprofits and NGOs to request that Tableau be donated for their use; you can find out more at `https://www.tableau.com/foundation`. The key to tracking and reporting is setting up case management appropriately to start and capture the data consistently. Creating the reports, whether you use Salesforce or Tableau, is a simple matter when the initial setup is done appropriately and the data is collected consistently.

Summary

Nonprofit Cloud's case management application is a paid addition that extends the capabilities of PMM. Case management provides tracking and reporting and case management for individual clients over some time. In the use case referenced at the beginning of this chapter, families are struggling with hunger. Case management picks up where program management leaves off; program management meets the immediate need of feeding a family, whereas case management creates a coaching and learning environment to teach families how to feed themselves better.

With case managers in mind, the critical record objects around goals and action items help create case plans so that case managers and clients can work together to move forward. The standard Salesforce Contact object acts as the center point of client work. As we discussed in *Chapter 3, Tracking Impact with the Program Management Module*, PMM adds Programs, Services, Service Schedules, Service Sessions, and Service Delivery to track attendance and engagement on behalf of the client. Client notes allow case managers to capture qualitative information, while assessments provide quantitative data.

The **Case Manager** home page places all the pertinent information a click away. Adding the advanced reporting and visualization capabilities of Tableau and Tableau's Dashboard Starters accelerates progress with actionable data for case managers and nonprofit executives.

Nonprofit Cloud provides the NPSP for fundraising and builds on that with the program management module and case management for programs. In the next chapter, we will look at an additional set of objects that provides the right tools for engaging with and managing volunteers.

Further learning

To learn more about the topics that were covered in this chapter, take a look at the following resources:

- Nonprofit Case Cloud Management Documentation: `https://powerofus.force.com/s/article/CM-Documentation`

- Human Services with Nonprofit Cloud Case Management: `https://trailhead.salesforce.com/content/learn/modules/human-services-with-nonprofit-cloud-case-management`

- You will need the following public data dictionary for case management: `https://quip.com/DiZCAUTDzh2Q#EFXACAPmpb3`

5
Tracking Volunteer Impact

Volunteers for Salesforce, sometimes abbreviated to **V4S**, helps nonprofits manage, engage, and track volunteer information. Almost every nonprofit that offers programs or services needs volunteers to power those programs and/or services. Sometimes, it is a few volunteers, while other times, it is hundreds or thousands of volunteers. V4S was designed to manage volunteer relationships at scale and record their interaction with your nonprofit organization. V4S is a free, open source, managed package from Salesforce that's designed to be used in conjunction with NPSP. V4S does not come with **Nonprofit Success Pack (NPSP)**; it must be installed separately.

In this chapter, we're going to cover the following main topics:

- Overview of Volunteers for Salesforce use cases

- How does Volunteers for Salesforce work in NPSP?

- The volunteer interface for Volunteers for Salesforce

In this chapter, we will explore several different use cases for Volunteers for Salesforce depending on the requirements a nonprofit might have; the actual data architecture of the Volunteers for Salesforce app; and the options for the volunteer interface for Volunteers for Salesforce.

Overview of volunteers for Salesforce use cases

Volunteers come in all shapes, sizes, ages, and colors. Nonprofit organizations utilize and engage volunteers in many ways. Because V4S is open source and it is native to Salesforce, it can be configured and customized to fit a myriad of organizational needs. There are several critical distinctions to make to apply the best V4S design for a nonprofit. Let's explore some of the specific use cases and considerations where V4S works best for nonprofit organizations.

How are volunteers assigned to jobs?

Just as volunteers are different, so are the organizations where they volunteer. Nonprofit organizations may prefer a level of control over which volunteer should be assigned to a particular job. Or, depending on the job, nonprofits may allow volunteers to assign themselves.

Big Brothers Big Sisters (`https://www.bbbs.org/`) is a nonprofit organization whose mission is to create and support one-to-one mentoring relationships that ignite the power and promise of youth. The process of becoming a Big Brother or a Big Sister includes meeting specific needs and criteria, completing an application, and interviewing. The entire application and verification process for a volunteer to become a big brother or a big sister happens before Big Brothers Big Sisters begins to search for a little brother or sister.

V4S can be configured to capture volunteer information to start the process of becoming a Big; then, when a match is made, the coordinator can assign you as a Big Brother or Big Sister so that they can track the hours you have spent mentoring little brothers and sisters in the program:

Volunteer coordinators can report on volunteers, shifts, jobs, and hours with one of the many reports that come in the V4S package:

Report	Description
Active Volunteers	List of contacts with Volunteer Status set to Active.
Available Volunteer Jobs	All Volunteer Jobs that are ongoing or still need volunteers.
Hours detached from their VRS	A list of Volunteer Hours that were created by a Volunteer Recurrence Schedule (VRS), but were detached because they no longer meet the VRS's criteria.
Inactive Volunteers	List of contacts with Volunteer Status set to Inactive.
New Sign Ups – Contacts	List of contacts with Volunteer Status set to New Sign Up.
New Sign Ups – Leads	List of leads with Volunteer Status set to New Sign Up.
Prospective Volunteers	List of contacts with Volunteer Status set to Prospect.
Recent Volunteers	List of volunteers whose Last Volunteer Date occurred in the past 120 days.
Shifts detached from their JRS	A list of Volunteer Shifts that were created by a Job Recurrence Schedule (JRS), but were detached from the JRS because they no longer meet the JRS's criteria.
Top Volunteers by Lifetime Hours	FOR DASHBOARD: List of total hours a volunteer has worked.
Top Volunteers by Recent Hours	FOR DASHBOARD: List of total hours a volunteer has worked during a specified period.
Unassigned Volunteers	Contacts with either Active, Prospect, or New Sign Up set as the Volunteer Status, who don't have current Volunteer Hours assigned.
Unique Volunteers	The total amount of unique volunteers by campaign and job.
Upcoming Shifts Needing Volunteers	A list of shifts in the future that don't have the desired number of volunteers signed up.
Upcoming Shifts with Volunteers	A list of upcoming shifts with volunteers that have been confirmed. This can be used as a check-in sheet.
Upcoming Volunteers	A list of volunteers who have upcoming Volunteers Hours (signed up for a shift or job) in the next 30 days.

Report	Description
Volunteer Hours by Account/Org	Total Volunteer Hours for all time, by account/org.
Volunteer Hours by Campaign	Total Volunteers Hours for all time, by campaign.
Volunteer Hours by Job	Total Volunteer Hours for all time, by volunteer Job.
Volunteer Hours by Month	FOR DASHBOARD: Total Volunteer Hours for the current and previous calendar years, grouped by month.
Volunteer Hours by Month Matrix	A matrix report that shows the sum of hours volunteered by month for each volunteer.
Volunteer Hours for Dashboard	FOR DASHBOARD: Total Volunteer Hours for each volunteer.
Volunteer Jobs with Shift Summary	Lists all jobs (grouped by campaign), their shifts, volunteers signed up, the desired number of volunteers, and the volunteers that are still needed.
Volunteer Roster	Lists all volunteers for the specified campaign, job, and shift (used by Roster buttons on the shift calendar).
Volunteers Active Last Month	List of volunteers who completed Volunteer Hours last month.
Volunteers by Account	List of all volunteers, grouped by account.
Volunteers by Availability	List of all volunteers, grouped by availability (the value in the Volunteer Availability field on the Contact record).
Volunteers by Skill	List of all volunteers, grouped by skill.
Volunteers Daily Roster	List of upcoming volunteers by shift start date and time.
Volunteers Last Month	FOR DASHBOARD: Volunteers who completed a Shift in the last month.
Volunteers This Year	FOR DASHBOARD: Volunteers who completed a shift this year.
Volunteers with a Volunteer Status	List of contacts that have Volunteer Status set to any value.

Table 5.1 – Standard reports included with the V4S package

These reports are the standard reports that come packaged with V4S. They can be edited to meet the specific needs of the organization or the organization can create new ones entirely.

Volunteers signup

A nonprofit community theatre is looking for a way to schedule volunteers who want to audition for parts in an upcoming play. They have specific dates and times that are available for volunteering and they can only accept 1-2 volunteers during any time block. Volunteers need to be able to sign up for a specific time slot. V4S's calendar functionality can be made available for volunteers to sign up:

Figure 5.1 – V4S calendar on a public web page

As volunteers sign up on the public web page, this information is captured in Salesforce. These volunteers and their activity can also be seen in the reports listed previously in this section.

When you have a few volunteers

Some nonprofit organizations have a small number of dedicated volunteers who come back week after week to do the same job that they love. Other nonprofits have disparate and different volunteer jobs that may have only one shift or may only volunteer rarely. Another group of nonprofit organizations may have Volunteer jobs of both types.

Doing the same job repeatedly

Meals on Wheels (`https://www.mealsonwheelsamerica.org/`) is a nonprofit organization designed to improve the health and quality of the life of the seniors they serve so that no one is left hungry or isolated. Local community volunteers deliver meals daily. Most Meals on Wheels volunteers deliver while going the same route every week. 59% of home-delivered meal recipients live alone, and for many of them, the volunteer delivering the meal is often the only person they will see that entire day.

V4S allows volunteers to sign up for recurring schedules to track the hours they contribute on an ongoing basis. This route can take a volunteer 2 hours to complete or 4 hours:

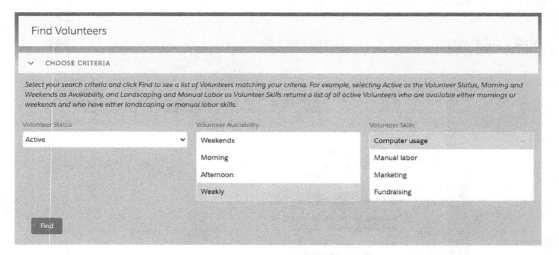

Figure 5.2 – Volunteers can indicate that they are available for long-term, weekly shifts

Doing random jobs on an ad hoc basis

Some nonprofit organizations have a variety of Volunteer jobs that range from pro bono assistance for a media campaign to answering telephones to sorting clothes or packing grocery boxes. Other nonprofit organizations have several programs that require different skills, depending on the volunteer job. V4S allows nonprofits to create different Volunteer jobs with different shifts and different skills, or even no skills at all:

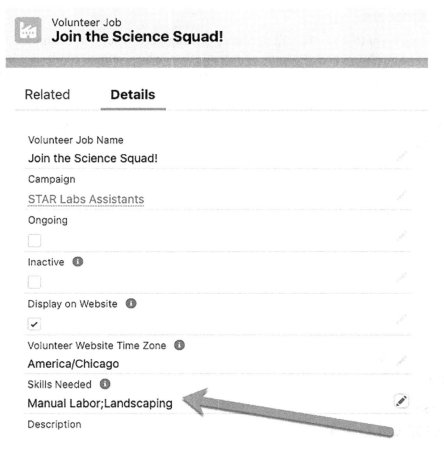

Figure 5.3 – V4S provides customizable options for Skills Needed, as well as whether the job is ongoing or not

When you have a lot of volunteers

Everything so far has involved a relatively small number of volunteers – probably less than 1,000 per year. But what happens when a nonprofit organization needs to scale? That is, when volunteer numbers grow exponentially, for whatever reason? Let's look at some use cases that nonprofits might have to use V4S in these situations.

Event volunteers

Any large-scale event that a nonprofit produces is going to require a large number of volunteers in a short period. Imagine an organization whose annual fundraiser is a triathlon. Just for the day of the event, volunteers are needed as safety marshals, at the hydration stations, as wetsuit strippers, in the athlete food tent, as timing assistants, at the aid stations, and even to check in on other volunteers. One such event required 700 volunteers on the actual day of the triathlon. If the event is over several days, the number of volunteers increases into the thousands very quickly. V4S helps organizers scale the volunteer effort by allowing volunteers to assign themselves to one or more shifts in the most needed areas:

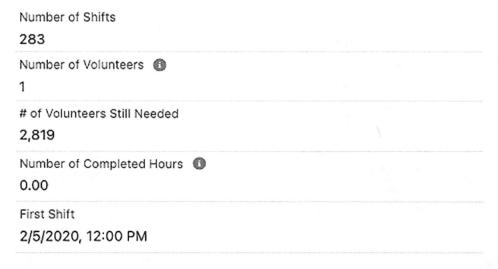

Figure 5.4 – V4S allows for shifts in volume and volunteer participation to scale

Disaster volunteers

Unfortunately, disaster volunteers are a common need in today's world. Everyone, from the American Red Cross to state volunteer agencies to local volunteer management centers, is called upon to manage volunteers in times of disaster. As soon as disaster strikes, volunteers want to help, regardless of the type of disaster. Generally, all those wonderful helpers pour into an area within the first 24-48 hours when the professionals are still working to assess the situation. Volunteers often don't understand why they can't be of assistance when they are ready, willing, and able. Three to six months after the hurricane or the tornado or the forest fire is when most volunteers are needed. V4S allows volunteers to share their desire to help so that nonprofits can capture that information, along with their specific skills, and reach back out to them when the time is appropriate. V4S uses the **Campaign** object to add volunteers (that is, **Campaign Members**) to the campaign:

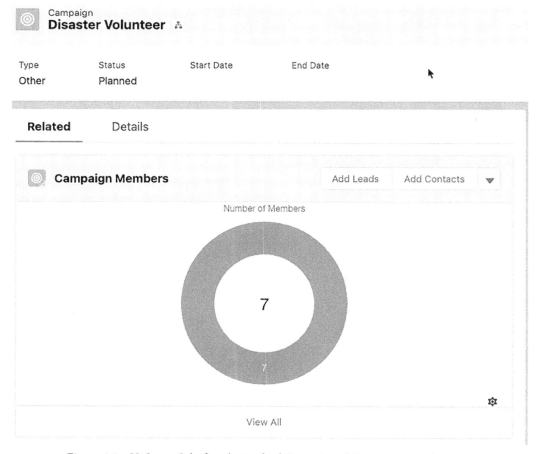

Figure 5.5 – V4S uses Salesforce's standard Campaign object to group volunteers

How does Volunteers for Salesforce work in NPSP?

V4S is not included in NPSP because it doesn't have to be. V4S utilizes the standard Salesforce objects; that is, **Contact**, **Lead**, and **Campaign**. Then, it adds a mere five more custom objects, plus a few fields, to the standard objects listed. There is a lot of power in a very simple application:

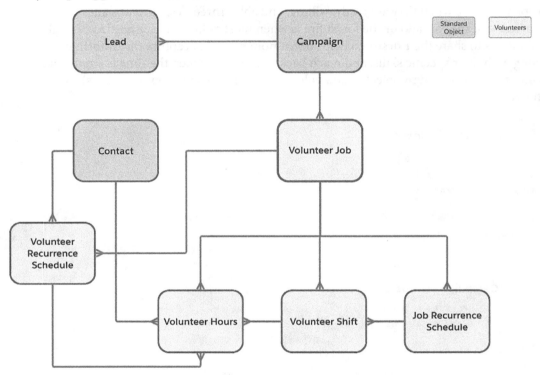

Figure 5.6 – V4S entity-relationship diagram

With this architecture, you can begin to see how V4S handles all the use cases we discussed earlier.

The standard Salesforce objects, **Contacts** and **Leads**, are used to track volunteers. A **Lead** is a volunteer who expressed interest in a specific volunteer campaign, such as the disaster volunteer. **Contacts** are volunteers who have signed up to perform a specific job or shift. **Campaigns**, another standard Salesforce object, is used to track volunteer engagements.

How does V4S use contacts?

V4S adds new fields to the **Contact** record. Each of the fields has a specific use in capturing and sorting information on volunteer engagement. Let's take a look:

- **Volunteer Status**: This is a picklist field that contains the standard options of **Active, Inactive, New Signup,** and **Prospective**.

- **Volunteer Hours**: This field is a rollup field where the volunteer's total completed hours are calculated.

- **Volunteer Organization**: If a volunteer is working on behalf of an organization, company, or group, this information is stored here.

- **Volunteer Skills**: This multi-picklist field is used to denote specific skills that a volunteer has indicated they possess.

- **First Volunteer Date**: This is another formula field that's used to capture the start of a volunteer's service.

- **Last Volunteer Date**: This is an additional formula field that's used to indicate the most recent date of the volunteer's service.

Additional picklist and multi-picklist values may be added to these fields based on the nonprofit's use case. Other custom fields may be added as well; see the following screenshot of a Contact record:

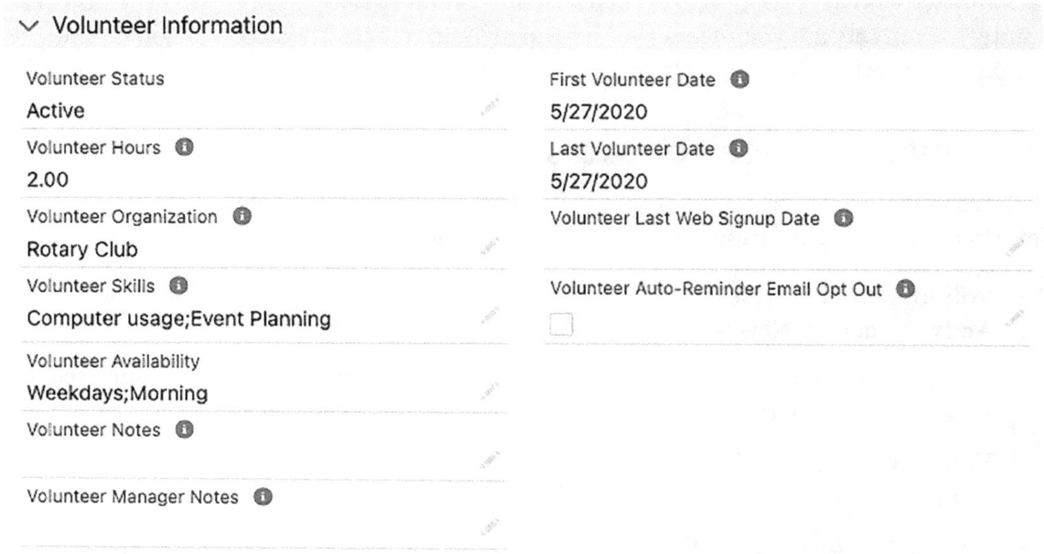

Figure 5.7 – Volunteer fields added by V4S to the Contact object

Volunteer coordinators can deactivate volunteers by changing their contact status. Volunteers and coordinators can also update their skills and availability. This functionality makes V4S more flexible to configure for specific use cases.

Campaigns and V4S

V4S has also added a few fields to campaigns to sum the data around volunteers into the Campaign record itself. These are almost all number fields. Let's take a look at these:

- **Number of Volunteers**: A rollup summary field (SUM Volunteer Job)
- **Volunteer Completed Hours**: A rollup summary field (SUM Volunteer Job)
- **Volunteers Still Needed**: A rollup summary field (SUM Volunteer Job)
- **Volunteer jobs**: A rollup summary field (COUNT Volunteer Job)
- **Volunteer Shifts**: A rollup summary field (SUM Volunteer Job)
- **Volunteer Website Time Zone**: Picklist values for time zones

The rollup summary values make it very easy to create reports and dashboards to easily see the level of engagement in volunteer campaigns. Rollups are not instantaneous; they are scheduled to run nightly:

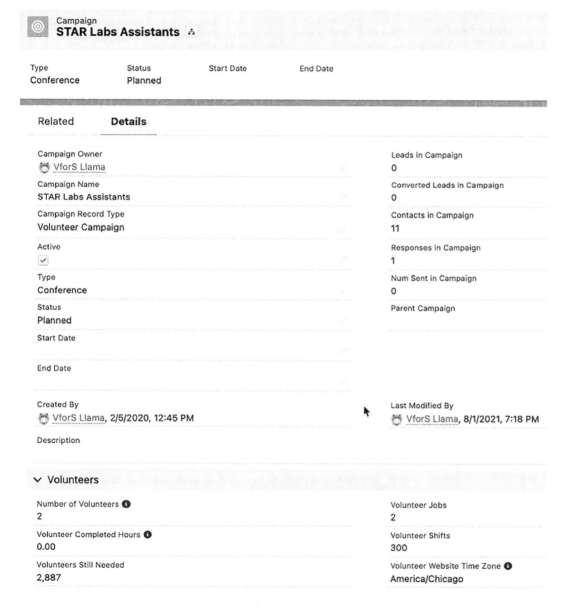

Figure 5.8 – Salesforce standard Campaign object with V4S custom fields

The custom objects of V4S

The objects that V4S adds to Salesforce via its open source package are as follows:

- **Volunteer Job**: Holds information about the high-level volunteer job itself and must look up to a campaign.

- **Volunteer Shift**: Holds information on date- and time-specific Volunteer jobs and looks up to a Volunteer Job.

- **Volunteer Hours**: Holds the quantitative information on the number of hours that have been volunteered for any given Volunteer Shift or Volunteer Job.

- **Job Recurrence Schedule** – Holds information on the Volunteer jobs that happen repeatedly.

- **Volunteer Recurrence Schedule**: Holds information on volunteers who sign up for the repeated, or recurrent, Volunteer jobs.

Jobs and shifts work together with campaigns to form the underlying framework for volunteers:

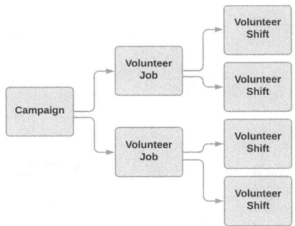

Figure 5.9 – Hierarchy of objects for V4S

The volunteer interface for Volunteers for Salesforce

There are two standard options for the volunteer interface for Volunteers for Salesforce:

- Website integration
- **Experience Cloud**

As we discussed earlier, providing volunteers with an easy-to-use interface is an important part of engaging volunteers, as well as disseminating the responsibility of signing up and tracking hours. If you don't have experience with website integration or with building out Experience Cloud, the volunteer interface can be the most difficult part of implementing V4S.

Website integration

There are detailed instructions in the V4S documentation concerning what and how you can integrate V4S pages into a nonprofit's website; we will look at this in more depth in *Chapter 11, Configuring Additional Features and Security*, when we go through all the configuration steps. The short story is that you can create an IFRAME tag and share that with the website developer, who will insert it into the nonprofit's web pages:

> **Note**
> Out-of-the-box functionality does not provide mobile responsive IFRAMEs for V4S.

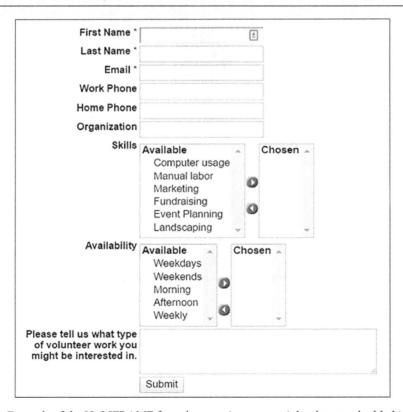

Figure 5.10 – Example of the V4S IFRAME for volunteer signup once it has been embedded into a website

V4S via Experience Cloud

V4S requires **Partner Experience Cloud** licenses for volunteers because campaigns are a part of the process. There is a new SKU for these Experience Cloud licenses from Salesforce for Nonprofit Cloud users. Be aware that there is an additional cost for the free V4S package if the nonprofit chooses to use Experience Cloud. Then, there is the additional effort of building out the Experience Cloud interface – that is another certification entirely. Additional information on Experience Cloud can be found here: `https://trailhead.salesforce.com/credentials/experiencecloudconsultant`.

Learning to build Experience Cloud interfaces is beyond the scope of the Nonprofit Cloud certification:

Figure 5.11 – Example of a V4S volunteer interface built into Experience Cloud

Summary

Although V4S is a relatively simple package, it is highly flexible and very customizable so that it can meet several different use cases and business processes that nonprofits have for volunteer engagement and management. V4S can automate standard processes, such as collecting contact information, providing a dynamic calendar of volunteer opportunities for volunteers to choose from, and sending volunteer notifications.

V4S is scalable within the standard Salesforce limits of API calls and records. It works best with NPSP but can be a standalone product as well. V4S pages for registration and signup and volunteer hour reporting can be integrated into an existing website, or nonprofits can use Experience Cloud to build a unique volunteer experience for their users.

V4S rounds out the triumvirate of nonprofits: fundraising, program management, and volunteers. We have covered a variety of use cases where a nonprofit might use Volunteers for Salesforce to engage with and manage volunteers, regardless of whether volunteers sign up for shifts or are assigned, whether there are many or few volunteers, and whether the volunteers sign up for one shift or ongoing shifts. You should now have a better understanding of the architecture of Volunteers for Salesforce and how it works to handle the data for recording volunteers, the shifts they work, and the hours they serve. Besides this, we discussed the two current Salesforce options for presenting this information to volunteers: IFRAMEs and Experience Cloud.

What else do nonprofits need? In the next chapter, we'll see what is available to round out the tools that nonprofits may need to automate their business processes. In *Chapter 6, What Else Is Needed from Nonprofit Cloud?*, we will look at Grantmaking and Grants Management, Marketing and Engagement, and Elevate and the Accounting Subledger.

Further reading

Take a look at the following resources to learn more about the topics that were covered in this chapter:

- Manage Volunteers for Nonprofits: `https://trailhead.salesforce.com/content/learn/trails/nonprofit_volunteer`
- Volunteers for Salesforce Documentation: `https://powerofus.force.com/s/article/V4S-Documentation`
- This book's GitHub repository: `https://github.com/SalesforceFoundation/Volunteers-for-Salesforce`
- The Data Dictionary for Volunteers for Salesforce: `https://salesforce.quip.com/FEp0AOdWp5tc`

6
What Else Is Needed from Nonprofit Cloud?

Nonprofit Cloud is designed to facilitate and automate a variety of nonprofit functions and support their missions. In this book, we have looked at use cases and functionality for **Nonprofit Success Pack** (**NPSP**), the foundation for Nonprofit Cloud, related to fundraising and program management. We have addressed how to extend program management for human services and how **Volunteers for Salesforce** (**V4S**) works for volunteer management. At this point, you might imagine we have covered all the use cases.

However, as we all know, Mr. Ron Popeil, the legendary advertising guru, often said, "*Hey! But wait, there's more!*" In this chapter, we're going to address use cases and overviews for the following:

- What facilitates grantmaking and grants management?
- Extended capabilities for fundraising and accounting for funds

There are over 1.5 million registered nonprofits in the **United States** (**US**). Thousands of those are grantmaking foundations, some are private family foundations, and others are publicly funded. Many foundations focus on one specific area of impact, while others cover a wide variety of causes. We will explore how the **grantmaking and grants management** tools in Nonprofit Cloud address this flexibility.

Marketing and engagement for nonprofits also vary significantly. No matter the form of communication, engaging constituents of all kinds is a critical need for nonprofits. The constituents may be donors, volunteers, or advocates; the goal may be moving prospects to givers, or it may be encouraging donors to move to a higher level of giving or volunteers to a high level of engagement. We will learn how marketing and engagement tools can automate much of the work that needs to be done in this area.

As a registered nonprofit, the **Internal Revenue Service** (**IRS**) requires the filing of appropriate documents each year for nonprofits to report on their financial activities. As such, nonprofits must have a formal accounting system. Nonprofits using Nonprofit Cloud and NPSP track giving data in Salesforce; however, actual cash income and/or donations are tracked using the accounting system. We will look at the value of syncing those two systems and **automating donations**.

What facilitates grantmaking and grants management?

Many nonprofits and most foundations administer, receive, or manage grants in some form or fashion. Whether making or receiving grants, there are always many data points to track and report on to continue funding or receiving grants. **OFM** is a basic grants management tool, and the **Nonprofit Cloud Grants Management** package is a more robust extension of this tool.

Managing grantmaking and outbound funds

OFM is a product of the Open Source Commons, a Salesforce community of mission-driven individuals working together to solve the world's most challenging problems. Through sprints that happen several times per year, OFM was conceived, created, and passed through the security review of Salesforce AppExchange to be made generally available for nonprofits.

The OFM logo is shown here:

Figure 6.1 – OFM logo from Open Source Commons

What is the use case?

Any nonprofit that manages outgoing funds, such as grants and scholarships, understands how many moving parts are involved. A local school foundation is a great example. They request information from teachers who are looking for small classroom grants for specific projects, and they administer scholarships. What is the best way to manage the collection of information from prospective grantees and scholarship recipients? Once they receive that information, it needs to be reviewed and funding requesters need to be notified. Then, the foundation decides what amount of money goes where and allocates and distributes it appropriately. However, most money comes with *strings*—those bits and pieces of information that the grantee or fund recipient must report back to the foundation to follow their funding guidelines.

How OFM helps

OFM helps organizations manage and track funding requests and outgoing funds by adding a new layer of custom objects and fields that work in conjunction with Salesforce and in both the NPSP and **Education Data Architecture (EDA)** environments.

You can see an **entity-relationship (ER)** diagram for OFM here:

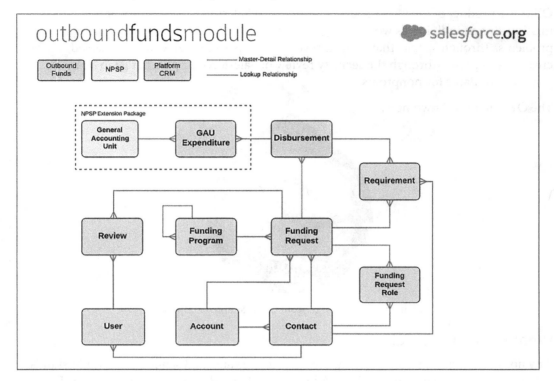

Figure 6.2 – OFM ER diagram

The custom objects, listed in green in the OFM ER diagram, work together in the following way for this application:

- **Funding Program**—The foundation of OFM, the program can be thematic or strategic and allows for a hierarchy of programs.

- **Funding Request**—This object contains the data gathered from an application requesting funds.

- **Funding Request Role**—This is a junction object that provides a way to relate one or more contacts to a funding request.

- **Review**—This object holds tracked information from reviewers on funding requests.

- **Requirement**—This object holds the deliverables that must happen in the approval or closing process of grantmaking.

- **Disbursement**—This object is where actual outgoing funds are tracked.

- **GAU Expenditure**—This is a junction object to connect a disbursement to a **general accounting unit** (**GAU**) to track the appropriate disbursement allocation.

> **Note**
> **GAU Expenditure** is available by installing the NPSP extension package.

To explore the use of OFM, consider a foundation that has funds available to impact the area of childhood hunger. The foundation invites a nonprofit to apply for funds to buy snacks for an after-school program. The status in the following screenshot shows that the nonprofit has been invited but not yet replied to. Notice that the foundation can track reviews when the nonprofits apply, the amount disbursed, and the requirements of the grant:

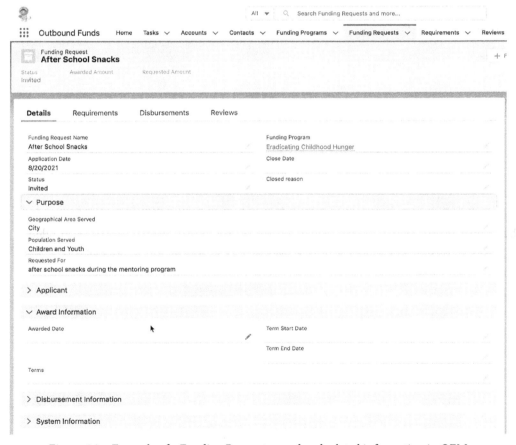

Figure 6.3 – Example of a Funding Request record and related information in OFM

Extending grantmaking capabilities

Grants Management is a paid offering from Salesforce to extend the capabilities of OFM with one additional custom object and an action plan template, an action plan, and document checklist objects from the Salesforce platform.

The additional custom object used by Grants Management is the **verification check** object. The verification check object allows you to track documents needed, requested, and received for an organization that is requesting funding. You can see an example of this in the following screenshot:

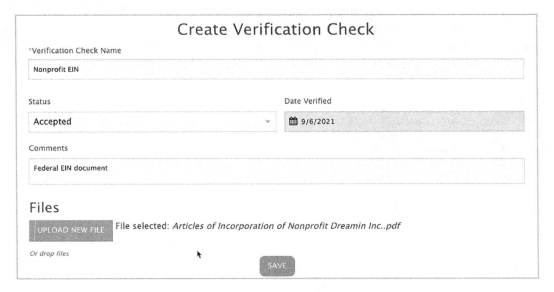

Figure 6.4 – Example of a verification check entry

If the grantmaking business process is particularly complex or information is compiled over a long period, the verification check checklist helps consistently manage the process.

Extended capabilities for fundraising and accounting for funds

To truly give a nonprofit a 360-degree view of constituents, Salesforce offers the following two additional paid products that are new as of 2020-2021:

- **Elevate**

- **Accounting Subledger**

Elevate extends fundraising capabilities, particularly in relation to Experience Cloud. The Accounting Subledger product helps prepare data for migration to external accounting sources.

Elevate – a new way to give to nonprofits

Elevate is a new paid product from Salesforce. It integrates with a variety of payment providers as well as with Salesforce NPSP (and with the Salesforce EDA as well). It has out-of-the-box donation forms called **Giving Pages** and is designed for mobile-first applications.

Accounting Subledger

Accounting Subledger is a paid product from Salesforce. The goal of Accounting Subledger is to prepare donor data for external accounting systems. This streamlines and deduplicates processes associated with donations and with accounting for those donations. As a nonprofit, fundraisers enter information regarding donations in Salesforce, whereas the financial team enters information in an accounting system; thus, the nonprofit information is not in sync. Accounting Subledger allows Salesforce to be the **single source of truth** (**SSOT**) while making it easy to export data to any accounting system that allows imports of data.

Summary

For grantmaking foundations, automating requests for grant proposals, grants requests, grant disbursements, and grant requirements can be handled by the Open Source Commons OFM and Grants Management. The flexibility of the OFM architecture allows grantmaking organizations to customize the system to meet their specific needs within its framework. The Grants Management package extends the functionality by providing verification checks.

Nonprofit Cloud offers a variety of levels for marketing and engagement, depending on the resources the nonprofit has and how complex the nonprofit's marketing and engagement plans are. From campaigns that come as a part of Power of Us donations, many nonprofits can do rudimentary email marketing campaigns. For more automation and more sophisticated emails and templates, Pardot provides nonprofits with those options. For nonprofits who need the highest level of marketing and engagement, Marketing Cloud for Nonprofits provides all the tools, including building personalized journeys for constituents, integration with Google Analytics, and all the true **business-to-consumer (B2C)** or, in this case, nonprofit-to-constituent moves management that is available, including integrating with the new payment system, Elevate.

Remember that at the beginning of the chapter, we discussed the fact that as a registered nonprofit, the IRS requires nonprofits to file the appropriate documents each year to report on their financial activities. Reconciling donor information in Salesforce with accounting information in another system has traditionally been a time-consuming manual process. With Accounting Subledger, we learned how this tool prepares Salesforce data for import into a variety of accounting systems. This one tool makes the donor and accounting process more efficient and diminishes entry errors. It also provides one SOT for a nonprofit organization and keeps fundraisers and accounting in sync.

We've explored the options that exist to help nonprofits automate their work in Salesforce. **Domain Expertise** counts for 20% of the **Nonprofit Cloud Consultant** exam.

In the next chapter, we will begin to learn about change management, governance, and tools for organizational alignment. These are critical pieces of the **Nonprofit Cloud Consultant** certification section on **Implementation Strategies and Best Practices**, which makes up 21% of the total questions.

Further reading

To follow along with this chapter, you will require the following:

- GitHub repository for **Outbound Funds Module (OFM)**:

```
https://github.com/SalesforceFoundation/OutboundFundsModule
```

- Data dictionary for OFM:

```
https://quip.com/z0hzAXpD8Da9#eDQACAp0LTt
```

Section 2: Get Set – Correlating Need with Nonprofit Cloud Tools

Now that you have a basic understanding of the building blocks of Nonprofit Cloud, let's dig a little deeper into how to work with an organization to tailor Nonprofit Cloud to its needs. This section contains the following chapters:

7
Is Change Difficult for an Organization?

The most difficult part of creating something new is often not the technology itself but creating an atmosphere that will welcome change. You may be asking why we are not jumping right into studying the installation, implementation, and configuration of all the great building blocks in Nonprofit Cloud. The fact that the certification weights the consultant work so heavily should give you a hint. Years of hands-on experience validate that setting the scene for success before we begin is critical.

In this chapter, we're going to address use cases and overviews for the following areas:

- Organizational alignment and change management
- Governance basics and **centers of excellence (COEs)**
- User adoption and metrics for success

In this chapter, we will learn to assist an organization with change management and create organizational alignment on the goals of implementing Nonprofit Cloud, examining how decisions will be made for Nonprofit Cloud and the overall Salesforce instance. We will also learn to assist with user adoption, as well as help establish metrics for the success of the implementation.

Organizational alignment and change management

During 2020 and 2021, the pandemic created vast amounts of change. The pandemic was an outside influence that exerted immense amounts of pressure on people and organizations to change—the way they worked, did business, entertained themselves, and more. At its worst, change can be painful and, at its best, it can be uncomfortable. Most organizations are willing to limp along with a system that is painful to use because they are familiar with it. If an organization has decided to implement something new, such as Nonprofit Cloud, the consultant has the unique opportunity to help make the transition less painful and more helpful.

Sometimes, change management can feel like pushing a boulder up a hill, as depicted here:

We'll now look at some best practices for managing change by aligning the organization's goals for successfully implementing Nonprofit Cloud.

Organizational alignment

First things first: how do you get a group of people aligned around what their goals and strategies are for a project? Nonprofits have worthwhile goals in mind when they begin. The goal might be to feed hungry children or provide support for people with leukemia or help families become homeowners. **Organizational alignment** means planning how the organization reaches that goal together as a team.

Nonprofit Dreamin case study

For **Nonprofit Dreamin** (https://nonprofitdreamin.org/), the goal was to present an online event for the folks in the Salesforce Nonprofit Cloud ecosystem. That sounds like a simple enough goal. However, when there are 24+ diverse members of the founding team, it takes a bit of alignment to establish direction and priorities. The answer was the **Salesforce V2MOM**. The Nonprofit Dreamin team worked through the V2MOM pack (https://developer.salesforce.com/files/V2MOMPack.zip) during three different team meetings that lasted about 45-60 minutes each. Here are the correlated pieces of the Nonprofit Dreamin V2MOM and what each part of the V2MOM stands for:

- **Vision**: Defines what you want to do or achieve, as illustrated here:

Figure 7.1 – Nonprofit Dreamin V2MOM: Vision

- **Values**: Principles and beliefs that define your vision, as illustrated here:

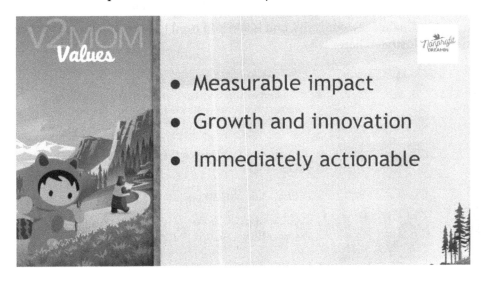

Figure 7.2 – Nonprofit Dreamin V2MOM: Values

- **Methods**: Actions and steps to accomplish your vision, as illustrated here:

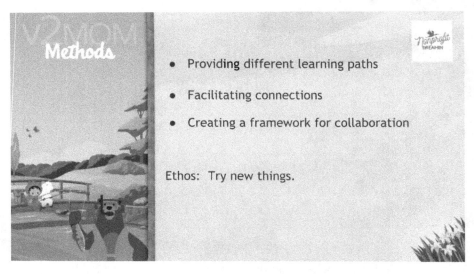

Figure 7.3 – Nonprofit Dreamin V2MOM: Methods

- **Obstacles**: Challenges, concerns, and issues you need to overcome to achieve your vision, as illustrated here:

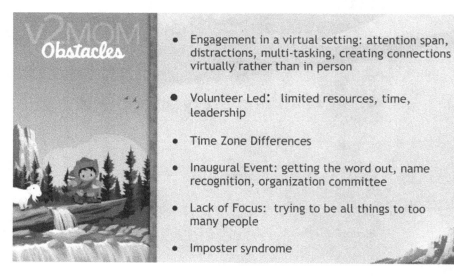

Figure 7.4 – Nonprofit Dreamin V2MOM: Obstacles

- **Measures**: Metrics for the success of achieving your vision, as illustrated here:

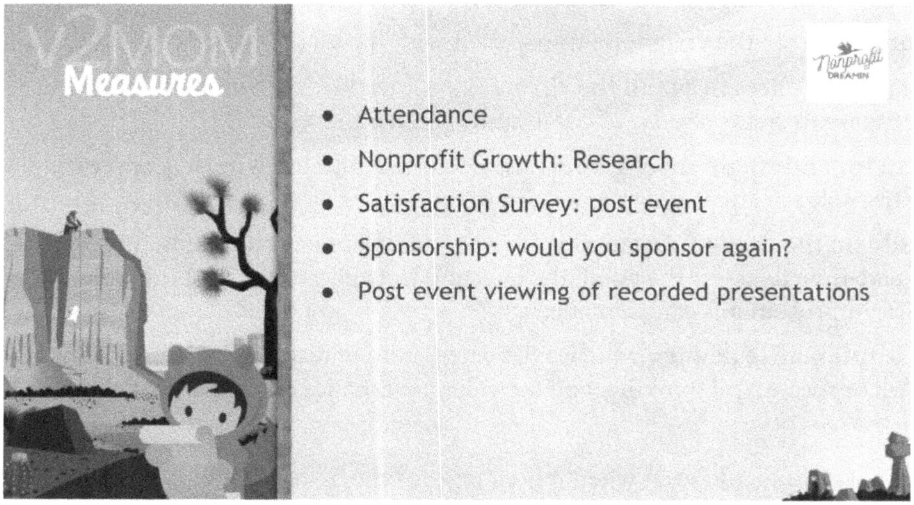

Figure 7.5 – Nonprofit Dreamin V2MOM: Measures

Once the Nonprofit Dreamin team created and agreed upon the V2MOM, every decision was weighed, and every priority was set against the vision, values, and methods as outlined.

Managing change

Once the V2MOM has been agreed upon and is in place, change management becomes a much simpler process. The V2MOM is an iterative and Agile document. It can inform a single project or be a part of a larger V2MOM for the entire organization. It also establishes a framework for managing the change that will be initiated by a V2MOM. Everything involved in managing change revolves around helping people transition through the changes. Kotter's *Eight Steps* is one way to address change.

Kotter's Eight Steps

In 2007, John Kotter, a professor at Harvard Business School, introduced the following eight steps for leading change, which Salesforce recommends as a tool for managing organizational change:

1. **Establish a sense of urgency**: This includes the timelines and milestones that are laid out in an implementation plan.

2. **Form a powerful guiding coalition**: More about this in the *User adoption and metrics for success* section later in this chapter, including champions and early adopters.

3. **Create a vision**: This step correlates with the first part of the V2MOM—the Vision statement.

4. **Communicate the vision**: Be transparent with the V2MOM; share it with everyone.

5. **Empower others to act on the vision**: Expect feedback when the V2MOM is transparent; create a sense of community around the V2MOM.

6. **Plan for and create short-term wins**: Celebrate milestones as they are reached and be transparent about progress toward the measures.

7. **Build on the change**: As mentioned in *Step 6*, celebrate milestones; however, be sure to take time to assess the good, the bad, and the ugly related to those milestones and what improvements can be made.

8. **Institutionalize new approaches**: Update the organization V2MOM appropriately to incorporate new thinking, and consider governance and a COE, as explained in the next section.

Change is always difficult, even when it is change for the better. The V2MOM exercise outlined in the *Nonprofit Dreamin case study* section is an excellent way to work with an organization to ensure everyone on the team is aligned and heading in the same direction. Kotter's Eight Steps help to maintain focus and alignment as changes are implemented so that iteration does not alter the agreed-upon priorities. Additional tools are presented in terms of more granular management in *Chapter 8, Requirements – User Stories – Business Processes – What Is Your Organization Trying to Achieve?*.

Governance basics and COEs

Preparing for success requires organizational alignment, common goals, and good change management. What does maintaining that success look like? Salesforce suggests a framework of governance and encourages a COE for nonprofits.

Governance for Salesforce Nonprofit Cloud

Technology changes with the speed of light (or lightning may be a more appropriate term in a Salesforce study). There are new products and there are products that are no longer supported. Technology has new releases and deprecates functionality. How is a nonprofit supposed to keep up, and how is a nonprofit's technology maintained without immense technical debt? Governance frameworks for any technology system strive to help meet compliance issues, assess and manage risks, improve **return on investment** (**ROI**) and efficiencies, and prioritize new initiatives.

Without a governance framework, a nonprofit may lack a technology vision or strategy; that lack can lead to misalignment going forward, as well as duplication of efforts. As already discussed, without alignment, implementation can be devastating, and users may refuse to adopt new processes. Identifying the stakeholders is a critical precursor to a governance framework. Establishing their roles (for example, **information technology (IT)**, **business units (BUs)**, and end users) and responsibilities can go a long way toward maintaining the hard-won success of the alignment process. The lean governance framework that Salesforce recommends consists of five distinct processes, as depicted in the following diagram:

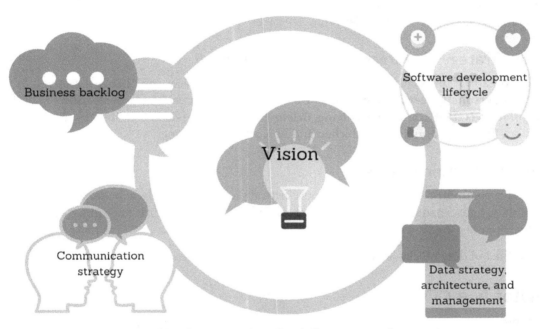

Figure 7.6 – Visual representation of an Agile governance framework

We'll now look at these processes in more detail.

Vision and strategy

Does this sound like an old, familiar tune? **Vision and strategy** are what align everyone on the same path working toward a common goal.

Business backlog

Business backlog sounds like a complicated term; however, as a consultant, you may relate to it more closely to requirements. Usually, a customer has a long list of "wants" that will require prioritizing to implement over time. How that happens is governed by the business backlog.

Software development life cycle

For a smaller organization, this may seem to be overkill. However, as the organization grows and new technology is added, already having a system in place to handle releases, migrations, and more is highly desirable.

Data strategy, architecture, and management

Every organization needs guidelines on data, particularly to meet compliance directives such as **personally identifiable information** (**PII**) or the **General Data Protection Regulation** (**GDPR**), and for archiving, deleting, and merging data, creating new data via custom fields and/or objects, and when and how all of this is done.

Communication strategy

Effective communication is the single most critical piece of any implementation and/or technology governance framework. Assure transparency and that direct communication is valuable rather than a worn-out "*all is well*" message.

With the building blocks of governance in place, the next stage is a COE.

What is a COE?

Nonprofits are notorious for siloing data and information within an organization. A simple way to think of a COE is as a committee with a representative from each program sitting at a table. The more formal definition of a COE states that a COE drives organizations to identify, prioritize, execute, and communicate while optimally leveraging people, processes, knowledge, and technology, and at the same time ensuring high value for all users and meeting overall organizational goals. A breakout of these groups might look like this:

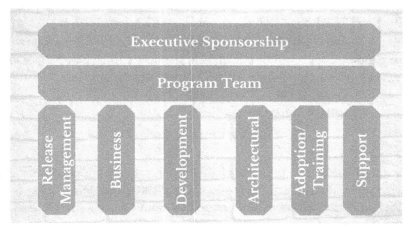

Figure 7.7 – Sample COE structure with a formal governance council

A COE can be small and informal to start and grow with the organization. Starting somewhere is the key. Nonprofit Dreamin utilized the organizing committee as the governance council; however, the team lacked clear lines of communication for governance. In its iterative process, the Nonprofit Dreamin team made a better governance structure a priority for the next year.

User adoption and metrics for success

User adoption is one of the best metrics for the success of a Nonprofit Cloud implementation project, but how do you get users to adopt something new and different? How do you encourage the users from the very beginning of the implementation? What will you measure as a benchmark to user adoption and success? Let's break this down.

Encouraging user adoption

The most important aspects of encouraging user technology adoption are people. Several key people need to be on board to ensure a successful implementation. Let's identify these important roles next.

Executive sponsor

An **executive sponsor** does not need to be the instigator of a project; however, they do need to be a champion of the project and be willing to go to bat for the team at executive levels. As an executive, they can help assemble the appropriate resources for the project, involve other key stakeholders, share a vision, rally the team, provide incentives, and support celebrations.

Champions

Champions are not necessarily the standard stakeholders. Champions may be those who just really like technology or are cultural leaders in the nonprofit. Champions can come from many areas and may even be volunteers. The most important characteristic in a champion is that they are excited about the benefits of the new technology and will help communicate that excitement to the rest of the organization.

Early adopters

Getting the right feedback is also important to the project. **Early adopters** are a great source of information and advocacy. Early adopters are those people who like to be the first to use new technology, test it out, and share their opinion and experience. Again, these folks come from a variety of sources.

Users

Don't forget to survey, observe, and include the actual users for the implementation. While executive sponsors may think they understand the work, the humans who will use the system provide the most critical feedback; they are the success of the project. We'll go into much more detail on testing in *Chapter 14, Testing and Deployment Strategies*, but don't forget that up to 80% of users today are on mobile as opposed to desktop or laptop, as depicted in the following screenshot. What they see or do in one as opposed to the other can drastically change the satisfaction level:

Figure 7.8 – As part of user surveys, don't forget that 80% of users work from mobile rather than desktop; this is an example of key testing criteria for user adoption

Add the critical transparency and communication necessary. Mix well. Follow the prescribed Agile methods of continuous testing and improvement. Keep it all hot during the implementation. And voilà! Successful user adoption.

How to measure user adoption

Before we talk about metrics for success, be sure to know that you can indeed measure user adoption of Salesforce. Salesforce Labs has created a free app called **Salesforce Adoption Dashboards** for this very purpose; it can be accessed at `https://appexchange.salesforce.com/listingDetail?listingId=a0N30000004gHhLEAU`. When creating your measures for success, consider the specific metrics you want to track for user adoption.

Creating the appropriate reports, based on your measures for success, allows you to create a dashboard similar to what you see here. This is a quick and easy way to track user login history and trending, which key features are being utilized, and more. Here is an example of how the **User Adoption** dashboard might look in a Salesforce instance:

Figure 7.9 – Sample dashboard for measuring user adoption

> **Note**
> Some users log in very infrequently. If they are not using the system, you need to know why. Perhaps they do not need a login to do their work, or perhaps they are not doing their work in the system.

Metrics for success

If a lot of this chapter seems redundant, that's because it is. We began by discussing organizational alignment and a tool called the V2MOM. Vision and strategy have been addressed several times in this chapter. How do you know that you have successfully achieved the vision the organization has?

Nonprofit Dreamin, in the initial use case at the beginning of this chapter, used SMART metrics to create its measures in the V2MOM.

SMART is an acronym that is outlined here:

- **S: Specific**. Clearly define your focus and what you're going to do.
- **M: Measurable**. Quantify an indicator of progress, such as percentages, numbers, targets.
- **A: Achievable**. Set the bar high yet make it achievable.
- **R: Relevant**. Ensure that the measure supports the organizations and the project's V2MOM measures.
- **T: Timely**. Set a specific and reasonable time frame for completion.

These were the original SMART goals defined by Nonprofit Dreamin:

- **Attendance**: 500
- **Nonprofit growth**: 25% survey response rate
- **Satisfaction survey**: 50 **net promoter score (NPS)**
- **Sponsorship**: 50%
- **Post-event viewing**: 30 average views per session

The following screenshot shows the actual outcomes of the Nonprofit Dreamin event based on the success metrics the V2MOM outlined:

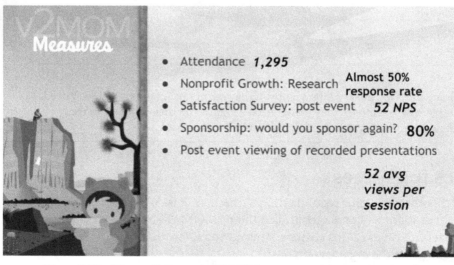

Figure 7.10 – Nonprofit Dreamin V2MOM measures with outcomes listed

At the end of the event, Nonprofit Dreamin met every measure of success.

Consultants can use this same tool, whether it is for a small project or for a large implementation, to gain alignment and set expectations. With SMART measures established, the organization and/or project team can measure and celebrate progress and a job well done for anything from project implementation to the success of an organization's overall goal.

Summary

As a Nonprofit Cloud consultant, this may be the most important chapter to read for actual implementation. This chapter also covers a wealth of information that is critical to the **Nonprofit Cloud Consultant Certification** exam. Here is a quick recap of our discussion so far.

Organizational alignment and change management are tools that cannot be overlooked. Without the stakeholders being in alignment as to the goals of even a simple project, the hope for success is slim. Understanding an easy-to-use tool such as Salesforce's V2MOM can make goal setting and alignment a much easier process. Preparing for success helps ensure success, as do managing change via Kotter's Eight Steps and understanding that a process can be a part of any implementation project.

Governance and COEs are natural progressions of organizational alignment and change management. In this section, we discussed the importance of a governance framework concerning compliance, strategy, efficiencies, risks, and new initiatives. A COE creates a more formal governance strategy, but it can start small and grow as the organization grows.

The last section explored user adoption and metrics for success. You learned how to accomplish user adoption via executive sponsors, champions, and early adopters, and how to measure user adoption using available reports and dashboards in Salesforce. Metrics for success should be SMART and established before the project begins to measure progress and success.

You are off to a great start in **Implementation Strategies and Best Practices**, 21% of the **Nonprofit Cloud Consultant Certification** exam.

In *Chapter 8, Requirements – User Stories – Business Processes – What Is Your Organization Trying to Achieve?*, we will expand the learning of implementation strategies and best practices around requirements, user stories, and business processes.

Further reading

- *Drucker School—Organization Change Leadership*: `https://trailhead. salesforce.com/content/learn/modules/drucker_org_change_ leadership?trailmix_creator_id=jfrichter&trailmix_ slug=nonprofit-cloud-consultants`

- *Drucker School Management Essentials program*: `https://www.cgu.edu/ academics/program/salesforce/resources/`

- *Create Strategic Company Alignment With a V2MOM*: `https://www. salesforce.com/blog/how-to-create-alignment-within-your- company/`

- *Why do I Need a Center of Excellence, Anyway?* `https://www.salesforce. org/blog/need-center-excellence-anyway/`

- *Leading Change: Why Transformation Efforts Fail*: `https://hbr. org/2007/01/leading-change-why-transformation-efforts-fail`

- *Governance Basics*: `https://trailhead.salesforce.com/content/ learn/modules/governance-basics?trailmix_creator_ id=sfdo&trailmix_slug=prepare-for-success`

8
What Is the Organization Trying to Achieve?

Once you have worked to create an atmosphere that will welcome change, the next step is to understand the organization's needs, resources, and what they are looking for in critical outcomes. This phase is what many call *discovery*—that is, discovering as much as possible about the organization and what it wants to accomplish by implementing new technology. Salesforce recommends an adaptive methodology that combines Waterfall and Agile approaches to meet expectations and retain the ability to adapt throughout the project. Here, we will explore the following topics:

- The iterative interrogative technique of five whys

- A case study interrogating a mentorship program to confirm the organization's needs

- A case study to define the organization's critical success factors for the mentoring program

- A case study defining business processes to capture the organization's needs and critical success factors

- An overview of defining success for the implementation

The aforementioned topics will appear in the following sections:

- Why five whys?
- Interrogating a mentorship program
- Defining program processes
- How does the organization define success?

By the end of this chapter, you will be able to define the organization's goals for implementing Nonprofit Cloud and its functionality. You will also be able to identify pain points that can be alleviated by Nonprofit Cloud and/or one of its components, as well as prioritizing goals and outcomes for the Nonprofit Cloud implementation.

As we work through each of these areas, remember how vitally important it is to truly understand the organization and what its goals are with the Nonprofit Cloud implementation. To do this well, you need to understand all the Nonprofit Cloud components we have already discussed and all the information around change management and discovery.

In the next chapter, when we begin with the installation of the **Nonprofit Success Pack** (**NPSP**) and other components, you will see the importance of what we will be doing in this chapter. So, let's begin.

Why five whys?

Organizations must address challenges when they start discussing new technology implementation. Sometimes, they are very certain that they know the solution to their problems, and sometimes, the only knowledge they have is they need a solution. Using the five whys is a great opportunity to better understand the organization's needs, pain points, and business processes. **Sakichi Toyoda** is credited with the development of the five whys methodology, and it is a part of the problem-solving skills used in the **Toyota Production System** (**TPS**). It is an interactive interrogative process to identify the root cause of a problem. By asking "why?", the cause and effect become apparent so that the problem itself can be solved instead of one or more of the effects of the problem. With a little adaptation for the specific circumstances, the five whys is a helpful discovery mechanism.

Here is a blank template of the progression of discovery using the five whys technique:

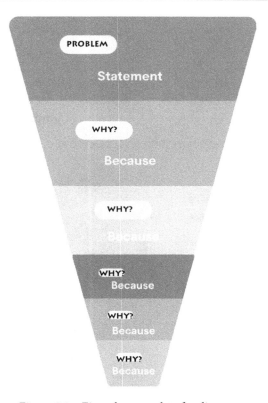

Figure 8.1 – Five whys template for discovery

Using this template, you can begin with whatever the organization states as a problem and refine the actual challenge from there. It may be a quick and easy process to get to the root cause, or it may require quite a bit of discussion for a larger team. Either way, the goal is to work through the process, dispel any assumptions, and learn as much as possible along the way.

Let's explore how this might work for a group that is working to define its mentorship program.

Interrogating a mentorship program

Mentors R Us (MRU), a nonprofit tasked with mentoring, are interested in leveraging Nonprofit Cloud to automate what they can for their local mentoring program. They have done a great job of selecting their partners and perfecting the matching process. They prepare mentees and mentors and keep their participants informed. The roadblock for their mentoring program is collecting data to share with their collaborators on the success of their program.

The problem

The first step is to have the organization state the problem in a concise and focused way. The problem statement should not be too broad, or the resolution will not be helpful because it will not be focused enough to implement a specific change. After some discussion with the mentorship program team, it becomes evident that they are struggling with showing impact because program participants are not reporting progress.

The problem: Participants do not report progress, as we can see from the updated template here:

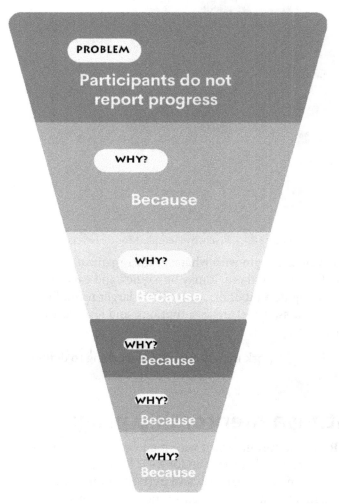

Figure 8.2 – Start with a concise problem statement

Ask the five whys

Next, you begin to ask why and fill in each step of the template, as follows:

1. **Why don't participants report on progress?**

   The program team responded that in the current training and business processes, participants were asked to email a progress report or to call regarding the progress report. The team got feedback from participants that it was too difficult to remember this, and they were not sure what to include in the progress report.

2. **Why do participants have to email or call?**

   The program team mentions that they did not have another way to get information from the participants. They do not have a form capability to outline specific information that should be submitted, and they do not have any consistent way to remind participants to submit information.

3. **Why doesn't the organization have a form capability?**

   The program team explored different ways to use forms last year—everything was cost-prohibitive and offered nothing that automatically populated Salesforce with the data from the forms. Additionally, there was no way to automate reminders.

4. **Why are forms too expensive?**

   Based on the cost involved, the program team believed that emails and phone calls would be more efficient. But participants said it was just too hard to remember to report and then create an email or make a phone call when the mentoring center was open.

5. **Why is it too hard to report progress?**

   Participants need reminders and a form that captures pertinent data rather than relying on mentors and mentees to cover everything freeform in an email or a call.

Here, you can see an updated version of the template with each step filled in:

Figure 8.3 – Template with five whys and answers filled in

As you can imagine, discussing this with the team would take much longer than reading the preceding outline. However, after the end of the discussion and asking the five whys, you will be able to find the root causes.

The root causes

If you have been paying attention throughout the entire conversation with the **MRU** program team, you will notice that each of the five times you asked "why?", the team delved a little deeper into a better understanding of why participants were not reporting their progress.

They worked through the idea that their assumptions about feedback costs were wrong. The team also acknowledged the feedback they were getting from participants and what they needed. The root cause of why participants were not reporting progress was simple: **participants need reminders and an easier way to share information**.

What is the goal of the mentorship program?

You have now successfully identified the root cause of the problem that the mentorship program is trying to solve. That was the first step.

Now, we need to look at the following areas:

- What are the goals of the mentorship program and why it is so important that participants report on progress?
- Which data will show progress toward the mentorship program goals?
- Who needs to see that data and why?
- What is the most effective way to collect that data?
- Most importantly, if the data is not actionable, why are you collecting it?

First goal

The first goal that **MRU** wants to measure is **mentee confidence** and **increased skills**. Sharing progress on this goal will require data from the mentee to start the program and combined data from the mentee and the mentor to show improvement in confidence and skills.

Creating user stories around this goal using *who, what, and why* will help us understand the ways that users may interact with the mentorship program, the data, and the Nonprofit Cloud implementation. The widely accepted format for a user story is: As a <**who**>, I want <**what**> so that <**why**>. This is *Step 1* of creating a user story.

Here are some example user stories around the first goal:

- **Example 1**: As the executive director, I want to pull a report once a month so that I can show the progress that our mentees are making in increasing their self-confidence and skills.

- **Example 2**: As a mentee, I want a simple way to share initial information on my confidence levels and skills so that my progress can be measured.

- **Example 3**: As a mentee, I want a simple way to share information throughout the mentor program on my confidence levels and skills so that my progress can be measured.

- **Example 4**: As a mentee, I want a reminder so that I can submit information on a timely basis.

The user stories should be small, independent, testable stories that provide value to the end user. The formula is simple; however, a story-writing workshop to develop those user stories can be time-consuming and inestimably valuable.

Second goal

The second goal for the **MRU** program is centered around specific tasks such as creating LinkedIn profiles and resumes/**curricula vitae (CVs)** and completing Trailhead modules and certifications. Mentors grade the quality of the LinkedIn profiles and resumes/CVs and monitor the number of Trailhead modules that are completed. The thought is that mentees who complete these tasks will gain confidence as well as skills. Tracking these quantifiable numbers against the more qualitative numbers in the first goal gives positive outcomes and refines the mentoring process.

The second part of a user story is the acceptance criteria. Let's look at some examples of user stories that the mentoring program team created and the acceptance criteria, a clear pass/fail statement, that goes with them, as follows:

- **Example 1**: As a mentor, I want a quick way to report a score for a mentee's LinkedIn profile so that the mentee can receive feedback.

  Acceptance criteria: A mentor can report a score on the mentee's profile with one click.

- **Example 2**: As a program director, I want up-to-date information on how many Trailhead modules a mentee has completed so that I can assist mentors in encouraging their mentees.

Acceptance criteria:

- A program director can see the current total number of completed Trailhead modules on the mentee profile.

- A program director can send an email to the mentor and/or mentee.

- A program director has access to mentee profiles where those mentees fall under the program director in the hierarchy.

> **Remember**
> *Acceptance criteria* should be specific and testable. If it is too vague, it is much more difficult to decide when that user story's work is completed.

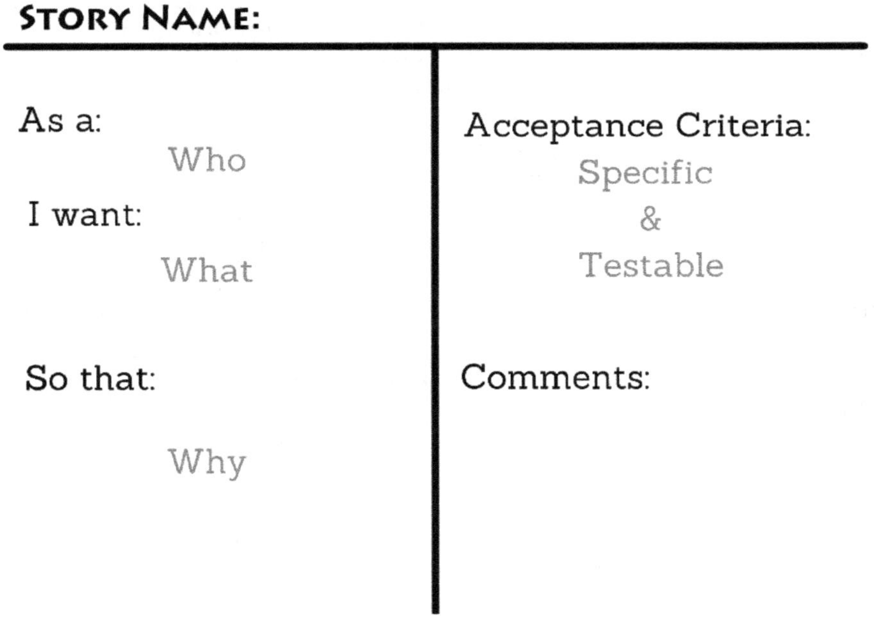

STORY NAME:

As a:	Acceptance Criteria:
Who	Specific
I want:	&
What	Testable
So that:	Comments:
Why	

Figure 8.4 – User story and acceptance criteria template

User stories and acceptance criteria do not require a complicated matrix or template. The simple template example shown in *Figure 8.4* is based on a user story template from Accenture, a global Salesforce partner.

Defining program processes

After the robust discussions around user stories, **MRU** are excited to get started implementing their new mentor program using Nonprofit Cloud. Before you start to create a solution, you need a set of directions to make certain that the functionality outlined in the user stories is present in the solution.

First, assign a **unique identifier** (**UID**) to each user story. Again, it does not have to be complicated. See the following example:

Mentoring Management system

Category	User Story ID	User Story
Mentoring Management	MM.1.0	The organization needs to measure and report on mentee confidence levels and skills improvement.
Mentoring Management	MM.1.1	As the Executive Director, I want to pull a report once a month so that I can show the progress our mentees are making in confidence and increased skills.
Mentoring Management	MM.1.2	As a mentee, I want a simple way to share initial information on my confidence levels and skills so that my progress can be measured.
Mentoring Management	MM.1.3	As a mentee, I want a simple way to share information throughout the mentor program on my confidence levels and skills so that my progress can be measured.
Mentoring Management	MM.1.4	As a mentee, I want a reminder so that I submit information on a timely basis.
Mentoring Management	MM.2.0	The organization needs to collect quantitative data on mentee progress and report on it.
Mentoring Management	MM.2.1	As a mentor, I want a quick way to report a score for a mentee's LinkedIn profile so that the mentee can receive feedback.
Mentoring Management	MM.2.2	As a program director, I want up-to-date information on how many Trailhead modules a mentee has completed so that I can assist mentors in encouraging their mentees.

Table 8.1 – Example of user story numbering and categorizing

With the user story IDs assigned, we can associate the functional requirements with those user stories. You see how the actual function correlates to the user story in the following example:

Category	ID	Function
Mentoring Management	MM.1.0	The organization needs to measure and report on mentee confidence levels and skills improvement.
Mentoring Management	MM.1.1	The system will provide a method for MRU to extract a report to aggregate performance data for each mentee.
Mentoring Management	MM.1.2	The system will provide a method for MRU mentees to easily enter their information.
Mentoring Management	MM.1.3	The system will provide a method for MRU mentees to easily update their information.
Mentoring Management	MM.1.4	The system will provide a method for MRU to set automated reminders for mentees to submit data.
Mentoring Management	MM.2.0	The organization needs to collect quantitative data on mentee progress and report on it.
Mentoring Management	MM.2.1	The system will provide a method for MRU mentors to submit scores for mentees.
Mentoring Management	MM.2.2	The system will provide a method for MRU program directors to view the current total of Trailhead modules completed for each mentee.

Table 8.2 – Example of functional requirements documentation

These functional requirements are a road map, especially for those stakeholders who create or configure the systems, to implement the processes that are needed to provide the organization with a successful implementation.

Another useful tool is a **business process map. Universal Process Notation (UPN)** is a helpful way to document the business processes for an organization so that all the stakeholders can easily understand each step and decision in a process from start to finish. See the following sample of UPN for NPSP:

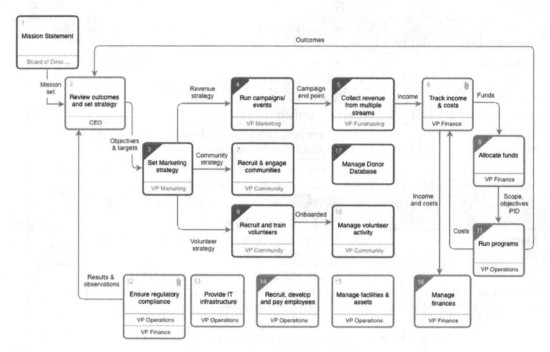

Figure 8.5 – Sample UPN for NPSP

Regardless of the tools you use, it is important to agree with stakeholders on what is needed.

How does the organization define success?

In *Chapter 7, Is Change Difficult for Your Organization?*, we covered the definition of success viewed from **Vision, Values, Methods, Obstacles, and Measures (V2MOM)** and the organization's alignment. We also talked about **SMART** metrics: **Specific, Measurable, Achievable, Relevant, Timely**.

In this section, the success we want to define is the success of the Nonprofit Cloud implementation itself. The Agile process promotes continual and iterative improvements. How do you and the organization know when the implementation is finished?

Everything we have discussed in this chapter so far helps with defining the success of the project. Using the five whys methodology, you should be able to eliminate assumptions and get to the root causes of problems. Creating user stories with the team brings into focus the goals for the implementation. The acceptance criteria associated with the user stories are what is used to test for the successful completion of each user story. When the acceptance criteria are met, the requirement itself can be checked off as completed. Understanding and documenting the business processes, decision points, and outcomes provides an overall picture for the implementation.

Additional help is a benchmark. A benchmark is a standard or a point of reference provided for assessment or comparison. Establishing benchmarks provides a way to measure success, incrementally, throughout the implementation instead of waiting until the very end of the project for an overall assessment. Benchmarks also provide decisions that will affect the project going forward—they are great tools for retaining focus. Examples of some initial benchmarks we want to set for the mentoring project are provided here:

- How long does it currently take a mentor to submit scores for a LinkedIn profile created by a mentee?
- Can you create a reliable average length of time?

If you can answer these questions, you can use them as initial benchmarks. When the requirements around mentors submitting these scores are ready for **user acceptance testing (UAT)**, you can time how long the new process takes. By using a benchmark this way, you offer quantifiable value to the organization.

Another form of measuring success is a timeline. Of course, much depends on how complex the implementation is, but even for a simple implementation, a written timeline helps manage expectations and keep everyone on track.

Here is an example of a timeline for the implementation of a managed package that requires little discovery:

Standard onboarding timeline

Date	Consultant	Customer
Week 1	Kickoff meeting (consultant & customer)	Kickoff meeting (consultant & customer)
	Review current Salesforce instance*	
	Create sandbox (if needed) *	
	Install mentoring managed package in sandbox and configure*	
Week 2	Create mentoring portal and attach to sandbox*	
Week 3		Begin sandbox review by customer*
		Content management system (CMS) training
		Begin customizing mentoring site
		Salesforce overview, organizations, & contacts training
		Mentoring opportunities, occurrences, & connections training
	Preliminary data meeting (consultant & customer)	Preliminary data meeting (consultant & customer)
Week 4		Submit completed data migration tables
		Tips & tricks training
		Reporting training
		Complete sandbox review by customer*
Week 5	Installation of mentoring managed package in production*	
	Data migration	
		Public site ready
	Data migration complete	
		Confirm data
Week 6	Launch the mentoring site (To ensure the highest levels of support, launches as scheduled for Monday, Tuesday, and Wednesday)	

Table 8.3 – Sample managed package implementation timeline

> **Note**
> This schedule may vary based on the complexity of an existing Salesforce implementation, the complexity of data to be migrated, and any customization or additional modules or functionality that may need to be applied (* *indicates that this may not apply to your onboarding*).

This simple timeline also serves to delineate who is responsible for the major steps in the implementation process and helps to keep the process moving.

Summary

This chapter and the preceding chapter (*Chapter 7, Is Change Difficult for Your Organization?*) covered a vast array of important information and techniques to pass the *Nonprofit Cloud Consultant Certification* and to successfully prepare to implement Nonprofit Cloud for an organization. In *Chapter 7, Is Change Difficult for Your Organization?*, we learned about organizational alignment and change management, the importance of governance and **Centers of Excellence** (**CoEs**), and user adoption and metrics for success.

In this chapter, we learned what the five whys methodology is and how to use it to interrogate pain points. Using the five whys, you can establish the root cause of problems. We also learned about user stories and how those stories define the functionality needed to achieve the goals of implementing new technology. The second half of the user story, the acceptance criteria, is a key part of defining the success of the implementation itself. With user stories and acceptance criteria in hand, we created simple requirements for stakeholders to implement and configure the new technology. UPN provides a way to see the business processes themselves and the decision points along the way to further document and confirm that all parts and pieces of the implementation come together to create a successful whole. UAT, benchmarking, and meeting timelines were introduced as ways to measure a successful implementation strategy.

Implementation Strategies and Best Practices make up 21% of the Nonprofit Cloud Consultant exam. We've covered a lot in *Chapter 7* and *Chapter 8, Requirements – User Stories – Business Processes – What Is Your Organization Trying to Achieve?* Next, in *Chapter 9, Installing Nonprofit Cloud Solutions*, we will get down to the nitty-gritty of implementing solutions from Nonprofit Cloud.

Resources and additional reading

- *Innovation Customer Discovery*: https://trailhead.salesforce.com/content/learn/modules/innovation_customer_discovery

- *Customer-Centric Discovery for Salesforce Partners*: https://trailhead.salesforce.com/en/content/learn/modules/customercentric-discovery-for-salesforce-partners

- *Project Management Plan Lite*: https://trailhead.salesforce.com/content/learn/modules/project-management-plan-lite

- *Salesforce Agile Basics*: https://trailhead.salesforce.com/en/content/learn/modules/salesforce-agile-basics

- *Salesforce.org Partner Network Basics*: https://trailhead.salesforce.com/content/learn/modules/salesforceorg-partner-network-basics

- *5 Whys Template*: https://miro.com/templates/5-whys/

- *Do These Data Spark Joy?*: https://thedataarealright.blog/2019/01/11/do-these-data-bring-me-joy/

- *Essential Business Analyst Skills*: https://trailhead.salesforce.com/content/learn/modules/business-analyst_skills-strategies

- *The evolution of process diagramming*: https://iangotts.medium.com/the-evolution-of-process-diagramming-266f8a447aab

9
Installing Solutions from Nonprofit Cloud

At last, we are ready to get down to the details of installing solutions from **Nonprofit Cloud**. Although you may not need every solution for your use case, this chapter will walk you through the installation of the standard solutions available.

By the end of this chapter, you will have this knowledge base:

- How to install **Nonprofit Success Pack (NPSP)** or upgrade it to the current version
- How to install Program Management Module
- How to install Volunteers for Salesforce
- How to implement Case Management

As we work through each of these areas, remember how vitally important it is to truly understand the organization and what its goals are with the Nonprofit Cloud implementation. To do this well, you need to understand all the Nonprofit Cloud components we have already discussed and the information about change management and discovery.

In this chapter, when we begin with the installation of NPSP and the other components, you will see where all of this must be done before the implementation can begin.

Technical requirements

- Nonprofit Success Pack 30-day trial:

  `https://www.salesforce.org/trial/npsp/`

- Metecho installation of NPSP:

  `https://install.salesforce.org/products/npsp/latest/install`

- Metecho installation of PMM:

  `https://install.salesforce.org/products/program-management/latest`

- Metecho installation of V4S:

  `https://install.salesforce.org/products/v4s/latest`

- Metecho installation of Case Management:

  `https://install.salesforce.org/products/case-management/latest`

First things first: Where do you install NPSP?

The first step for installing NPSP is the decision of where to install it. Here is a quick way to identify what needs to be done next:

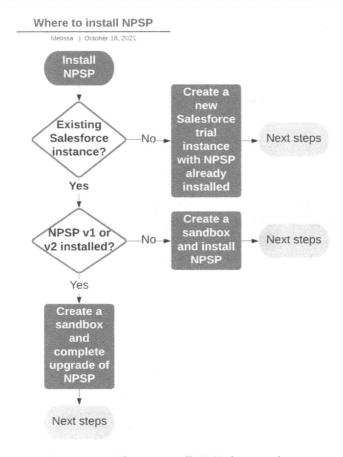

Figure 9.1 – Where to install NPSP decision chart

Let's walk through the thought process for where to install NPSP by following these recommendations:

1. Does a Salesforce instance already exist?

    If the answer is *No*, create a new **Salesforce trial** instance with NPSP already installed. The 30-day free trials are available at https://www.salesforce.org/trial/npsp/. Then you can skip to the section on **configuring NPSP** in your Salesforce instance.

2. If you already have a Salesforce instance, there are additional questions that need to be answered before you create a sandbox and install the latest version of NPSP:

    I.   Have you enabled My Domain?

    You must enable My Domain before you install NPSP.

    II.   Is your Salesforce instance an Enterprise edition?

    Enterprise-level or above is required for NPSP to work as expected. You can check from the Salesforce Setup menu by going to **Company Information** and looking at the **Organization Edition** field.

3. If you have a Salesforce instance without any version of NPSP installed, create a sandbox, preferably a **Full Copy Sandbox**, so you have readily available native data to test and install NPSP using the installer listed in the *Technical requirements* section. If a full copy sandbox is not available or feasible, a **Partial Copy Sandbox** is acceptable and would be the next best option. Then you are ready for the section on configuring NPSP.

4. If you have a Salesforce instance with a previous version of NPSP installed, there is no need to uninstall any of the older versions. **Create a sandbox**, preferably a **Full Copy Sandbox**, so you have readily available native data to test and install NPSP using the installer listed in the *Technical requirements* section. The installation process will update any older versions and add any missing sections. An in-depth **NPSP Upgrade Guide** is available with detailed instructions at `https://s3-us-west-2.amazonaws.com/sfdo-docs/npsp_upgrade_guide.pdf` thanks to the Open Source Commons Sprint team.

The installation of NPSP is handled very simply through the install page. You will need to log into the Salesforce instance where you want to install NPSP. The installer will run a pre-install validation and prompt you to begin the actual installation.

Figure 9.2 – NPSP installer with pre-install validation example

Because every case where you do an install into an existing Salesforce instance can be different, for this case we will start with a brand-new trial instance of Salesforce Nonprofit Cloud.

Starting with a 30-day trial Salesforce instance and NPSP

To get started, go to `https://www.salesforce.org/trial/npsp/` and fill in the required information. You will receive an email for the new trial you have created; click to verify and reset your password and password hint. The new Salesforce instance will open at the **Get Started with NPSP – Admin** page.

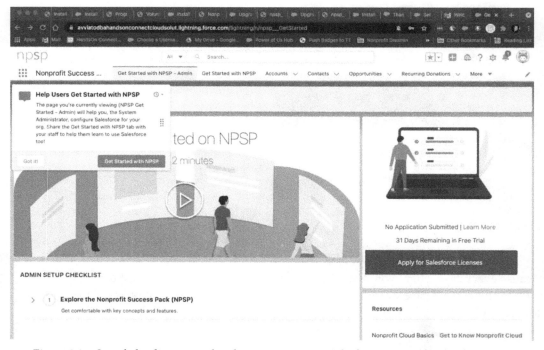

Figure 9.3 – Sample landing page when logging into a new Salesforce Nonprofit Cloud instance

Whether you are using a new instance as just created or whether you are installing NPSP in an already existing instance of Salesforce, check to make sure that the post-installation configuration is done. We will come back to this interesting-looking page in *Chapter 10, Configuring Fundraising Features*.

Permissions configurations

First, you will need to grant the appropriate access to manage the NPSP settings. Add the following system permissions to the profile that will be managing the **NPSP Settings**. Go to **Setup** > **Profiles** > **System Permissions** and confirm that the boxes are checked for the following:

- **Author Apex**
- **Customize Application**
- **Modify All Data**

If the boxes are not checked, you may need to clone the profile. If it is a standard Salesforce profile, check the boxes, and reassign the appropriate users.

> **Remember**
> **Modify All Data** applies to all the data in the Salesforce instance. Assigning this permission makes it possible for users to edit and delete data.

Required configurations

Because we created a Salesforce instance from the trial signup form, most of the configuration has already been done in advance. However, when installing NPSP, whether it is a new Salesforce instance or an established one, there are several post-installation configurations to be considered. Let's walk through the post-installation configurations that are required and compare them to the trial instance we just created.

Organization record types

In NPSP, there are two **Account Record** types:

- **Household Account**
- **Organization**

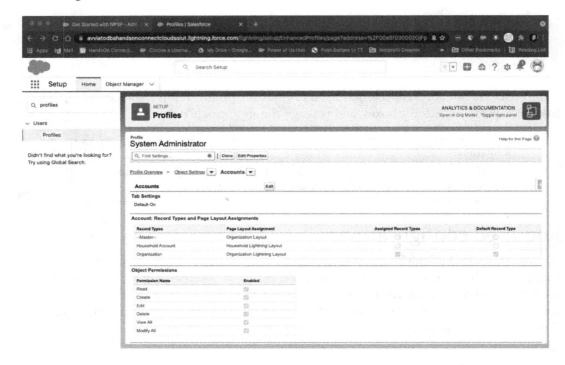

Figure 9.4 – This is a view of the Accounts settings in a profile using NPSP

NPSP automatically creates a **Household Account** for any new contact where the account name is left blank.

You need to remember the following steps:

1. You must confirm that the record types are available in the **Account** object.
2. Then, confirm that the profiles using NPSP are set with the **Organization** record type as the default by going to **Setup** > **Profiles** > **Accounts**.

As a rule, the Organization record type should be set as the default for users in NPSP. Household accounts are created automatically for **Contacts**.

Page layouts

NPSP also comes with preconfigured page layouts. A general recommendation is to assign the standard NPSP page layouts now based on **Profile** and **Record** types. As we continue the process of implementing NPSP for specific use cases, we will look at how those page layouts may be redefined or changed.

The recommendation is to assign standard page layouts for **Account, Opportunity, Contact,** and **Campaign** objects. Go to **Setup** > **Object Manager** > **Account** > **Page Layout** > **Page Layout Assignment** and edit as shown:

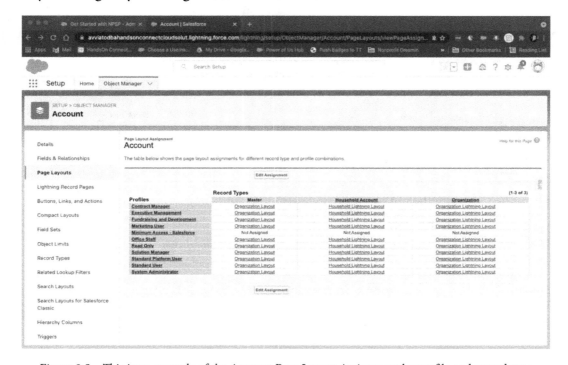

Figure 9.5 – This is an example of the Account Page Layout Assignment by profile and record type for NPSP

Repeat these same steps for **Opportunity, Contact,** and **Campaign** objects to make the NPSP standard page layouts available.

Account View, Edit, and Manage Household buttons

If you are working in an existing Salesforce instance, you need to confirm that the **Account View** and **Edit** buttons are set to **No override**, if you intend to use the Salesforce Lightning Experience:

1. Check by going to **Setup** > **Object Manager** > **Account** > **Buttons, Links, and Actions**.

2. After confirming the **View** and **Edit** buttons, confirm that the **Manage Household** button is enabled.

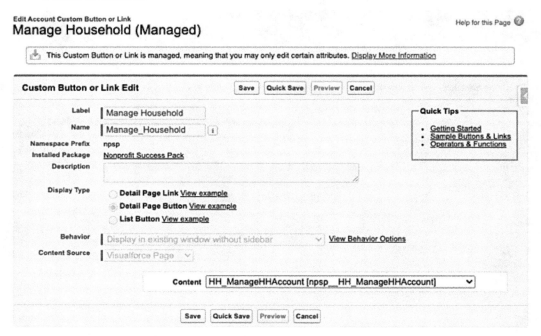

Figure 9.6 – This is how the Management Household configuration looks on the Account object in NPSP

If you do not see the **Manage Household** button on your **Household Account** page layout, you may need to add the button in the page layout itself.

Lead Convert override

Confirm that the **Convert** button on the Lead object is set to the **Visualforce page** override.

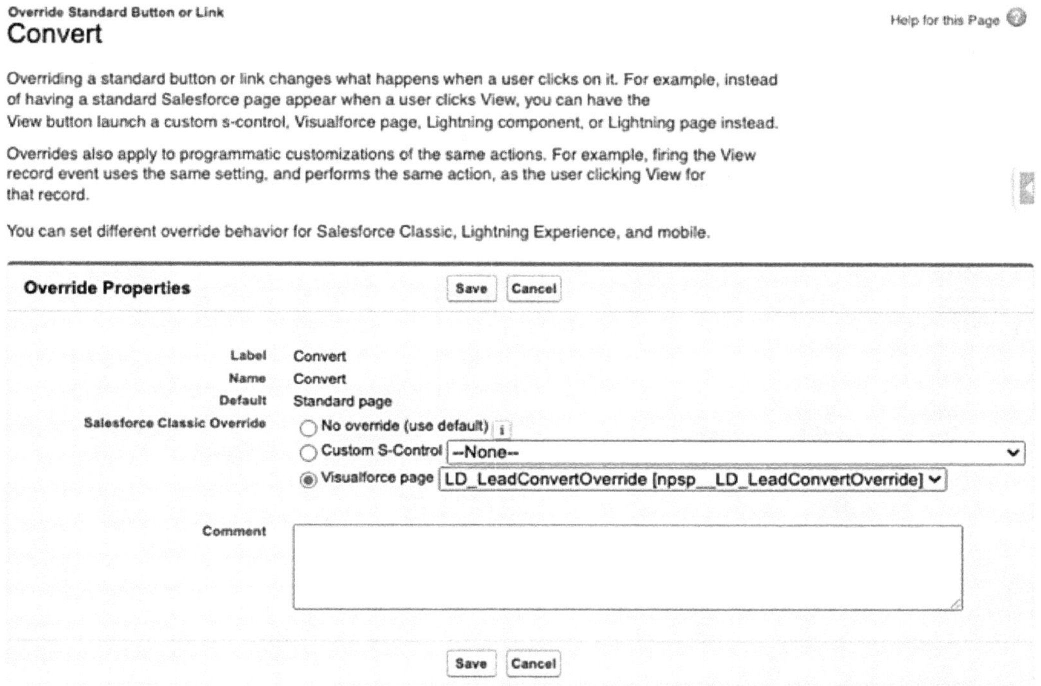

Override Standard Button or Link   Help for this Page

Convert

Overriding a standard button or link changes what happens when a user clicks on it. For example, instead of having a standard Salesforce page appear when a user clicks View, you can have the View button launch a custom s-control, Visualforce page, Lightning component, or Lightning page instead.

Overrides also apply to programmatic customizations of the same actions. For example, firing the View record event uses the same setting, and performs the same action, as the user clicking View for that record.

You can set different override behavior for Salesforce Classic, Lightning Experience, and mobile.

Override Properties   Save   Cancel

Label	Convert
Name	Convert
Default	Standard page
Salesforce Classic Override	○ No override (use default) ⓘ
	○ Custom S-Control --None-- ▼
	⦿ Visualforce page LD_LeadConvertOverride [npsp__LD_LeadConvertOverride] ▼
Comment	

Save   Cancel

Figure 9.7 – Convert button override in Lead in NPSP

The **VisualForce page** provides a much better user interface for users in the Salesforce instance.

Contact Delete button

Confirm that the **Contact Delete** button is set to the **Visualforce page** with the following text: CON_DeleteContactOverride[npsp__CON_DeleteContactOverride].

Override Standard Button or Link

Help for this Page

Delete

Overriding a standard button or link changes what happens when a user clicks on it. For example, instead of having a standard Salesforce page appear when a user clicks View, you can have the ng page instead. View button launch a custom s-control, Visualforce page, Lightning component, or Lightning page instead.

Overrides also apply to programmatic customizations of the same actions. For example, firing the View record event uses the same setting, and performs the same action, as the user clicking View for that record.

You can set different override behavior for Salesforce Classic, Lightning Experience, and mobile.

Override Properties	Save Cancel

Label	Delete
Name	Delete
Default	Standard page
Salesforce Classic Override	◯ No override (use default) ℹ
	◯ Custom S-Control --None--
	⦿ Visualforce page CON_DeleteContactOverride [npsp__CON_DeleteContactOverride]
Comment	

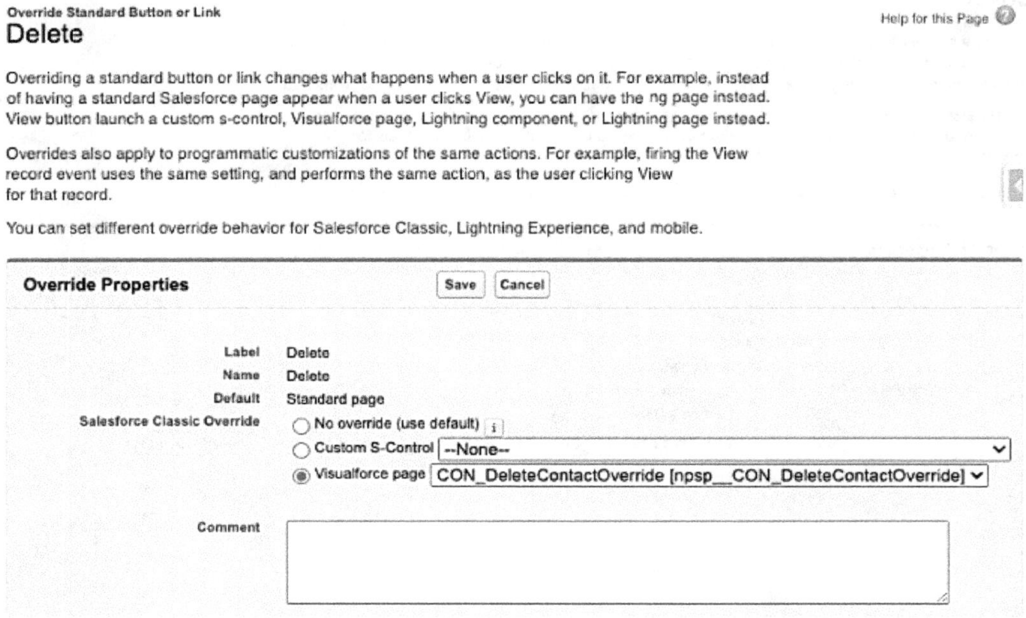

Figure 9.8 – Contact Delete button override screenshot

Unless the **Contact Delete** button is configured this way, it is possible to delete the **Contact** and leave a **Household** with no members.

Relationship settings

Relationships are custom objects in the NPSP package. Relationships show how two people (or contacts) are connected to each other. Following are the standard reciprocal relationship records from NPSP:

NAME	MALE	FEMALE	NEUTRAL
Aunt	Nephew	Niece	Sibling's Child
Child	Father	Mother	Parent
Cousin	Cousin	Cousin	Cousin
Daughter	Father	Mother	Parent
Employee	Employer	Employer	Employer
Employer	Employee	Employee	Employee
Father	Son	Daughter	Child
Grandchild	Grandfather	Grandmother	Grandparent
Granddaughter	Grandfather	Grandmother	Grandparent
Grandfather	Grandson	Granddaughter	Grandchild
Grandmother	Grandson	Granddaughter	Grandchild
Grandparent	Grandson	Granddaughter	Grandchild
Grandson	Grandfather	Grandmother	Grandparent
Husband	Husband	Wife	Spouse
Mother	Son	Daughter	Child
Parent	Son	Daughter	Child
Partner	Partner	Partner	Partner
Son	Father	Mother	Parent
Spouse	Spouse	Spouse	Spouse
Uncle	Nephew	Niece	Sibling's Child
Wife	Husband	Wife	Spouse

If these do not exist in your Salesforce instance, you can create them. You can use some or all of these or create your own:

1. Click the App Launcher and find **NPSP Settings**.

2. Click **Relationships** and then click **Relationship Reciprocal Settings** to see the following interface:

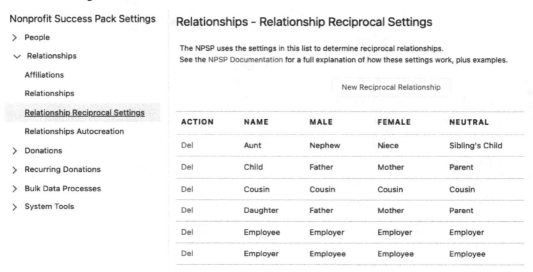

Figure 9.9 – Relationship Reciprocal Settings page in NPSP

> **Note**
>
> This is for **Contact-to-Contact** relationships and **not** for **Contact-to-Account** or **Account-to-Account** relationships.

The only additional required configurations are in conjunction with the fundraising functionality of NPSP. Those configurations will be covered in *Chapter 10, Configuring Fundraising Features*.

Installing Program Management Module

Once you have NPSP installed and the required configurations are done as noted in the previous section, you can begin to install the other Nonprofit Cloud modules.

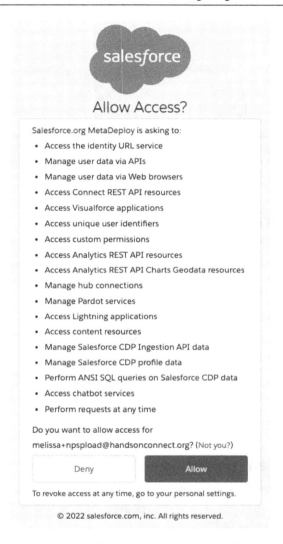

Figure 9.10 – Allow access screen for installation

Steps for installing PMM

We will start with **Program Management Module (PMM)**. The same guidelines apply as with NPSP regarding where you should install Program Management Module. In this case, we are working with a brand-new trial instance that has NPSP installed in production, so we install PMM in production as well:

1. The install is found at `https://install.salesforce.org/products/ program-management/latest`.

2. When you click the blue bar to begin the installation, you will be asked to log into the instance where you want to install the PMM package.

3. Once you are logged in, a page will open requesting you allow several Salesforce accesses to a variety of resources.

4. Confirm you are installing in the appropriate location and click **Allow**.

5. When the pre-install validation is completed, the **Install** button will appear. Click it and PMM will be installed in an average of 3 minutes.

This will complete the installation of PMM itself.

Post-installation required configuration

There are a few post-installation configurations that are required for PMM to function as expected. These need to be done before any other additional setup, configuration, or customization.

Program Management Standard User

PMM installs a **Program Management Standard User** profile. Users who will be accessing PMM need to be assigned the **User** profile.

Go to **Setup** > **Users** > **Profile** > **Program Management Standard User** and click **Assigned Users**.

Assign the appropriate users to the profile.

Program Management permission sets

There are three different levels of permissions that can be assigned to users in relation to PMM. Permission sets should be assigned depending on how the user will interact with PMM. The permission sets are as follows.

PMM Manage

Assign this permission set to the Salesforce admin as well as other users who will be configuring programs, services, and engagements. These users are generally program managers or directors:

1. Go to **Setup** > **Users** > **Permission Sets** > **PMM: Manage** and click **Manage Assignments**.

2. Choose the users who need this level of permission and add them.

3. See the following figure:

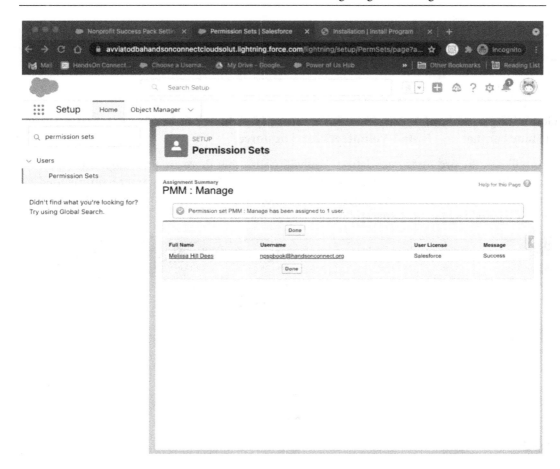

Figure 9.11 – PMM: Manage permission set example for the system administrator assignment

Repeat this process for any users who need **PMM Deliver** or **PMM View**.

PMM Deliver

This permission set is for users who normally fulfill the role of **Case Manager** or deliver services. These users have limited capabilities for creating and editing.

PMM View

Assign this permission set to those users who need to view information but have no need to modify any of the PMM data.

In *Chapter 11, Configuring Additional Features and Security*, additional configuration work will be outlined depending on the use case for PMM.

Installing Volunteers for Salesforce

Installing V4S is very similar to installing PMM. Let's get started.

Steps for Installing V4S

Go to https://install.salesforce.org/products/v4s/latest and click the blue bar that says **Install Volunteers for Salesforce**.

This will run the pre-install validation. You will notice that there are four different steps that the installation can take; **Install Page Layouts (NPSP)** is optional but recommended. Unless you already know that you will *not* be using the preconfigured page layouts, install all four by clicking the blue **Install** button.

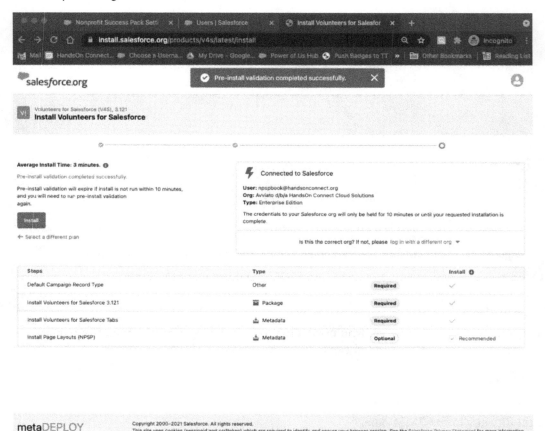

Figure 9.12 – Options for steps to install V4S using metaDEPLOY

The average installation time is approximately 3 minutes. There are no additional post-install configurations; optional configurations can be found in *Chapter 11, Configuring Additional Features and Security.*

Installing Case Management

Because Case Management is a paid product, the licenses for it must be provisioned and available in the Salesforce instance before you begin the installation.

> **Note**
>
> Case Management **only** works in Lightning Experience, therefore, it is not available in Salesforce Classic.

Once you have confirmed that the Nonprofit Cloud Case Management licenses are available, install Case Management from `https://install.salesforce.org/products/case-management/latest/install` by clicking the blue button to start the pre-installation validation as done for the previous installs in this chapter.

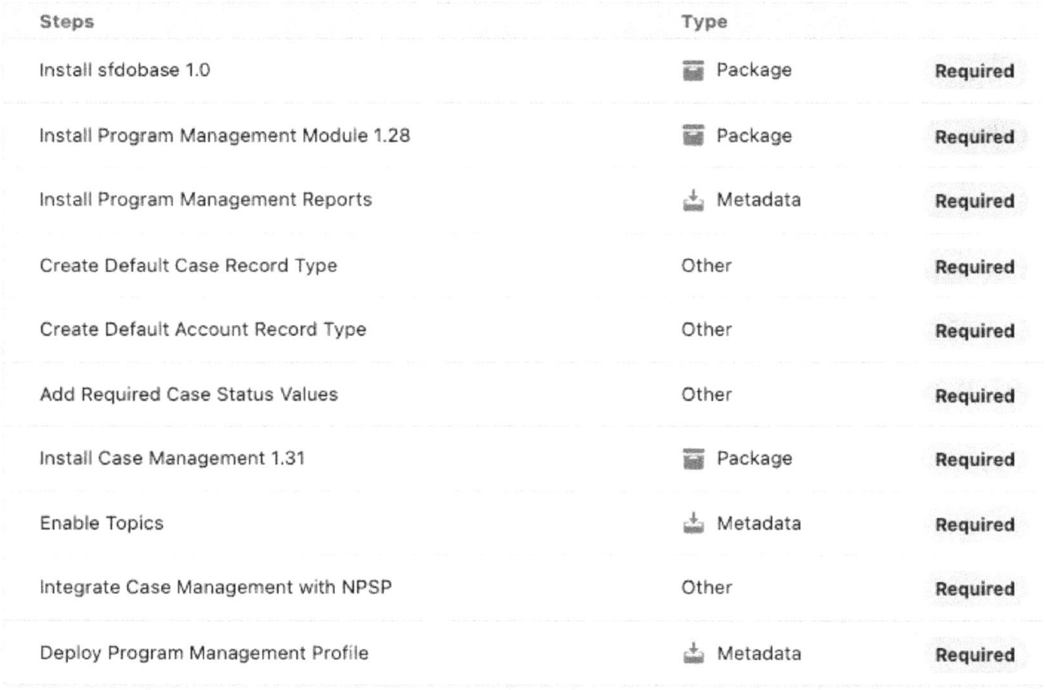

Steps	Type	
Install sfdobase 1.0	Package	Required
Install Program Management Module 1.28	Package	Required
Install Program Management Reports	Metadata	Required
Create Default Case Record Type	Other	Required
Create Default Account Record Type	Other	Required
Add Required Case Status Values	Other	Required
Install Case Management 1.31	Package	Required
Enable Topics	Metadata	Required
Integrate Case Management with NPSP	Other	Required
Deploy Program Management Profile	Metadata	Required

Figure 9.13 – Case Management installation page

Once the pre-install validation is done, click the blue bar that says **Install Nonprofit Cloud Case Management** to complete the installation.

Post-installation required configuration

There are only two required post-installation configurations for Case Management.

User access

Grant users access to Case Management by assigning them the **Case Management Permission** set. This permission gives users access to the Case Management app.

Additionally, there are three levels of permission sets to be assigned to users based on the functionality the user will need. They are very similar to the permission sets in PMM and follow the same pattern:

- **Manage**: This is the highest level of permission and generally is assigned to the Salesforce Administrator and Program Managers.
- **Deliver**: This level is assigned to case managers with less create and edit permissions.
- **View**: This level is view-only.

Assigning page layouts

Installing Case Management provides three pre-configured page layouts. Assign the following page layouts to the appropriate Case Management users:

- **Account**: Branch page layout
- **Contact**: Case Management page layout
- **Case**: Incident layout

With this, we have completed the required configurations for Case Management.

Summary

This chapter and the next two chapters – *Chapter 10, Configuring Fundraising Features*, and *Chapter 11, Configuring Additional Features and Security* – cover installing and configuring the most common Nonprofit Cloud components in a Salesforce instance. In this chapter, we installed components in a Salesforce instance and went through the required post-installation configurations.

Chapters 9 to *Chapter 11* comprise the bulk of the work on implementing and configuring the various Nonprofit Cloud components we explored in the early chapters of this book. You have learned how to ascertain where to install the Nonprofit Cloud components depending on whether there is an existing Salesforce instance or if a new trial instance is being created that already has NPSP installed. Armed with the knowledge of what NPSP, PMM, V4S, and Case Management features provide, we have taken a hands-on look at getting those components installed and configured in a Salesforce instance.

In *Chapter 10, Configuring Fundraising Features*, we will focus solely on the additional configurations and practical uses cases for the fundraising features found in NPSP. This chapter will call on all the areas of knowledge gained up to this point to make decisions about which configurations will be necessary and how to make the fundraising features work best.

Resources and additional reading

- *Nonprofit Success Pack Upgrade Guide*: `https://s3-us-west-2.amazonaws.com/sfdo-docs/npsp_upgrade_guide.pdf`

- *Convert to the Nonprofit Success Pack Household Account Model*: `https://s3-us-west-2.amazonaws.com/sfdo-docs/npsp_account_model_conversion.pdf`

- *Feature Configuration Overview*: `https://powerofus.force.com/s/article/NPSP-Feature-Configuration-Overview#topic-3670`

- *NPSP Basics*: `https://trailhead.salesforce.com/en/content/learn/modules/nonprofit-success-pack-basics?trail_id=explore-nonprofit-success-pack`

- *Program Management with Nonprofit Cloud*: `https://trailhead.salesforce.com/en/content/learn/modules/program-management-with-nonprofit-cloud`

- *V4S Basics*: `https://trailhead.salesforce.com/en/content/learn/modules/nonprofit_volunteer_basics`

- *Human Services with Nonprofit Cloud Case Management*: `https://trailhead.salesforce.com/content/learn/modules/human-services-with-nonprofit-cloud-case-management?trailmix_creator_id=pwhite39&trailmix_slug=get-started-nonprofit-cloud-case-management`

10
Configuring Fundraising Features

In *Chapter 9*, *Installing Nonprofit Cloud Solutions*, we installed NPSP and did the required configurations for everything except the fundraising features.

Why did we do so? We did this because fundraising is at the very heart of NPSP. There are many ways to configure NPSP, as can be seen from the variety of use cases we have already discussed. Although we may not cover every configuration in detail, in this chapter, we will walk through the configurations of the most common use cases.

By the end of this chapter, we will have the following knowledge base:

- How to implement the required configurations in NPSP for fundraising
- How to implement the recommended configurations in NPSP for fundraising
- How to configure the most commonly used NPSP features for fundraising
- Use cases for other commonly used NPSP fundraising features

As we work through each of these areas, it is a good practice to remember how vitally important it is to truly understand the organization and what its goals are as regards the Nonprofit Cloud implementation. In *Chapter 9*, *Installing Nonprofit Cloud Solutions*, we began with the installation of NPSP and the post-installation configuration. Here, in *Chapter 10*, *Configuring Fundraising Features*, we will complete the configuration of NPSP and discuss any use cases for the features that we are implementing.

Required configurations for NPSP fundraising

Since you have already installed NPSP in *Chapter 9*, *Installing Nonprofit Cloud Solutions*, you will need to complete these additional configurations to adequately set up and test NPSP for your use cases. These steps are required before we can begin to refine what is required:

> **Note**
>
> Whether you are using a new instance or are installing NPSP in an already existing instance of Salesforce, check to make sure the post-installation configuration is done.

1. Log in to your Salesforce instance and you should be back at the **Get Started with NPSP - Admin** page.

2. You can refer to the following screenshot:

Figure 10.1 – Get Started with NPSP – Admin landing page when you log in to Salesforce

Once you are done with this, let's finish up the required configurations.

Opportunity stages

As a Salesforce administrator, you are already familiar with the standard object, **Opportunity**. In a Salesforce instance with NPSP, you should confirm that the following picklist values exist for opportunities based on the use cases you will use.

Go to **Setup** > **Object Manager** > **Opportunity** > **Fields & Relationships** to edit or add new stages as per the recommended stages list in the following table:

Recommended Stage Name	API Name	Type	Probability	Forecast Category
Application Submitted	Application Submitted	Open	30%	Pipeline
Awarded	Awarded	Closed/Won	100%	Closed
Closed Lost	Closed Lost	Closed/Lost	0%	Omitted
Closed Won	Closed Won	Closed/Won	100%	Closed
Cultivation	Cultivation	Open	30%	Pipeline
Declined	Declined	Closed/Lost	0%	Omitted
Identification	Identification	Open	10%	Pipeline
In-Kind Not Yet Received	In-Kind Not Yet Received	Open	50%	Omitted
In-Kind Received	In-Kind Received	Closed/Won	100%	Omitted
LOI Submitted	LOI Submitted	Open	20%	Pipeline
Pledged	Pledged	Open	50%	Pipeline
Posted	Posted	Closed/Won	100%	Closed
Proposal/Review	Proposal/Review	Open	60%	Best Case
Prospecting	Prospecting	Open	10%	Pipeline
Qualification	Qualification	Open	10%	Pipeline
Solicitation	Solicitation	Open	40%	Pipeline
Verbal Commitment	Verbal Commitment	Open	80%	Commit
Withdrawn	Withdrawn	Closed/Lost	0%	Omitted

Table 10.1 – Recommended settings for the stage value in the Opportunity object

These are the suggested stages for opportunities when using NPSP. Additional stages may be required depending on specific use cases.

Sales processes

NPSP has four different **sales processes** that come as part of the standard package:

- Donation
- Grant
- In-Kind Gift
- Major Gift

You need to confirm that they are available in your Salesforce instance by going to **Setup** > **Sales Processes**, as shown in *Figure 10.2*:

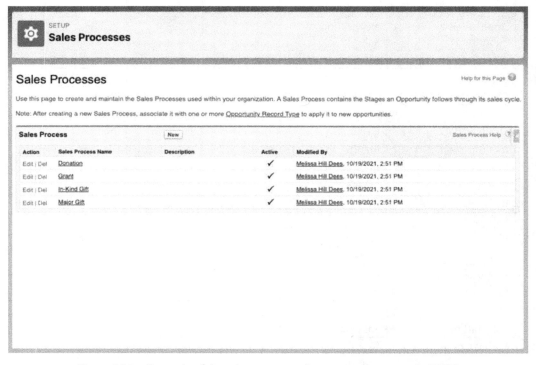

Figure 10.2 – Example of the sales processes that are present to use in NPSP

Each sales process may use a specific set of opportunity stages based on the business process the organization has shared. The recommended settings are listed here:

Sales Process	Recommended Opportunity Stages
Donation	Pledged, Closed Won, Declined, Closed Lost
Grant	Prospecting, LOI Submitted, Application Submitted, Awarded, Withdrawn, Declined
In-Kind Gift	Prospecting, In-Kind Not Yet Received, In-Kind Received, Withdrawn
Major Gift	Identification, Qualification, Cultivation, Solicitation, Proposal/Review, Verbal Commitment, Awarded, Closed Won, Withdrawn, Declined

Table 10.2 – Sales process examples with correlating recommended opportunity stages

Additional sales processes may exist in the Salesforce instance for reasons outside of NPSP, while additional sales processes may be added to NPSP if the business processes are required.

Opportunity record types

NPSP also comes with six different **opportunity record types** as part of the standard package. Check to confirm that each of the six record types exists in the Salesforce instance by going to **Setup** > **Object Manager** > **Opportunity** > **Record Type**:

Record Types
6 Items, Sorted by Record Type Label

| | | Quick Find | New | Page Layout Assignment |

RECORD TYPE LABEL ▲	DESCRIPTION	ACTIVE	MODIFIED BY	
Donation	Donation Received	✓	Melissa Hill Dees, 10/19/2021, 2:51 PM	▼
Grant	Grant Received	✓	Melissa Hill Dees, 10/19/2021, 2:51 PM	▼
In-Kind Gift	Goods or Services received as In-Kind	✓	Melissa Hill Dees, 10/19/2021, 2:51 PM	▼
Major Gift	Large Donation from a Major Donor	✓	Melissa Hill Dees, 10/19/2021, 2:51 PM	▼
Matching Gift	Matching Donation from an Donor's Employer or other Organization	✓	Melissa Hill Dees, 10/19/2021, 2:51 PM	▼
Membership	A membership record type	✓	Melissa Hill Dees, 10/19/2021, 2:51 PM	▼

Figure 10.3 – Recommended Opportunity record types for standard NPSP

For each record type, you can create unique page layouts, picklist values, and business processes and enable those record types as the default for users of various profiles in Salesforce. There may be additional opportunity record types in the Salesforce instance, particularly if it has been in use for some time.

> **Note**
> This is an excellent reason to create a sandbox in an existing Salesforce instance. Some Opportunity record types may be duplicates in what they accomplish. Also, be aware of the Opportunity record type that is set as the default for existing users.

New button on the Opportunity-related list

Confirm that the **New** button on the opportunity-related list is working as expected by following these configuration steps:

1. Click **Setup** > **Object Manager** > **Accounts** > **Page Layout** > **Organization** (or Account) **Layout**. Scroll down through the related list to **Opportunities**.

2. Click the **wrench** and then scroll down to the section marked **Buttons**.

3. Click the + sign to open this section.

4. Be sure that the **New** button is checked and move the **New Account Donation** to the **Selected Buttons** section.

Figure 10.4 – This figure shows how the setup should look when you are finished

Once you have updated or confirmed these configurations, click **OK**.

New and Edit buttons on Contact

You need to confirm that the following button lists exist on the **Contact** record:

- New Donation
- New In-Kind Gift
- New Major Gift
- New Membership
- New Open Recurring Donation

There may be additional buttons on the page layout. The buttons listed here are the ones that are necessary for the fundraising feature configuration:

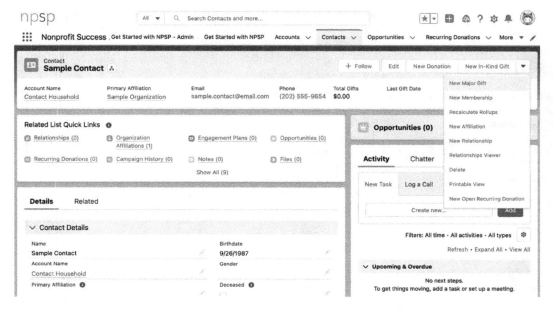

Figure 10.5 – Buttons that should exist on the Contact record

If these buttons do not exist in the Salesforce instance, you may need to create **Quick Actions** for each Opportunity record type and add these buttons to the Contact record.

Opportunity Contact Roles

Opportunity Contact Roles are used to connect **Opportunities** and **Contacts**. Although you can create whatever is appropriate for the nonprofit, the most commonly used roles are as follows:

- Donor
- Household Member
- Soft Credit
- Matched Donor
- Honoree
- Notification Recipient
- Grant Manager

- Decision Maker

- Influencer

- Solicitor

- Workplace Giving

- Other

To add, edit, or deactivate any **Contact Roles**, go to **Setup** > **Feature Settings** > **Sales** > **Contact Roles** on **Opportunities**.

Enabling Opportunity workflow rules

There are two helpful workflow rules in NPSP that are inactive by default when NPSP is installed. The workflow rules are as follows:

Opportunity Copy FMV to Amount:	Enable this rule to copy the fair Market Value to the Amount field, when the amount is zero or blank.
Opportunity Email Acknowledgment:	Emails an acknowledgment to the primary Contact for an Opportunity when the Acknowledgement Status is set to Email Acknowledgement Now.

Table 10.3 – Opportunity workflow rules that need to be activated during configuration

To enable these workflow rules, go to **Setup** > **Process Automation** > **Workflow Rules**. Activate these two workflow rules. These two automations streamline the work done in fundraising and conclude the required configurations. Next, we begin the recommended configurations.

Recommended configurations for NPSP fundraising features

Now that the required and standard configurations for NPSP fundraising features are complete, the next step is to apply the recommended configurations. Applying some of these configurations will depend on the nonprofit's use case. Let's get started and look at what can be configured.

Helpful list views

One of the most helpful configurations is the list view. Salesforce comes with default list views already created. For Nonprofit Cloud users, the following list views are recommended for **Accounts** and **Opportunity**:

The table shows the recommended name of the list view, the record type to be used as a filter (if applicable), and the fields to be included in the list view.

List view	Record type	Fields to be included
Organization Accounts	Account Record Type = Organization	Account Name, Account Site, Billing State/Province, Phone, Type, Account Owner Alias
All Accounts	N/A	Account Name, Billing State/Province, Phone, Total Gifts, Total Gifts Last N Days, Average Gift, Type, Account Record Type
Household Accounts	Account Record Type = Household	Account Name, Formal Greeting, Informal Greeting. Total Gifts, Average Gift, Best Gift Year, Household Phone
All Donations	Opportunity Record Type = Donation	Opportunity Name, Account Name, Amount, Close Date, Stage, Opportunity Owner Alias

Table 10.4 – Recommended list view names, record types, and included fields for helpful list views

1. Create the list views from the object list view page.

2. Click the **Accounts** object tab.

Figure 10.6 – This is what you should see when you click the Accounts object tab in NPSP

3. Click **List View Controls cog** and then click **New**.

4. Enter the appropriate name. Salesforce will automatically create the API name. Allow all users access.

5. Click **Save**.

6. Next, update the display fields for the list view.

7. Open the list view and click **List View Controls cog**.

8. Click **Select Fields to Display** and move the appropriate fields from **available** to **visible**.

9. Click **Save**.

10. Finally, open the list view and click the filter. Click **Add Filter**.

    The All-Accounts list view does not require a filter. For the rest of the list views, select record type as the field, `equals` as the operator, and `appropriate record type name` as the value.

11. Click **Done**.

12. Click **Save**.

Your helpful list views should now be configured appropriately. Don't forget that you can pin the single most used list view so that the page automatically opens on that list view. Let's continue to **Compact Layouts**. List views that are filtered by one record type make inline editing available for many fields.

Configuring Compact Layouts

Already in this chapter and in *Chapter 9, Installing Nonprofit Cloud Solutions*, page layouts have had some updates. NPSP also adds new **Compact Layouts** to the Salesforce instance. Some of the Compact Layouts installed by NPSP are as follows:

- **Contact**: NPSP Contact Compact Layout
- **Account**: NPSP Household Account, NPSP Organization Account
- **Opportunity**: NPSP Donation Compact Layout
- **Campaign**: NPSP Compact Layout

These can be used as they are installed, or you can clone them to create more customized versions that work better for the use case.

Configuring fundraising features for specific use cases

As of the time of publication of this book, NPSP offers 20 different features that can be configured for specific use cases. The features are listed here. We are going to look at the most common features used in fundraising:

NPSP Feature	Description
Acknowledge Donations by Email	Email acknowledgments to donors.
Address Management	Enter different types of addresses for Accounts (specifically Household), such as home, work, and seasonal addresses.
Advanced Mapping	Import to fields directly related to Accounts, Contacts, or Opportunities.
Automated and Manual Soft Credits	Configure NPSP to assign soft credit automatically or manually by creating Opportunity Contact Roles records based on Relationships, Affiliations, and Opportunity fields.
Batch Data Import	Advanced data import strategies.
Customizable Rollups	Highly customizable rollups from Opportunities, Payments, or Soft Credits.
Data Importer	NPSP data import tool.
Donation Allocations	Track donations using General Allocation Units.
Engagement Plans	A set of tasks to engage constituents and lead them toward a specific outcome.
Gift Entry	Gift entry templates for consistent data entry of single gifts or many gifts.
Grants	Manage incoming grant data.
Household Naming	Create appropriate naming conventions for automatically created Households.
In-Kind Gifts	Differentiate in-kind donations from monetary donations.
Levels	Track engagement based on data such as total donations or total volunteer hours this month.
Matching Gifts	Record corporate donations made as a match triggered by a donation from an employee.
Memberships	Manage memberships in NPSP by individual or household, length, and level of membership.

NPSP Feature	Description
Recurring Donations (Enhanced)	Pledged donations given over a period.
Recurring Donations (Legacy)	Pledged donations given over a period.
Reports & Dashboards Package	67 reports and 4 dashboards contributed by community members.
Relationships	Relationships connect one Contact to another and can be automated or manual.
Tribute Opportunities	Track donor data related to honorees and memorials and the individual who should be notified of the donation.

Table 10.5 – Fundraising features available in NPSP

Of these features, the most commonly used are as follows:

1. Automated and manual soft credits

2. Donation allocations

3. Gift entry

4. Recurring donations

Let's address configuring each of these in the next section.

Configuring automated and manual soft credits

In *Chapter 2, What Is NPSP?*, we discussed soft credits to track a donor's influence on donations that are made to the nonprofit. We outlined a situation where Diana, a board member with a nonprofit, donates to the nonprofit. Her employer matches her donation. For the donation from the employer, Diana should receive soft credit for that donation. So how do we configure NPSP to make that happen? Let's see.

Firstly, we need to confirm that the **Advanced Mapping for Data Import** and **Gift Entry system** tools are enabled.

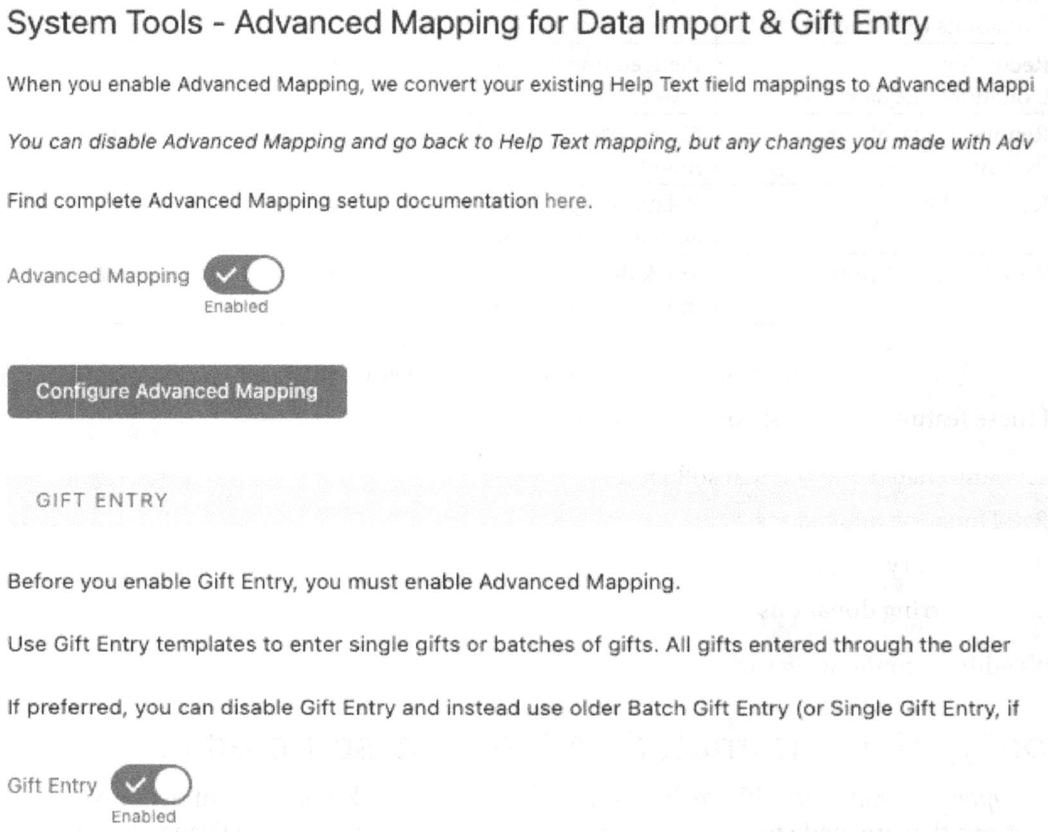

System Tools - Advanced Mapping for Data Import & Gift Entry

When you enable Advanced Mapping, we convert your existing Help Text field mappings to Advanced Mappi

You can disable Advanced Mapping and go back to Help Text mapping, but any changes you made with Adv

Find complete Advanced Mapping setup documentation here.

Advanced Mapping   ☑◯
                   Enabled

[Configure Advanced Mapping]

GIFT ENTRY

Before you enable Gift Entry, you must enable Advanced Mapping.

Use Gift Entry templates to enter single gifts or batches of gifts. All gifts entered through the older

If preferred, you can disable Gift Entry and instead use older Batch Gift Entry (or Single Gift Entry, if

Gift Entry   ☑◯
             Enabled

Figure 10.7 – NPSP Settings page where the Advanced Mapping and Gift Entry settings are enabled

With these tools enabled, there are several steps yet to confirm:

1. Confirm the appropriate roles have been activated on the **Opportunity Contact Role** object based on the nonprofit's use case. For Diana's soft credit, the **Matched Donor** role should be available and assigned.

2. Confirm that the soft credit fields are enabled on **Contacts**, **Relationships**, and **Affiliations** by checking the field-level security and the page layouts.

3. Confirm that the **Manage Soft Credits** button is available on the **Opportunity** page layout for the profiles who need access to the feature.

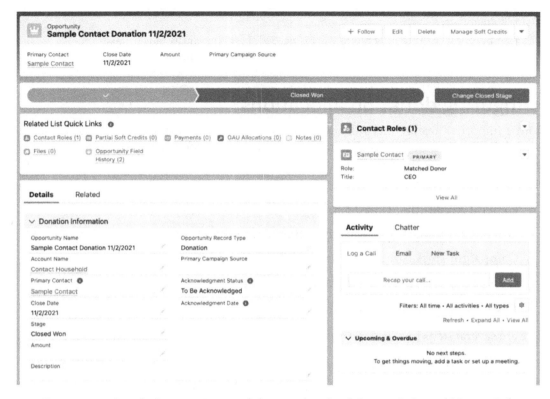

Figure 10.8 – Sample Opportunity record showing the related Contact Roles and Manage Soft Credits dropdowns

Other available configurations include the following:

- Enabling automated household member soft credits

- Enabling contact role for organizational opportunities

- Enabling relationship and affiliation soft credits

- Enabling partial soft credits

- Enabling account soft credits

Determine which of these will be needed using the tools for discovery as discussed in *Chapter 8, Requirements - User Stories – Business Processes – What Is Your Organization Trying to Achieve?*. Resources for additional configurations are listed at the end of this chapter.

> **Remember**
>
> A best practice is to only reveal what is needed. Less complexity aids in easy user adoption. Additional features can be configured as demand requires.

Configuring donation allocations

Another important feature that will automate manual processes is the ability to define **General Accounting Units (GAUs)** that correlate to a nonprofit's chart of accounts. Donations are then assigned and tracked based on the allocation. The objects involved in donation allocations are as follows:

- **General Accounting Unit**: Chart of accounts represented
- **GAU Allocation**: Connects the donation to the GAU
- **Campaign**: Tracks groups of donations
- **Opportunity**: Tracks the amount for each donation
- **Recurring Donation**: Tracks the amount for recurring donations

There are several steps involved in confirming configurations for donation allocations:

1. Confirm that every profile that needs access to GAUs has access to the GAU tab.
2. Confirm that every profile that needs access to GAUs has access to the objects, fields, and, specifically, the `visualforce` page entitled `npsp.ALLO_ManageAllocations`.
3. Confirm that the GAU Allocations-related list has been added to the appropriate page layouts.
4. To use donation allocations, you need to create at least one GAU.
5. Additionally, you can add custom fields via the **Manage Allocations** and **Additional Fields** fieldset if the nonprofit's business processes require them to manage allocations.

Let's now see the steps to automate allocations:

1. Go to **NPSP Settings** > **Donations** > **GAU Allocations** and click **Edit**.
2. Select the **Default Allocations Enabled** checkbox and select **GAU** for the default.
3. Click **Save**.

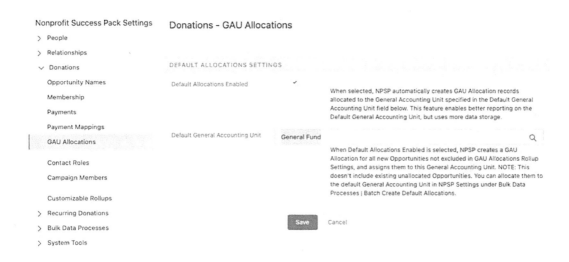

Figure 10.9 – Example of a standard GAU Allocation configuration

With this configuration, all incoming donations are automatically allocated to **General Fund**. Rollups for Allocations in NPSP are pre-defined. If you choose to customize allocation rollups, you can exclude specific **Opportunity record** types using filters and set day values or fiscal years. These settings are available to edit in **NPSP Settings** > **Donations** > **Customizable Rollups**.

Configuring gift entry

Gift Entry is an important tool for facilitating the entry of donations in Salesforce and maintaining consistent data integrity. By default, **Gift Entry** is disabled in NPSP.

To enable **Gift Entry,** you can follow these four steps:

1. Go to **NPSP Settings** > **System Tools** > **Advanced Mapping for Data Import & Gift Entry**.

2. Confirm that **Advanced Mapping** is enabled.

3. Then, enable **Gift Entry**.

4. Replace the **New Donation** button in page layouts with the **New Gift** button or add the **New Gift** button in the **Mobile & Lightning Actions** section of the page layouts for **Accounts** and **Contacts**.

Confirm that the users have the **Gift Entry Recommended** permission set assigned so they can access the appropriate tools. There is an extensive list of standard permissions that should be confirmed for the **Gift Entry Recommended** permission set; see the *Resources and additional reading* section at the end of this chapter. Additional permissions may be granted based on the nonprofit's specific use cases.

In the **Gift Entry** tab, you can update the list view for **Batches**. You can also edit or create a new template for **Gift Entry**, which is specifically based on the nonprofit's business processes.

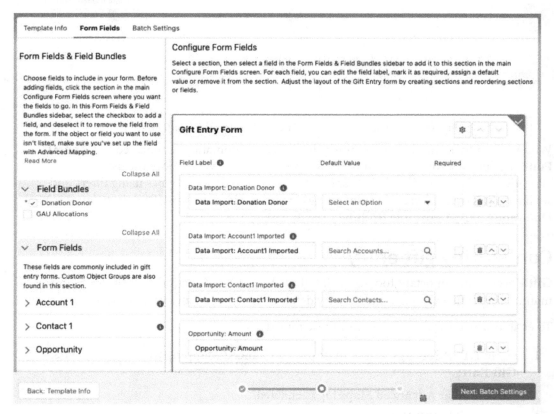

Figure 10.10 – New gift entry template creator in NPSP

Advanced options for configuration include adjusting **Gift Entry** and advanced mapping so that a contact's address field is autopopulated in the **Gift Entry** form. Advanced options are documented in the **Resources** section for **Configure Gift Entry**.

Configuring recurring donations

Recurring donations are what every nonprofit hopes for – donors who pledge to give over and over on a recurring basis. NPSP needs to be configured to accept and track those recurring gifts. Because recurring donations are so important, NPSP introduced **Enhanced Recurring Donations** in March 2021. To configure the ability to track gifts that donors have pledged (monthly, quarterly, yearly, and even custom schedules), the **Recurring Donation** and **Opportunity** objects are used.

The **Recurring Donation** object is where the donation schedules and amounts are set; this object also related the donor to the donation. The **Opportunity** object tracks each installment paid per the schedule and amount set in the **Recurring Donation** field.

To configure **Recurring Donations**, review the settings in **NPSP Settings** > **Recurring Donations** > **Recurring Donations**.

The settings are editable based on the nonprofit's business processes; however, NPSP does provide default settings. You will also need to confirm that **Recurring Donations** users have the appropriate object, field, and Apex class permissions, specifically for the **Recurring Donations** and **Opportunities** objects. There is no default **Recurring Donation** permission set installed; you may want to create your own based on the detailed information supplied in the **Resources** section of this chapter.

You also need to confirm that the **Active Schedules** and **Upcoming Installments** components are visible on the **Recurring Donations** lightning record pages.

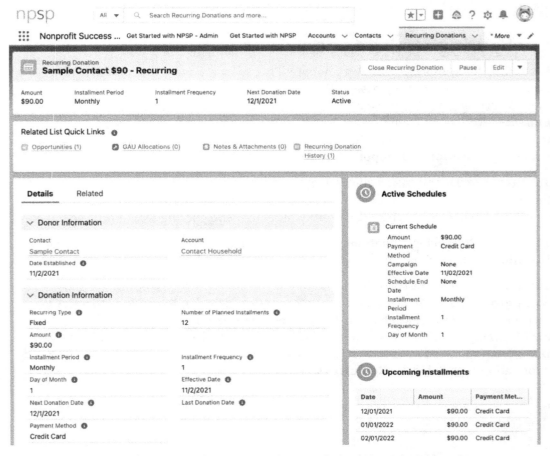

Figure 10.11 – Sample recurring donation record page with the Active Schedules and Upcoming Installments components

Recurring Donations is a simple way to visualize these vital gifts as well as project future income based on pledged funds.

Summary

In this chapter, we have gone much deeper into the actual setup and configuration of the fundraising features of NPSP. The commonly used features include applying soft credits, donation allocations, gift entry, and recurring donations. We have outlined how to enable and configure each of those fundraising features in general.

There are additional, more self-explanatory, configurable settings in the NPSP settings based on the nonprofit's use cases and business processes. There are also additional configurations documented for less-used features. In *Chapter 12, Declarative Tools and Modules*, we will take a deeper dive into **Customizable Rollups and Matching Gifts** that we touched on in this chapter. And then, in *Chapter 13, To Customize or Not to Customize*, we will learn the advanced configuration of **Table-Driven Trigger Management (TDTM)** and its use cases.

Before we start more advanced studies, let's finish configuring the standard PMM, case management, and V4S applications, and address data management and security in *Chapter 11, Configuring Additional Features and Security*.

Resources and additional reading

- *Nonprofit Success Pack Upgrade Guide*: https://s3-us-west-2.amazonaws.com/sfdo-docs/npsp_upgrade_guide.pdf

- *Convert to the Nonprofit Success Pack Household Account Model*: https://s3-us-west-2.amazonaws.com/sfdo-docs/npsp_account_model_conversion.pdf

- *Feature Configuration Overview*: https://powerofus.force.com/s/article/NPSP-Feature-Configuration-Overview#topic-3670

- *Create Global Quick Actions*: https://help.salesforce.com/articleView?id=creating_global_actions.htm

- *Configure Automated and Manual Soft Credits*: https://powerofus.force.com/s/article/NPSP-Configure-Automated-Soft-Credits

- *Configure Gift Entry*: https://powerofus.force.com/s/article/NPSP-Configure-Gift-Entry#topic-9135

- *Configure Recurring Donations*: https://powerofus.force.com/s/article/NPSP-Configure-Recurring-Donations

11

Configuring Additional Nonprofit Cloud Features and Security

In *Chapter 9, Installing Nonprofit Cloud Solutions*, we installed NPSP and the additional features that are available for PMM and V4S. In *Chapter 10, Configuring Fundraising Features*, we configured the fundraising features for NPSP. In this chapter, we will finish configuring PMM and V4S. Although we may not perform every configuration in detail, we will walk through the configurations for the most common use cases. **Case Management** is a paid add-on for PMM where we will make these configurations.

After completing this chapter, you will know about the following:

- Configuring permission sets in PMM
- Implementing configurations in V4S for volunteers and staff
- Setting up Case Management

The last two sections in this chapter will be about data management and security and any additional permissions considerations that are relevant to implementing Nonprofit Cloud. Here, we will do the following:

- Maintaining data integrity and security
- Understanding additional permissions for NPSP administrators and other profiles and roles in NPSP

So, let's start by looking at the permission sets for PMM.

Configuring Program Management Module (PMM)

For a detailed recap of the functionality of PMM and its use cases, see *Chapter 3, Tracking Impact with the Program Management Module*. The following diagram shows the data structure of PMM before we begin configuring it:

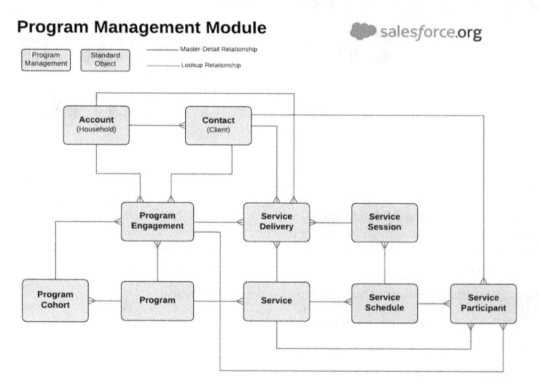

Figure 11.1 – PMM entity relationship diagram

Wherever you installed NPSP and PMM in *Chapter 9, Installing Nonprofit Cloud Solutions*, you will need to complete these additional configurations to adequately set up PMM. Upon logging into your Salesforce instance, you should be back at the **Get Started with NPSP – Admin** page.

Let's complete the required configurations.

Required post-installation configurations

As a Salesforce administrator, you should already be familiar with **Profiles** and **Permission Sets**. Post-installation configuration for PMM involves these two settings. Let's take a look at them in more detail.

Profiles

When we installed PMM, **Program Management Standard User Profile** was installed alongside it. At this point, profiles need to be assigned to users who want to use PMM:

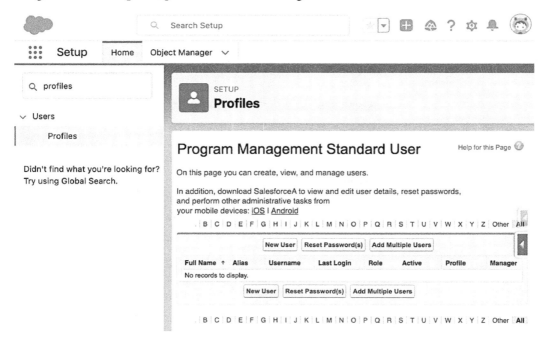

Figure 11.2 – Program Management Standard User profile management

Let's understand the steps for user management:

1. To add new users or assign one or more users to the profile, click **Setup** > **Users** > **Profiles** > **Program Management Standard User** > **Assigned Users**.

2. Assign the appropriate users to this profile.

One additional consideration for the **Program Management Standard User** profile is to add the functionality to **View Dashboards** in public folders and **View Reports** in public folders. This can be done in the profile itself by checking the appropriate boxes under **System Permissions**. Alternatively, create a **Permission Set** with the desired access and settings. Permission sets are gaining popularity as the best way to provide access to users regardless of their profile or role.

Permission sets

Next, the appropriate **Permission Set** for PMM's functionality needs to be assigned. The PMM package provides three different permission sets based on the tasks a user needs to complete. You can access these permission sets by clicking **Setup** > **Users** > **Permission Sets**, as shown in the following screenshot:

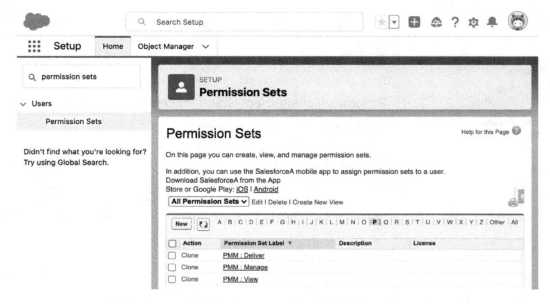

Figure 11.3 – PMM Permission Sets to be assigned as part of the post-installation configuration

Each permission set provides different levels of access in PMM. You can assign these permission sets to the appropriate users based on the access they need:

- **PMM: Manage** is the least restrictive level of access. This permission set is normally assigned to the Salesforce administrator, directors, and managers. It gives create, read, edit, and delete access to the **Programs, Services, Program Engagements, Program Cohorts, Service Deliveries, Service Participants, Service Schedules,** and **Service Sessions** objects and fields.

- **PMM: Deliver** is the level of access that most of the staff who deliver programs will need. It can also apply to case managers. It provides create, read, and edit access to the **Program Engagements, Services Deliveries,** and **Service Participants** objects and fields; read and edit access to the **Service Sessions** objects and fields; and read-only access to the **Programs, Program Cohorts and Services,** and **Service Schedules** objects and fields.

- **PMM: View** provides read-only access to the custom objects that make up PMM. This permission set is helpful for executives who need visibility for PMM.

> **Note**
> These permission sets only apply to the custom objects that make up PMM. Ensure that read, create, edit, and delete access is granted for standard objects for **Accounts, Contacts, and Cases**.

Configuring sharing rules for PMM

As a Salesforce administrator, sharing rules are an important part of configuration and security in a Salesforce instance. The same is true if you're using sharing rules for PMM and the task is just as simple. Follow these steps:

3. Create a public group by clicking **Setup** > **Users** > **Public Groups** > **New**, filling in the group's **Label** and **Group Name,** and specifying the appropriate users under **Available Members**:

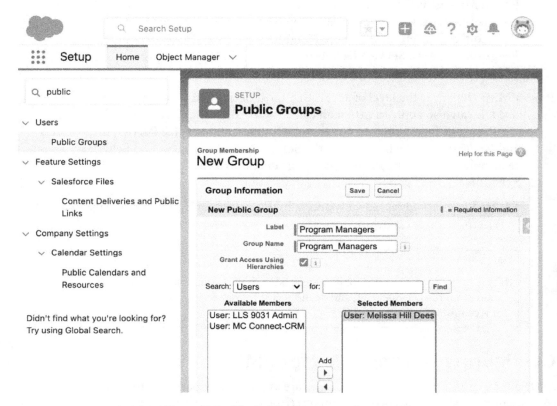

Figure 11.4 – The Public Groups creation page

4. Then, create the sharing rules for the public group by clicking **Setup** > **Sharing Settings**. Choose **Program** from the dropdown list and click **New** under **Program Sharing Rules**.

5. See the recommended configuration that's shown in the following screenshot:

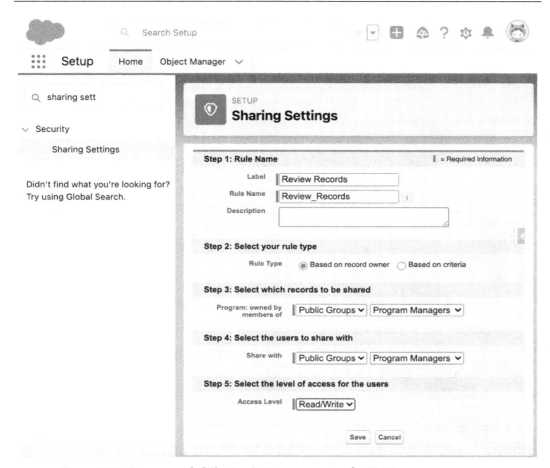

Figure 11.5 – Recommended Sharing Settings page setup for PMM program managers

6.   Click **Save**.

Repeat these steps to define the sharing rules for other objects in the PMM, such as **Program Engagements**, **Program Cohorts**, **Services**, and **Service Deliveries**.

Experience Cloud configurations (optional)

If you wish to use Experience Cloud for the PMM audience to engage and interact with Salesforce, then you will need to build an **Experience Cloud** site, as we discussed in *Chapter 5*, *Tracking Volunteer Impact*. Experience Cloud is another certification altogether; learning how to build out Experience Cloud will not be addressed here. However, it is important to note that when you are configuring PMM, additional configurations are required if you wish to use Experience Cloud.

Let's look at some of these configuration options:

- You will need to assign the appropriate permission set to Experience Cloud user licenses. A quick way to make sure they have the access they need to do this is to do the following:

  - Clone the **PMM: View** permission set.

  - Name the cloned permission set `Site Participant: View`.

  - Assign it to users as needed.

- **Attendance** and **Service Schedule** are two components that are available in Experience Cloud. Use **Sharing Rules** to further define and refine what your external Experience Cloud users will see.

PMM can be used without a participant interface, depending on the organization's specific use cases.

Customizable configurations for PMM

PMM is a very robust and flexible tool that can be configured and customized to fit almost any program. Let's take a high-level look at some of the ways PMM can work with different use cases.

Who are the recipients of programs and services?

Two of the use cases that we looked at in *Chapter 3*, *Tracking Impact with the Program Management Module*, involved recipients who were not individuals or contacts; they were entire households and animals. So, how do we configure PMM to work in those cases? For both cases, where a **Client (Contact)** is not served, the first step is to remove the **Client** field from the **Program Engagements** and **Service Deliveries** objects.

The configurations that are required for households include adding a new field to the **Program Engagements** and **Service Deliveries** objects. The field will be a lookup field to **Account**, for a household, or to a custom object that has been created, such as **Animal**. This process will not relate the appropriate object to the programs and services you are tracking.

> **Note**
>
> Be sure to include these new fields in the appropriate page layouts and include the related lists on **Accounts** and custom objects.

Additionally, you will want to customize the **Bulk Service Delivery** object to reflect the change in the related service recipient, as well as customize **Quick Actions** and **Record Naming**.

Automating Program Engagement and Service Delivery naming

PMM also includes two process builders that can be updated or customized to reflect the specific use cases for PMM. As an administrator, you should already be familiar with process builders and how to access them. The two PMM process builders are called **Program Engagement Object** and **Service Delivery Object**:

Figure 11.6 – PMM process builders installed

The default formula for the `Update Name` part of the **Program Engagement Object** process builder can be edited by cloning the process builder and making the necessary adjustments. Depending on the use case, you may want to remove `Anonymous` from the auto-naming process or replace it with an account name or a custom object, such as `Animals`. The default formula is as follows:

```
IF(
    NOT(
```

```
    ISBLANK(
      [pmdm__ProgramEngagement__c].pmdm__Contact__c
    )
  ),
  IF(
    LEN(
      [pmdm__ProgramEngagement__c].pmdm__Contact__c.FirstName
+ ' ' + [pmdm__ProgramEngagement__c].pmdm__Contact__c.LastName
+ ' ' +
      IF(
        NOT(
          ISBLANK(
            [pmdm__ProgramEngagement__c].pmdm__StartDate__c
          )
        ),
        TEXT(
          [pmdm__ProgramEngagement__c].pmdm__StartDate__c
        ),
        LEFT(
          TEXT(
            [pmdm__ProgramEngagement__c].CreatedDate
          ),
          10
        )
      ) + ': ' + [pmdm__ProgramEngagement__c].pmdm__
Program__c.Name
    ) > 77,
    LEFT(
      ( [pmdm__ProgramEngagement__c].pmdm__Contact__c.FirstName
+ ' ' + [pmdm__ProgramEngagement__c].pmdm__Contact__c.LastName
+ ' ' +
        IF (
          NOT(
            ISBLANK(
              [pmdm__ProgramEngagement__c].pmdm__StartDate__c
            )
          ) ,
```

```
            TEXT (
              [pmdm__ProgramEngagement__c].pmdm__StartDate__c
            ) ,
            LEFT (
              TEXT (
                [pmdm__ProgramEngagement__c].CreatedDate
              ),
              10
            ) ) +  ': ' + [pmdm__ProgramEngagement__c].pmdm__
Program__c.Name ),
      77
    ) + '...',
    [pmdm__ProgramEngagement__c].pmdm__Contact__c. FirstName +
' ' + [pmdm__ProgramEngagement__c].pmdm__Contact__c.LastName +
' ' +
    IF (
      NOT (
        ISBLANK (
          [pmdm__ProgramEngagement__c].pmdm__StartDate__c
        )
      ),
        TEXT (
          [pmdm__ProgramEngagement__c].pmdm__StartDate__c
        ),
        LEFT (
          TEXT (
            [pmdm__ProgramEngagement__c].CreatedDate
          ),
          10
        )
    ) + ': ' + [pmdm__ProgramEngagement__c].pmdm__Program__c.
Name
    ),
  IF (
    LEN (
      $Label.pmdm__Anonymous + ' ' +
      IF (
```

```
    NOT (
     ISBLANK (
        [pmdm__ProgramEngagement__c].pmdm__StartDate__c
     )
    ),
      TEXT (
       [pmdm__ProgramEngagement__c].pmdm__StartDate__c
     ),
     LEFT (
      TEXT (
         [pmdm__ProgramEngagement__c].CreatedDate
       ),
        10
      )
    ) + ': ' + [pmdm__ProgramEngagement__c].pmdm__
Program__c.Name
  ) > 77,
   LEFT (
    ( $Label.pmdm__Anonymous + ' ' +  IF (          NOT (
         ISBLANK (
           [pmdm__ProgramEngagement__c].pmdm__StartDate__c
         )
        ) ,
        TEXT (
          [pmdm__ProgramEngagement__c].pmdm__StartDate__c
        ) ,
        LEFT (
         TEXT (
            [pmdm__ProgramEngagement__c].CreatedDate
          ),
          10
        ) ) + ': ' + [pmdm__ProgramEngagement__c].pmdm__
Program__c.Name ),
     77
  ) + '...',
  $Label.pmdm__Anonymous + ' ' +
   IF (
```

```
    NOT (
      ISBLANK (
          [pmdm__ProgramEngagement__c].pmdm__StartDate__c
      )
    ),
      TEXT (
        [pmdm__ProgramEngagement__c].pmdm__StartDate__c
      ),
      LEFT (
        TEXT (
          [pmdm__ProgramEngagement__c].CreatedDate
        ),
        10
      )
    ) + ': ' + [pmdm__ProgramEngagement__c].pmdm__Program__c.
Name
  )
)
```

Update this formula to automate the appropriate name without Anonymous or with the account or custom object name for the **Program Engagement** object.

Similarly, for **Service Delivery** naming, clone the process builder and update the AutoName formula. The default formula is as follows:

```
IF (
  NOT (
    ISBLANK (
      [pmdm__ServiceDelivery__c].pmdm__Contact__c
    )
  ),
  IF (
    LEN (
      [pmdm__ServiceDelivery__c].pmdm__Contact__c.FirstName + '
' + [pmdm__ServiceDelivery__c]. pmdm__Contact__c.LastName + ' '
+ IF (
        NOT (
          ISBLANK (
```

```
                [pmdm__ ServiceDelivery__c].pmdm__DeliveryDate__c
            )
        ) ,
        TEXT (
            [pmdm__ ServiceDelivery__c].pmdm__DeliveryDate__c
        ) ,
        LEFT (
            TEXT (
                [pmdm__ ServiceDelivery__c].CreatedDate
            ),
            10
        ) ) + ': ' + [pmdm__ServiceDelivery__c].pmdm__
Service__c.Name
    ) > 77,
    LEFT (
        [pmdm__ServiceDelivery__c].pmdm__Contact__c.FirstName +
' ' + [pmdm__ServiceDelivery__c].pmdm__Contact__c.LastName + '
' + IF (
            NOT (
                ISBLANK (
                    [pmdm__ServiceDelivery__c].pmdm__DeliveryDate__c
                )
            ) ,
            TEXT (
                [pmdm__ServiceDelivery__c].pmdm__DeliveryDate__c
            ) ,
            LEFT (
                TEXT (
                    [pmdm__ServiceDelivery__c].CreatedDate
                ),
                10
            ) ) + ': ' + [pmdm__ServiceDelivery__c].pmdm__
Service__c.Name,
        77
    ) + '...',
    [pmdm__ ServiceDelivery__c].pmdm__Contact__c.FirstName + '
' + [pmdm__ServiceDelivery__c].pmdm__Contact__c.LastName +  '
```

```
' + IF (
    NOT(
      ISBLANK(
        [pmdm__ServiceDelivery__c].pmdm__DeliveryDate__c
      )
    ),
    TEXT(
      [pmdm__ServiceDelivery__c].pmdm__DeliveryDate__c
    ),
    LEFT(
      TEXT(
        [pmdm__ServiceDelivery__c].CreatedDate
      ),
      10
    ) ) + ': ' + [pmdm__ServiceDelivery__c].pmdm__Service__c.
Name
  ),
  IF(
    LEN(
      $Label.pmdm__Anonymous +  ' ' + IF (          NOT(
          ISBLANK(
            [pmdm__ServiceDelivery__c].pmdm__DeliveryDate__c
          )
        ),
        TEXT(
          [pmdm__ServiceDelivery__c].pmdm__DeliveryDate__c
        ),
        LEFT(
          TEXT(
            [pmdm__ServiceDelivery__c].CreatedDate
          ),
          10
        ) ) + ': ' + [pmdm__ServiceDelivery__c].pmdm__
Service__c.Name
    ) > 77,
    LEFT(
      $Label.pmdm__Anonymous + ' ' + IF (          NOT(
```

```
        ISBLANK(
            [pmdm__ServiceDelivery__c].pmdm__DeliveryDate__c
        )
    ),
    TEXT(
        [pmdm__ServiceDelivery__c].pmdm__DeliveryDate__c
    ),
    LEFT(
        TEXT(
            [pmdm__ServiceDelivery__c].CreatedDate
        ),
        10
    ) ) + ': ' + [pmdm__ServiceDelivery__c].pmdm__
Service__c.Name,
    77
) + '...',
$Label.pmdm__Anonymous + ' ' + IF (      NOT(
        ISBLANK(
            [pmdm__ServiceDelivery__c].pmdm__DeliveryDate__c
        )
    ),
    TEXT(
        [pmdm__ServiceDelivery__c].pmdm__DeliveryDate__c
    ),
    LEFT(
        TEXT(
            [pmdm__ServiceDelivery__c].CreatedDate
        ),
        10
    ) ) + ': ' + [pmdm__ServiceDelivery__c].pmdm__
Service__c.Name
    )
)
```

Updating the value in the **Service Delivery Name** field in the process builder automates the auto-naming process to reflect the specific use case. Don't forget to activate the new version!

Initial setup for Service Delivery summary data

Attendance and the most recent date of service for a client are contained in rollup fields and are automatically calculated on the **Contact**, **Program Engagement**, **Service**, and **Service Session** objects. However, PMM requires these automations to be set up for them to work as expected. Follow these steps:

1. The first step is to make the appropriate triggers active. Go to **Setup** > **Custom Code** > **Custom Metadata Types** and click **Manage Records** for **Feature Gate**. Four rollups will be listed, as follows:

    - `ServiceDeliveriesToContact`
    - `ServiceDeliveriesToService`
    - `ServiceDeliveriesToServiceSession`
    - `ServiceDeliveriesToProgramEngagement`

    Click **Edit** next to the features and click **Active** for the summary features you want to see. Then, click **Save**.

2. The second step ensures that the summary fields stay up to date. Go to **Setup** > **Apex Classes** and click **Compile All Classes**. This may take some time to complete. Once it has, click **Schedule Apex**. Again, four Apex classes correlate with the features in *Step 1*; they are as follows:

    - `ContactRollupsSchedulable`
    - `ProgramEngagementRollupsSchedulable`
    - `ServiceRollupsSchedulable`
    - `SessionRollupsSchedulable`

    Choose the appropriate name and Apex class and schedule; best practice is to schedule the job when the fewest users will be working with **Service Delivery** records – perhaps every Saturday at 2:00 A.M.

3. Confirm that the summary fields are available on the appropriate page layouts and that they are **Read Only**.

4. The attendance statuses, by default, are as follows:

    - **Present**
    - **Excused Absence**
    - **Unexcused Absence**

If your use case requires additional or different statuses, add the status(es) to the picklist values in the **Attendance Status** field in the **Service Delivery** object. Then, go to **Setup** > **Custom Metadata Types** and click **Manage Records** in the row for the bucketed value. Click **New** and create each picklist value and indicate whether the bucket it belongs in is **Absent** or **Present**. Then, click **Save**.

Additional optional configurations

PMM is highly configurable from both a Salesforce administrator standpoint and from the Nonprofit Cloud view. Examples of additional administrator configurations that you may make based on the use case include customizing the home tab, buttons, and picklist values. From a Nonprofit Cloud viewpoint, you can enable mass program cohort updates and mass creation of program engagements, as well as customize bulk service deliveries. Each of these configurations will vary based on the specific use case.

> **Note**
>
> PMM is also available in Dutch, English (UK), French, German, Japanese, Spanish, and Spanish (Mexico) during the org-wide setup. Alternatively, you can use the Translation Workbench to override translations.

Setting up Case Management for NPSP

Case Management is a paid add-on. It works with or without NPSP. The following diagram shows the data architecture for Case Management and how it expands PMM and NPSP:

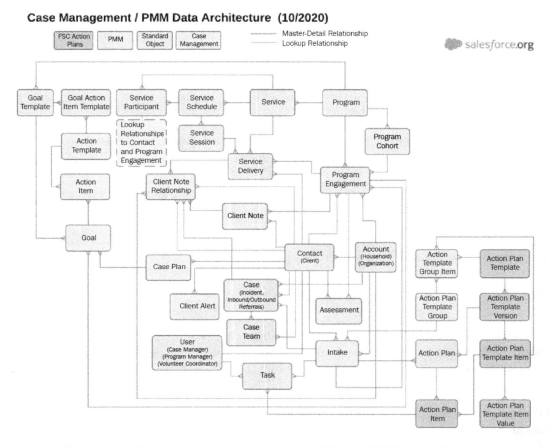

Figure 11.7 – Case Management extension for the PMM and NPSP data architecture

Setting up Case Management for the first time requires very few steps and is like setting up PMM. Let's take a look:

1. Assign users the Case Management permission set that comes installed with Case Management.

2. To refine these permissions, there are three functional permission sets that we can use with similar use cases to the permission sets in PMM. Assign these to the appropriate users:

    - **Case Management: Manage**
    - **Case Management: Deliver**
    - **Case Management: View**

3. Confirm that users have the correct page layouts assigned to their profiles. Best practice suggests the following:

- **Account layout = Branch page layout**
- **Contact layout = Case Management page layout**
- **Case layout = Incident layout**

These are the basic setup steps. Now, let's look at other ways Case Management may need to be configured for an organization's specific business processes.

Additional configurable elements of Case Management

With the new objects introduced by Case Management, there are additional configurations that can be used to automate and streamline the user experience. Case Management also introduces new interfaces.

The client card and client notes

As a Salesforce administrator, editing page layouts is something you already have experience doing. The client card component allows you to configure the client details that appear on the **Contact** page. These details may include the client's photo, mailing address, alerts, ID, pronouns, badges, and watchlists. What is shown will depend on the business processes and use cases.

Likewise, as a Salesforce administrator, you can configure the **Client Note** layout to add custom fields, display fields based on record types, and maintain **Client Note** relationships.

Configuring and customizing additional Nonprofit Cloud Case Management features

Because we are using a brand-new instance of Salesforce Nonprofit Cloud, referrals and intakes should already be configured. Just be aware that older instances may need some additional setup. Be sure to check the **Intake Checklist** configuration. If no intake checklist exists, one can be created under **Action Item Templates**.

Incidents and assessments can be customized using standard Salesforce administrator skills. Here, you can add custom fields, assign the fields to page layouts, and create field sets. Assessments are based on the organization's business practices and use cases. Customizing case plan goals and action items follows a similar pattern.

V4S configurations for staff and volunteers

As we explore the configurations that are available for staff and volunteers in V4S, let's review the underlying data structure, which consists of **Contacts**, **Leads**, **Campaigns**, **Volunteer Jobs**, **Volunteer Shifts**, **Volunteer Hours**, **Job Recurrence Schedules**, and **Volunteer Recurrence Schedules**:

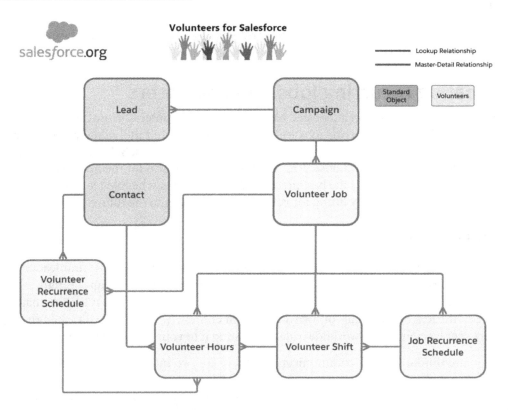

Figures 11.8 – The V4S data architecture

From here, we can begin to configure specific aspects of V4S based on the business processes of the organization.

Leveraging volunteer skills

Volunteer skills are an important part of matching the right volunteer to the right job. Matching those volunteers to the right time slot is also important. **Volunteer Skills** are picklist values in the **Contact** and **Lead** objects. Adding new skills that you can choose from is as easy as updating those two fields. Although you may think that updating the **Availability** field is also a good plan – it isn't!

In the next section, you will see that recurring schedules rely on the **Availability** values just as they are. Just say no to changing them.

Automating recurring jobs and volunteers

Some volunteer jobs happen on a repeated basis with repeat volunteers. How can you automatically create those recurring jobs without creating each shift individually? Use your Salesforce administrator skills to go to **Setup** > **Apex Classes** and click **Schedule Apex**. Give the job a descriptive name and choose VOL_BATCH_Rucurrence for the Apex class. Running this job once a week is the best practice. By creating this scheduled job, the system automatically does all the heavy lifting for you, up to 4 months into the future.

Notifying volunteers

V4S provides out-of-the-box email templates for the most used volunteer communications such as reminders, notifications, and thank you emails. Be sure to go to **Setup** > **Email Templates** and select the **Volunteers Email Templates** folder to review the available emails. You can edit the text of the emails or turn an email off entirely. You can also edit when the emails are sent by cloning the workflow rule and editing it to your desired preference.

While you are thinking about communications, there are two more things you will want to confirm:

- **Organization-Wide Address**: Do you have an org-wide email address configured for the volunteer coordinator (or your choice of display name)? This will ensure that volunteers receive emails from the appropriate email address rather than an individual's email address.

- **Brand Consistency**: Do you need to update the letterhead for your volunteer emails? Are the subject lines consistent in your email templates? Are you addressing emails to {!Contact.FirstName} for all volunteers? This is a quick check that will present a unified, friendly experience for your communication.

Configuring for your staff's ease of use

V4S makes use of **field sets** to align with the organization's use case and business processes more closely. Review the following three pages to provide an optimal user experience:

- The **Volunteers' wizard** page displays a group of **Campaign** fields; edit the `VolunteersWizardFS` field set to meet the business processes.

- The **Mass edit volunteer hours** page provides an interface where you can mass edit volunteer hours. Edit the `MassEditVolunteerHours` field set to match the use case.

- The **Find volunteers** page can be used to search for volunteers and display contact fields. Depending on the use case, edit the `VolunteersFindCriteriaFS` and `VolunteersFindFS` field sets to surface the appropriate fields.

> **Note**
> There are two important limitations regarding V4S: it requires that a user license has, at a minimum, read access to the object, and V4S is not optimized for mobile devices.

What are the best practices for data integrity and security?

The discovery discussions that we provided in *Chapter 7, Is Change Difficult for Your Organization?*, encompass the security model. This includes profiles and how **sharing rules** and **permission sets** are assigned to them. But, wait! There's more. Let's look at additional ways to secure your data.

Multi-factor authentication

Multi-factor authentication (MFA) is the next iteration of **two-factor authentication (2FA)**. Salesforce has made it easy to implement with its **Multi-Factor Authentication Assistant**, which is built right into **Setup**. MFA will be available in the Spring 2022 release. Multi-factor means that users prove their identity in multiple ways – a username and password combination, plus an authenticator app:

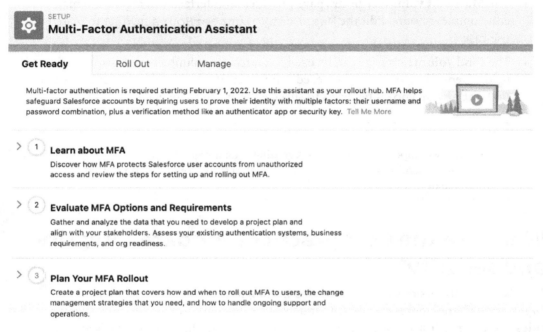

Figure 11.9 – Multi-Factor Authentication Assistant in Salesforce's setup

As you can see, there is a vast amount of documentation on MFA within the Salesforce instance itself. It just takes a bit of time to go through it all. Some of this will depend on how many users your organization contains and how many system admins there are.

How many system admins do you need?

As you're aware, the Salesforce administrator has all the superpowers. The **System Administrator** profile should only be assigned to trained Salesforce users. Depending on the size of the organization and the business use case, there may be more than one Salesforce administrator. However, best practices stipulate reserving the **System Administrator** profile for those users who set up, configure, and maintain the Salesforce system. It is never a best practice for every user to have a **System Administrator** profile.

What about users who leave your organization?

The appropriate steps to take when a user is no longer active are dependent on the permissions the user has. The more permissions and dependencies that are related to a user, the more time it takes to deactivate that user. This is another excellent reason to limit system admins to those who truly need those permissions.

The following are two important best practices around users that are no longer part of your organization:

- Deactivate the users' Salesforce account. Do not simply change the user's name so that it's different.
- Be sure to migrate ownership of records to an active user in your Salesforce instance. Leaving records to be owned by inactive users can cause your applications to stop functioning as expected.

There are many additional ways to encourage data integrity and secure your data in Salesforce. NPSP provides **Health Check**, a no-code tool that's designed to identify challenges that may affect the integrity of your data. Health Check can be accessed in NPSP by going to **Settings** > **System Tools** > **Health Check**. Data privacy laws in your area may affect how you set up security. Salesforce offers features such as field encryption, field history tracking, and paid features such as Salesforce Shield to help you protect your data.

Summary

In this chapter, we configured PMM, Case Management, and V4S. We looked at various customizable standard options for each of the three applications. We also looked at the most important best practices for data integrity and security.

As with all Salesforce tools, many new options and updates are made available in every release to help you configure and customize applications so that they suit business processes and use cases. This chapter has also illustrated how important a Salesforce administrator's knowledge of standard Salesforce functionality is for configuring profiles, permissions, sharing rules, and streamlining the user interface for the best results.

In *Chapter 12, Declarative Tools and Modules*, you will require your Salesforce administrator skills to understand the options for customizable rollups, matching gifts, and the Open Source Commons Outbound Funds module.

Further reading

- Who sees what video: `https://salesforce.vidyard.com/watch/kXk6BaNlWJP27UyFO8vNUg`

Section 3: Go! – Data for Impact

The solution is Nonprofit Cloud and some, or all, of its components are based on the requirements of a client nonprofit organization. Let's build the solution. This section contains the following chapters:

12
Declarative Tools and Modules

In the previous three chapters, we installed NPSP and the additional features available for PMM and V4S, configured the fundraising features for NPSP, and completed the configuration for PMM and V4S. Declarative tools and Open Source Commons modules are additional ways to extend the functionality of NPSP based on a nonprofit's specific use cases and business processes.

In this chapter, we will learn the following:

- What customizable rollups are and when they should be used
- **Matching gifts** – how and when they apply to donations
- Grantmaking capabilities and how to use the Open Source Commons' Outbound Funds Module

None of these tools are required for NPSP to work; however, when they are needed, understanding what they do and how they do it will make NPSP tremendously better.

Technical requirements

All we need for this chapter is the Outbound Funds installer: `https://install.salesforce.org/products/outbound-funds/latest`.

What are customizable rollups?

NPSP customizable rollups give us the ability to adapt out-of-the-box NPSP rollups and create new rollups. As a Salesforce administrator, you are familiar with rollup summary fields that roll up information from related records to another record. More than 80 rollup summary fields come already created in NPSP when you install it. However, each organization has specific metrics and business processes they are trying to measure. Customizable rollups provide a way to create a newly defined rollup field and the filter to use on that rollup field:

> **Note**
> There are two types of rollups: **aggregate rollups**, which sum, average, or count data; and **single-result operation rollups**, which find a specific record that is the smallest, largest, most recent, or oldest.

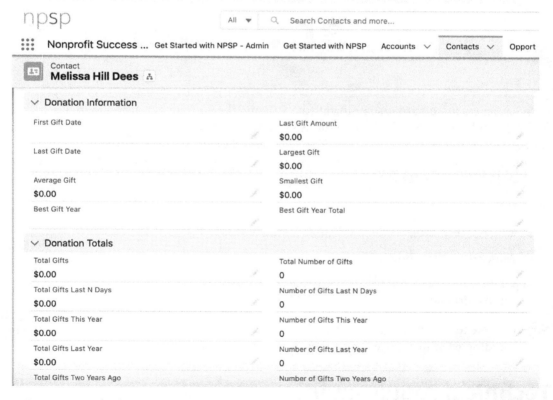

Figure 12.1 – The donation information and donation totals fields on a contact page are examples of standard rollup fields.

What do you do when you need a rollup field that does not already exist?

When do you need a customizable rollup?

Because you have installed NPSP, you might never need a customizable rollup. However, consider these user stories. We will also look at how to configure each one.

A custom rollup to sum data

As a program manager, I want to see which family has provided the most in-kind donations so that I can thank them on social media:

1. To configure this customizable rollup, create a new custom field on the **Account** record to hold the information. This should be a currency field.

2. Next, go to **NPSP Settings** > **Donations** > **Customizable Rollups**.

3. **Customizable Rollups** should already be enabled. (If it is not, enable it now.) Here, you should see the list of all **Customizable Rollups** that come already created as a part of NPSP:

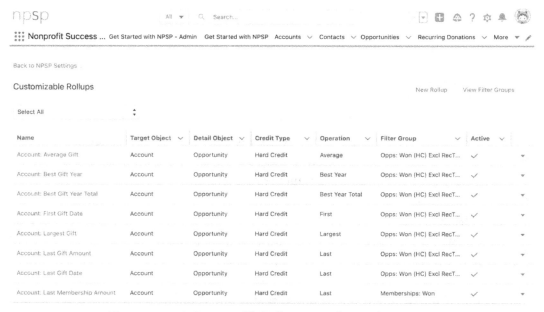

Figure 12.2 – A Customizable Rollups example page from NPSP

4. Click **View Filter Groups**. Since we are creating a new filter group, click **New Filter Group**. Name the filter group and give a description.

5. Next, create two filters for this rollup. In this story, we want to filter the rollup by opportunities that are **Closed Won** and whose record type is **In-Kind Gift**. Click **Save**:

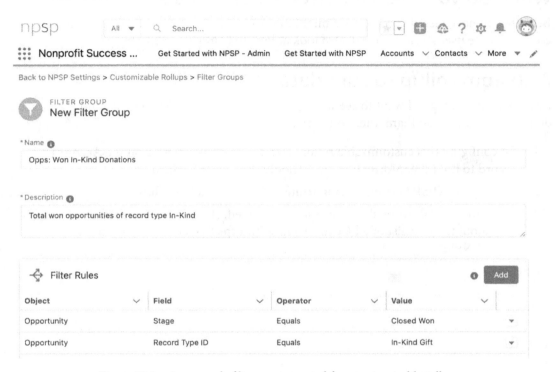

Figure 12.3 – An example filter group created for a customizable rollup

6. Next, we will create the customizable rollup itself. Go back to the **Customizable Rollup** page and click **New Rollup**.

7. Enter the target object where you want the rollup to show, and select the target field where the data should appear.

8. Fill in the description.

9. Choose **Operation**; because we want a sum of all the in-kind donations here, choose **Sum**. The timeframe defaults to **All Time**. Designate the rollup type; we want to roll up opportunities with hard credits using the filter group we just created – **Opps: Won In-Kind Donations**. Leave **Amount Field** as **Opportunity: Amount**. Click **Save**. Your entries should look like *Figure 12.4*:

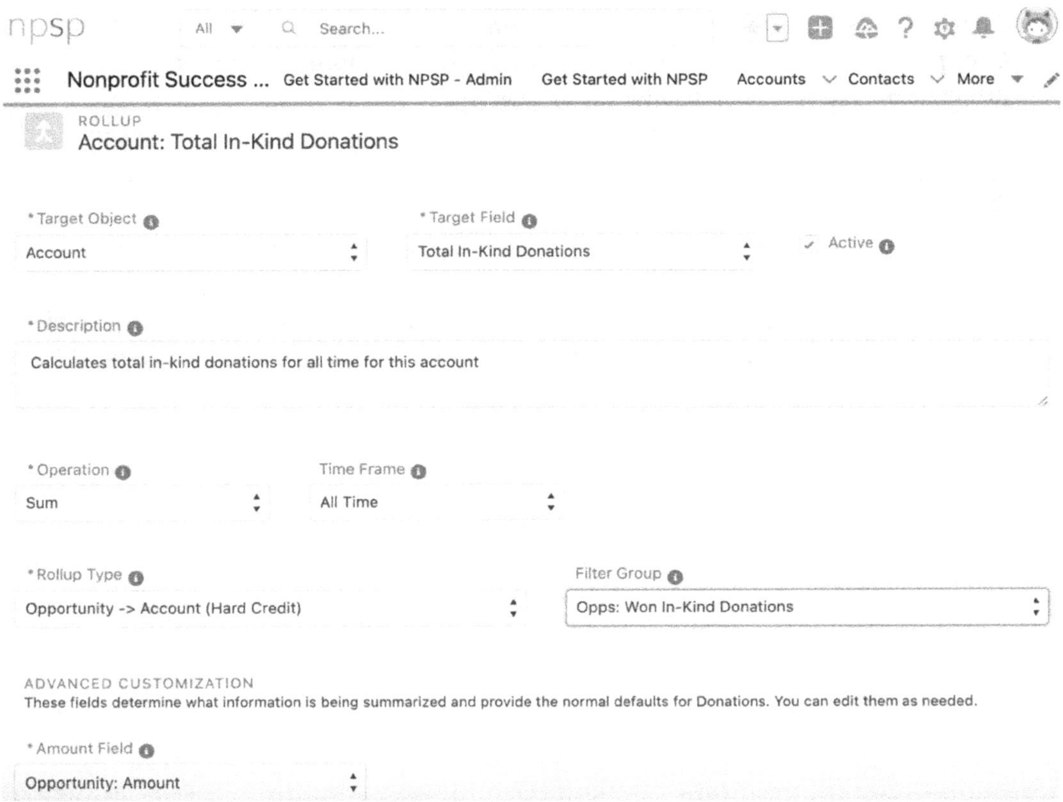

npsp   All ▼   Q Search...   ▼ ➕ ☁ ? ⚙ 🔔 😺

⣿ Nonprofit Success ... Get Started with NPSP - Admin   Get Started with NPSP   Accounts ∨ Contacts ∨ More ▼ ✏

ROLLUP
Account: Total In-Kind Donations

* Target Object ℹ   * Target Field ℹ   ✓ Active ℹ

Account   ⬍   Total In-Kind Donations   ⬍

* Description ℹ

Calculates total in-kind donations for all time for this account

* Operation ℹ   Time Frame ℹ

Sum   ⬍   All Time   ⬍

* Rollup Type ℹ   Filter Group ℹ

Opportunity -> Account (Hard Credit)   ⬍   Opps: Won In-Kind Donations   ⬍

ADVANCED CUSTOMIZATION
These fields determine what information is being summarized and provide the normal defaults for Donations. You can edit them as needed.

* Amount Field ℹ

Opportunity: Amount   ⬍

Figure 12.4 – An example of customizable rollup creation to sum in-kind donations

Now that everything is configured, the rollup will run overnight each night. If you need to immediately see the rollup summary information, go to **NPSP Settings** > **Bulk Data Processes** > **Rollup Donations Batch** and click **Run Batch**. This will automatically process rollups in the queue.

A custom rollup for the last or most recent date

As a **program manager**, I need to see the date of the most recent in-kind donation that a family has contributed to prioritize asks for new in-kind donations.

This **custom rollup** is configured very similarly to the previous one:

1. First, create the field where you want to view the data on the **Account** record – for example, create a data field titled **Last In-Kind Donation**.

2. Go to **NPSP Settings** > **Donations** > **Customizable Rollups** and click **View Filter Groups**. You should see the **Opps: Won In-Kind Donations** filter group that we just created. We can use this filter group again.

3. Go back to **Customizable Rollups** and click **New Rollup**. The target object will again be **Account** and the target field is the field just created – **Last In-Kind Donation**. Add a description.

4. The operation this time will be **Last**, and the time frame is **All Time**. The rollup type is still **Opportunity -> Account (Hard Credit)**, and we reuse the filter group we created – **Opps: Won In-Kind Donations**. In advanced customization, the field to roll up is **Opportunity: Close Date**. Your work should look similar to *Figure 12.5*:

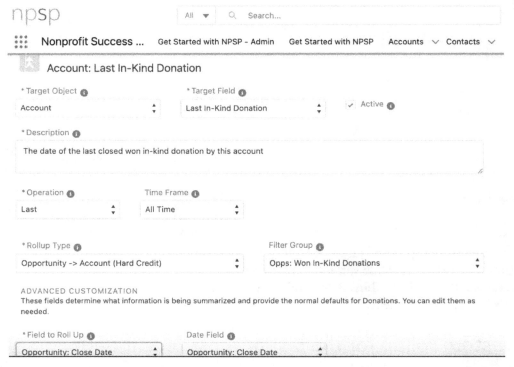

Figure 12.5 – An example of the creation of a customizable rollup to show the last date that an in-kind donation was made

5. Don't forget to click **Save**.

Again, the rollup batch will run overnight unless you force the updates via the batch process. There are a wide variety of use cases for customizable rollups, and there is a great deal of documentation to help with more complex filters and options. Helpful links are listed in the *Resources* section at the end of this chapter.

Apply matching gifts to donations

Matching gifts are a fundraiser's best friend. It's like shopping with *buy one, get one free*. It's the easiest money you can possibly raise. How do you track all the lovely donations that come in with the possibility of a matching gift? And, when that matching gift arrives, how do you make certain the right donor gets credited? Let's get started on learning more about matching gifts.

Confirm the matching gifts configuration

Depending on when your Salesforce instance was created, these configurations may already be in place. Be sure to confirm each step:

1. First, be aware that matching gifts uses standard objects that are already available: **Opportunity, Opportunity Contact Role, Account**, and **Contact. Configuration** is quick and simple.

2. Second, we configure soft credits, as we did in *Chapter 10, Configuring Fundraising Features.*

3. Third, add the matching gift fields in **Accounts, Contacts**, and **Opportunities**. The fields and related lists should also be added to the appropriate page layouts in a section entitled **Matching Gifts**:

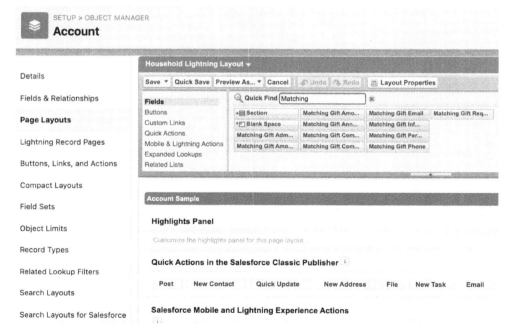

Figure 12.6 – The matching gift fields to be added to the Account page layouts

Once the fields are added and the page layouts are complete, we can look at how to create the gifts appropriately.

Creating matching gifts

For companies or organizations that will contribute matching gifts, be sure to check the **Matching Gift Company** checkbox on the relevant **Account** record:

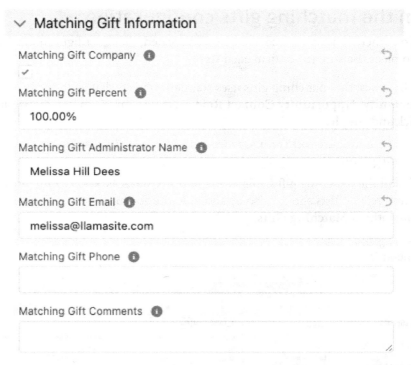

Figure 12.7 – An account record sample for a company that provides matching gifts

Now, a new donation that is eligible for a matching gift can be created when the donation from a contact arrives:

1. Create a donation, a standard **Donation** record type, and in the **Matching Gift** section, indicate two pieces of important information:

    I. The **Matching Gift** account.

    II. The **Matching Gift** status should be either **Potential** or **Submitted**.

2. Save the donation.

When the matching gift arrives from the donor's company, you will want to create the donation appropriately:

1. Go to the **Account** record of the company.
2. Click **New Matching Gift** to create a new donation of the record type matching gift.
3. Complete the information and click **Save**.
4. Go to the opportunity just created and click **Find Matched Gifts**.
5. Select the **opportunity** that should be matched and click **Save**.

The rest is automated for you by NPSP:

1. You can see the donation by the company on the related list for the company.
2. Contact roles are automatically created.
3. Soft credits are created.
4. The contact original donation is listed in the matching gifts-related list.

> **Note**
> Soft credits are not seen immediately. These calculations are populated overnight.

How to leverage Outbound Funds Module

Outbound Funds Module is another special extension of NPSP because it was community-inspired and created through the Open Source Commons Community sprints. The module was designed to meet the needs of nonprofit organizations that work with grants and scholarships. There are four main areas where Outbound Funds Module is useful:

- Managing requests for funding
- Tracking an applicant journey
- Scheduling payments
- Maintaining relationships

In *Chapter 6, What Else Is Needed from Nonprofit Cloud?*, we took a high-level look at the data architecture and use cases of Outbound Funds Module. Now, let's install and configure the module based on some specific use cases.

Installing and configuring Outbound Funds Module

In *Chapter 6, What Else Is Needed from Nonprofit Cloud?*, we learned that NPSP is not required for Outbound Funds Module to work, **unless** the connection object, GAU Expenditure, is needed to connect the disbursements with the general account unit. For our purpose, we will assume that NPSP has already been installed and configured.

Outbound Funds Module is available to install from Salesforce's AppExchange, `https://appexchange.salesforce.com/appxListingDetail?listingId=a0N3u00000OMYvzEAH`, or via the installer at `https://install.salesforce.org/products/outbound-funds/latest`.

Before we install the module, let's confirm these steps:

1. The Salesforce instance is at the minimum an Enterprise edition.
2. Lightning Experience is enabled.
3. My Domain is enabled.
4. Chatter is enabled.
5. (Optionally) Digital Experiences is enabled.

Because Outbound Funds Module is from Open Source Commons, there is no cost to install or use it. However, if an organization is interested in using the fund seeker starter portal template, digital experience must be activated, and digital experience partner community plus licenses must be purchased from Salesforce before the template can be installed.

There are only two configurations left to do:

1. Page assignments:

    I. Go to **Setup** > **Object Manager** > **Disbursement** > **Page Layouts** > **Page Layout Assignment**.

    II. Click **edit assignment**.

    III. Assign the profiles to use the **Disbursement NPSP Layout** page and click **Save**.

    IV. Repeat the steps for the **General Accounting Unit** object and assign **GAU Outbound Funds Layout** to the appropriate profiles. Don't forget to click **Save**.

2. Lightning record pages:

    I. Go to **Setup** > **Object Manager** > **Disbursement** > **Lightning Record Pages** > **Disbursement NPSP Record Page** and click **Edit**.

    II. At the right-hand corner, click **Activation** and assign it as the app default for Outbound Funds. No other changes are needed; just remember to save.

    III. Follow the same steps for the **GAU Outbound Funds Record** page and the **GAU Expenditure Record** page.

Now, you are ready to use Outbound Funds Module.

Using Outbound Funds Module

From *Chapter 6, What Else Is Needed from Nonprofit Cloud?*, you will remember that the funding foundation for our use case has funds available for organizations working to make an impact in a situation where cases were rising due to childhood hunger. To get started, we will create a funding program, the highest level in the fund's hierarchy, and use additional records to track the necessary information.

Setting up the funding program

To understand the functionality and test the configuration, start by creating a new funds request:

1. Go to **Outbound Funds** > **Funding Programs** > **New**; the only required field is the name of the program:

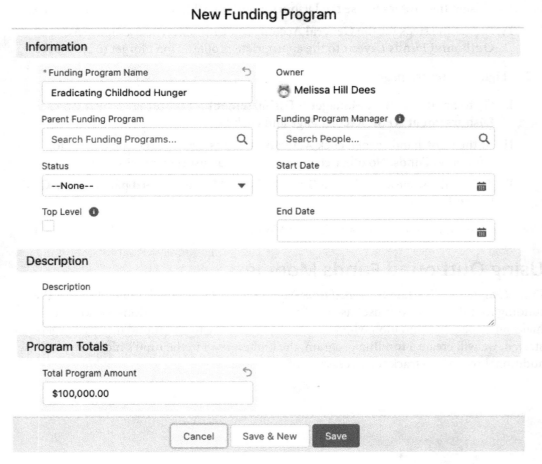

Figure 12.8 – An example of the creation of a new funding program in Outbound Fund Module

2. Next, we need to create a funding request to track the applications from organizations. Still in the Outbound Funds app, go to **Funding requests** and click **New**. Fill in the appropriate name, and the funding program is a lookup field, as shown in *Figure 12.9*. In this example, the funding program is **Eradicating Childhood Hunger**:

New Funding Request

Information

* Funding Request Name	* Funding Program
After School Snacks	🏛 Eradicating Childhood Hunger ×
Application Date	Close Date
11/30/2021 📅	📅
Status	Closed reason
Invited ▼	

Purpose

Geographical Area Served

City   ▼

Population Served

Available		Chosen
People with Diseases and Illnesses	▶	Youth at Risk
Religious Groups	◀	
Veteran		
Victims and Oppressed People		
Women		

Requested For

Applicant

Applying Organization

Cancel   Save & New   Save

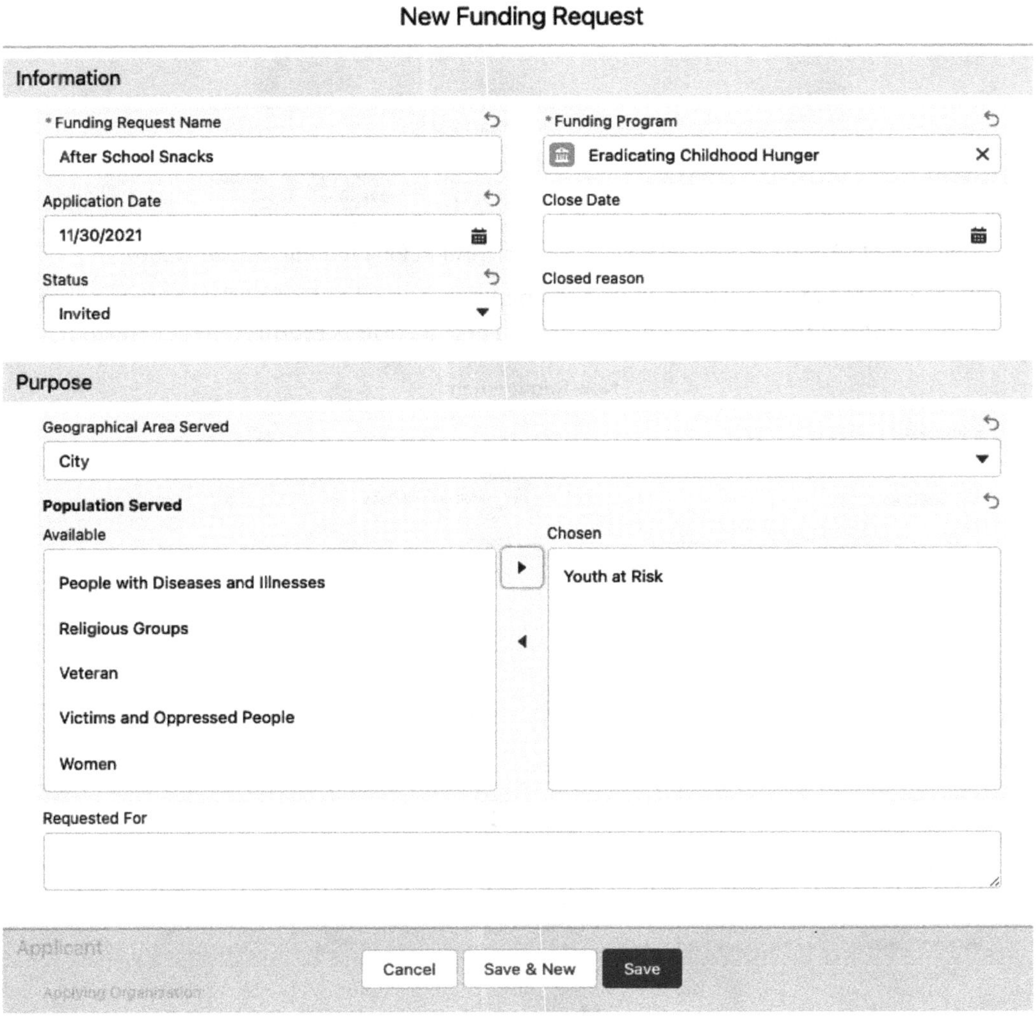

Figure 12.9 – An example of the form to create a funding request in Outbound Funds

3. Additionally, you can create funding request roles for contacts associated with the funding request. On the funding request record page, click **Create Funding Request Role** and fill in the appropriate information:

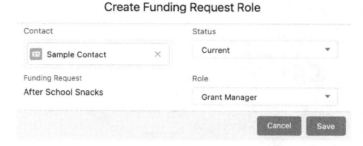

Figure 12.10 – A sample funding request role creation for a funding request record

4. You may also have step-by-step requirements that need to be fulfilled in the request for the funding process. In this use case, an application is required to get started:

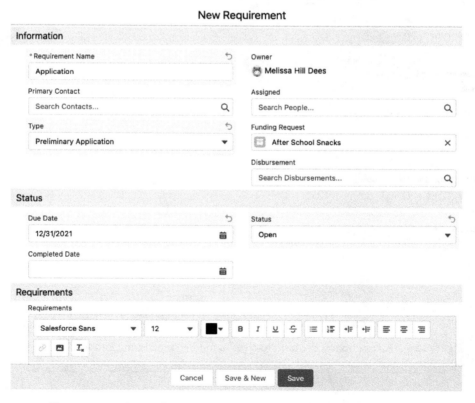

Figure 12.11 – A sample requirement creation for a funding request record

5.   Separately, the organization's letter from the government stating that they are a registered nonprofit, a **501(c)3** from the IRS in the United States, is required, as well as a roadmap of how the organization intends to use the funds specifically:

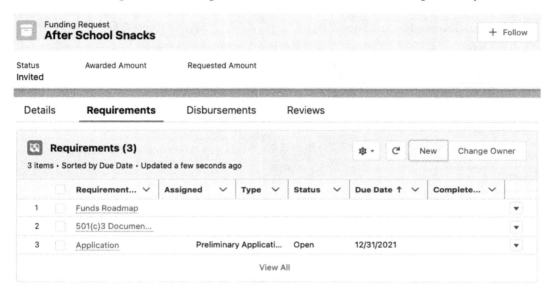

Figure 12.12 – A sample requirements listing for a funding request in Outbound Funds

Once the requirements are completed, the request needs to be reviewed.

Creating reviews

Create a review and assign it to a reviewer to understand the review process and its configurations:

1. Click **Reviews** in the Outbound Funds app and click new to request feedback from a reviewer on a funding request. The **Review Name** and **Funding Request** fields are all lookup fields from information already in your Salesforce system, and the **Assigned To** field is a lookup to a user record:

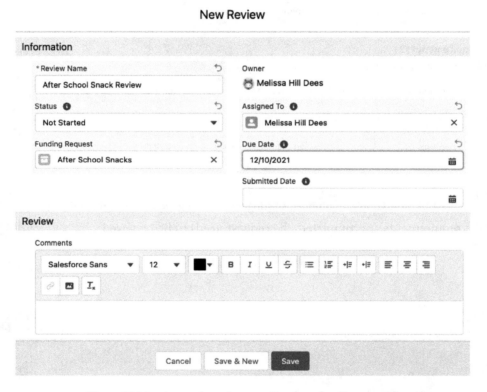

Figure 12.13 – A sample review creation for a funding request

2. Now, you are ready to share the review with the appropriate reviewer for their feedback. Go to the review record that you just created and click **Share**. Select the user you are inviting to review the funding request and give them the appropriate level of access to complete the review:

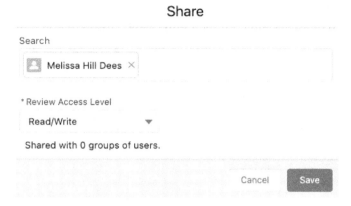

Figure 12.14 – A sample of sharing with a reviewer for a funding request

3. Now, the reviewer can complete and submit the review simply by clicking **Submit Review**:

Figure 12.15 – A sample review submission for a funding request

Once all the requirements are met and the reviews are submitted, the foundation can decide which organizations should be awarded the funding they've requested.

Disbursing the funds

Now comes the fun part – parceling out the money itself. To create a disbursement, there is a button on the funding request page called **Create Disbursements**. Click that button to schedule the disbursements:

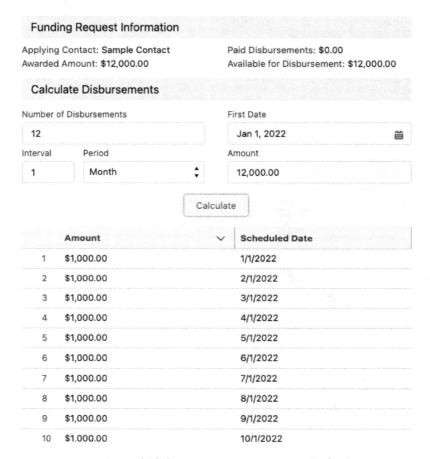

Figure 12.16 – A sample disbursement creation page in the funding request

All the information is on the funding request record to track the request itself, the organization and contact, the fulfilled requirements, the reviews, the award, and the disbursement of the awarded funds. Outbound Funds Module also comes with 10 helpful reports already created for the organization, including the following:

- Awarded Requests Sorted by Program Codes
- Funding Requests by Program and Status
- Awarded Requests by Year by Program

- Requests with Open Disbursements
- Parent Funding Program Analytics
- Funding Program Analytics
- Requests with Upcoming Milestones
- Overdue Disbursements
- Unscheduled Disbursements
- Upcoming Disbursements

These reports make it simple and streamlined to share information in real time with the foundation's stakeholders.

Summary

In this chapter, we have configured customizable rollups, applied matching gifts, and explored the grantmaking capabilities of Outbound Funds Module. Each of these is unique and individual and is called for in the specific use cases we discussed in this chapter.

Salesforce releases updates for standard functionality such as customizable rollups and matching gifts every two weeks, and new features are released three times per year. Open Source Commons applications such as Outbound Funds Module may require some manual updates, since it is not a standard part of the Nonprofit Cloud package. This is where your skills as a Salesforce administrator are important as well.

Throughout the previous chapters, what we have done is configuration. In *Chapter 13, To Customize or Not to Customize*, the emphasis will be less on configuration and more on customizing Salesforce itself, using the TDTM, including disabling code or creating custom code. As a part of this process, we will review the order of execution of operations in a Salesforce instance. Sometimes, it just takes some Apex code to automate at the scale that is needed.

Resources and additional reading

- *Create a Customizable Rollup*:

  `https://powerofus.force.com/s/article/NPSP-Create-Customizable-Rollup#topic-7412`

- *Customizable Rollups Recipes*:

  `https://powerofus.force.com/s/article/NPSP-Custom-Rllps-Recipes`

- *Donation Soft Credit Management with Nonprofit Success Pack*: `https://trailhead.salesforce.com/en/content/learn/modules/donation-soft-credit-management-with-nonprofit-success-pack`

- Outbound Funds Module documentation: `https://powerofus.force.com/s/article/OFM-Meet-Outbound-Funds-Module`

13
To Customize or Not to Customize?

Everything we have learned so far has been standard NPSP functionality, configuration of NPSP, or extending the functionality of NPSP. What if none of those options provides the solution the organization needs? To keep technical debt at a minimum and still meet the organization's business process needs, how can we customize NPSP?

Table-Driven Trigger Management (**TDTM**) is another tool in the structure of NPSP that gives Salesforce administrators more control over what happens and more options to customize the way NPSP works in any given Nonprofit Cloud implementation.

In this chapter, we will learn the following topics:

- What is TDTM and how is it useful?
- Disabling triggers using TDTM
- Creating custom triggers using TDTM
- Order of execution

TDTM was designed for Salesforce admins so that administrators are not required to rewrite code to disable triggers. However, the triggers that TDTM references are written in Apex code; Apex code is the standard programming language for Salesforce, so you may find that understanding how to read Apex code is helpful. TDTM is available by default in NPSP. Knowing how and why to use TDTM, in conjunction with the standard order of execution, provides additional tools to streamline processes and simplify data imports.

What is TDTM and how is it useful?

NPSP has many objects that connect with each other, so there are many automations coded into the NPSP package. TDTM provides an *admin-friendly* declarative interface to reorder coded triggers or to disable triggers entirely. Your first question may be: *what is a trigger?*

Let's do a quick overview of triggers and how they function.

Triggers are snippets of code that run in response to something that happens and are a part of the programmatic side of NPSP that is Apex code-based. When you do programming with Apex code you can do almost anything within Salesforce as long as the functionality stays within the governor limits. It can also be more performant than declarative tools. However, changes usually require a developer, a sandbox instance, and unit tests.

So, TDTM is really a set of records within an object (**trigger handler**) managing automations related to triggers. In accordance with best practices, TDTM provides one trigger per object with multiple trigger handlers. TDTM allows you to control the order of when the triggers fire. The logic itself is all stored in Apex classes instead of triggers. Also, you can work with all of this declaratively without writing Apex code.

A quick look at how to use TDTM

Let's look at TDTM. Go to the waffle menu and open **NPSP Settings > System Tools > Trigger Configuration**.

System Tools - Trigger Configuration

Trigger Handlers contain the actual business logic that needs to be executed for a particular trigger event.

⚠ Warning: These triggers control core functionality in the Nonprofit Success Pack, so please exercise extreme caution when creating or modifying them.

New Trigger Handler

OBJECT	CLASS	LOAD ORDER	TRIGGER ACTION	ACTIVE	ASYNCHRONOUS AFTER EVENTS	USER MANAGED	USERNAMES TO EXCLUDE
Account	ACCT_Accounts_TDTM	1	BeforeInsert; BeforeUpdate; AfterUpdate				
Account	ACCT_CascadeDeleteLookups_TDTM	1	BeforeDelete; AfterDelete; AfterUndelete				
Account	ACCT_AccountMerge_TDTM	1	AfterDelete				
Account	ADDR_Account_TDTM	1	BeforeInsert; BeforeUpdate;				

Figure 13.1 – A first look at TDTM in NPSP Settings

You will notice that each class ends in **TDTM**. You also see the order in which the trigger fires, when the trigger fires, and whether the trigger is currently active. Also, notice the **New Trigger Handler** button, which lets you create a new trigger in TDTM.

> **Note**
> None of the standard NPSP triggers are designed to run asynchronously. So, use **ASYNCHRONOUS AFTER EVENTS** with caution and test thoroughly.

A quick look at the why of TDTM

For Salesforce administrators, Apex code can be a bit intimidating, so why would we even want to delve into TDTM?

Well, let's see the benefits:

- **Scale**: TDTM manages large numbers of trigger handlers.
- **Order**: TDTM controls logic ordering.
- **Flexibility**: TDTM provides options to turn off functionality or triggers.
- **Extensibility**: TDTM allows the integration of new trigger handlers.
- **Performance**: TDTM optimizes **Data Manipulation Language** (**DML**) usage.

By using TDTM in NPSP, these benefits can be realized. Plus, TDTM reduces the amount of maintenance required within the Salesforce instance. With this covered, let's now go and explore some more details.

Disabling triggers using TDTM

Disabling triggers using TDTM is a quick and easy three-step process. The more difficult part—understanding when to disable triggers—follows these steps:

1. To disable triggers for NPSP, go to the waffle menu and open the **Trigger Handlers** tab.

2. A quick recommendation to make it easier to use is to go to the **All** list view and add the **Active**, **Class**, **Object**, **Load Order**, and **Trigger Action** fields. This will make it much easier to find what you need.

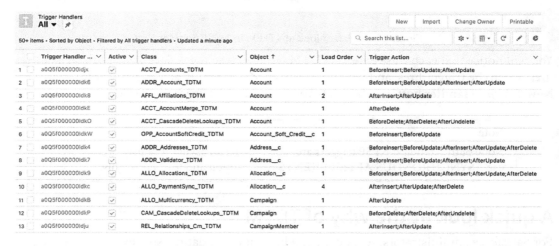

Figure 13.2 – Recommended format of the All list view for Trigger Handlers

3. Clicking on the trigger handler name will open the record for editing.

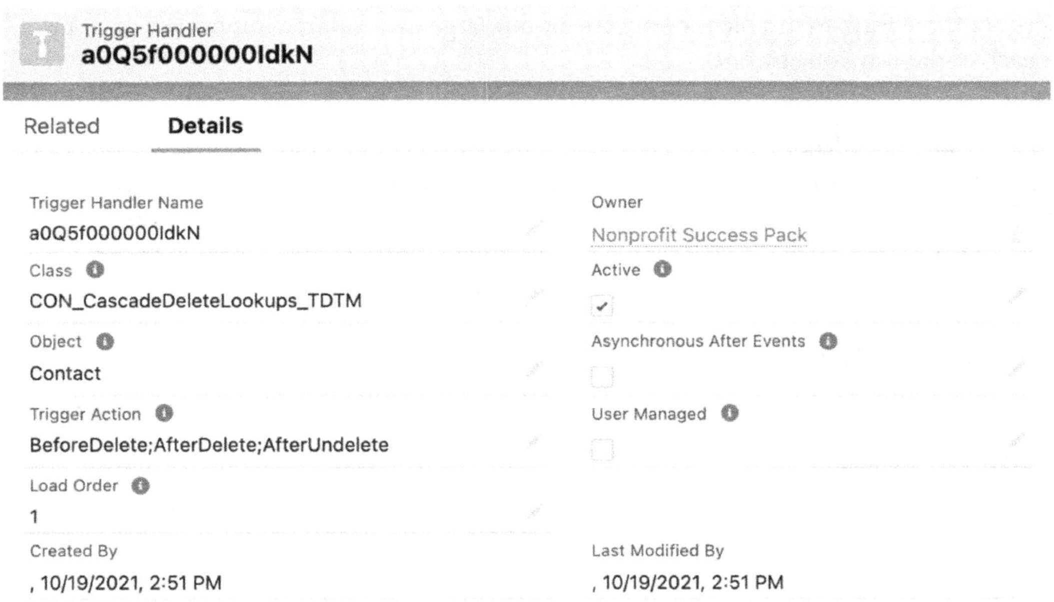

Trigger Handler
a0Q5f000000IdkN

Related   **Details**

Trigger Handler Name   Owner
a0Q5f000000IdkN   Nonprofit Success Pack

Class ⓘ   Active ⓘ
CON_CascadeDeleteLookups_TDTM   ✓

Object ⓘ   Asynchronous After Events ⓘ
Contact   ☐

Trigger Action ⓘ   User Managed ⓘ
BeforeDelete;AfterDelete;AfterUndelete   ☐

Load Order ⓘ
1

Created By   Last Modified By
, 10/19/2021, 2:51 PM   , 10/19/2021, 2:51 PM

Figure 13.3 – Trigger Handler record in NPSP

Each field is editable in the record; however, the most useful fields are the **Active** checkbox
and **Load Order**. Other edits may not have the desired effect since these triggers are part
of the NPSP managed package.

When to disable triggers using TDTM

Let's explore a use case for disabling triggers using TDTM. Imagine that you are
importing a large amount of data into NPSP. The more automations that are running
when you import large volumes of data, the more likely it is that errors will occur with
Apex CPU timeouts or row locks. Making the triggers inactive reduces the opportunity
for these types of errors.

Conversely, remember that the NPSP triggers are designed to work with each other to
accomplish the desired automations. Before disabling a trigger handler, it's important
to understand how it will affect your data import. A list of descriptions for each **Trigger
Handler** class is available in the *Resources and additional reading* section at the end of
this chapter.

> **Warning**
> Only disable triggers after testing thoroughly in a sandbox! Also, be sure to
> create the same process when you do the work in production.

There are three ways to disable the triggers for our large data volume import use case. Let's see each of the ways one by one.

Disabling the trigger handler entirely

To disable the **trigger handler entirely**, uncheck the **Active** checkbox in the **Trigger Handler** record. This will cause the trigger not to run until the **Active** checkbox is rechecked. This affects all users, so while you are importing data, the trigger does not work for other Salesforce users who may be working in the system.

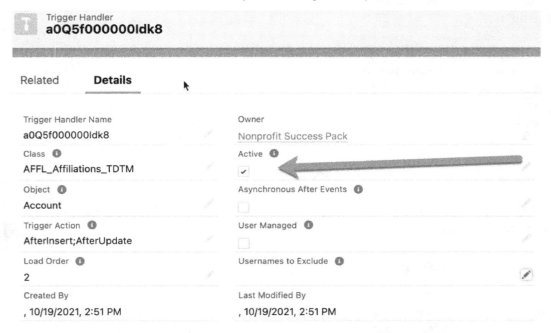

Figure 13.4 – Uncheck the Active checkbox to disable the trigger handler

Once the data is imported, be sure to reactivate the trigger handler.

Disabling the trigger handler for one or more users

In the previous scenario, you noticed that deactivating the trigger handler turns off the functionality for everyone in the system. To avoid undesired behavior across the system, you can disable the trigger handler for the one user for whom the data is being imported:

1.   First, find the username of the user that you wish to exclude.

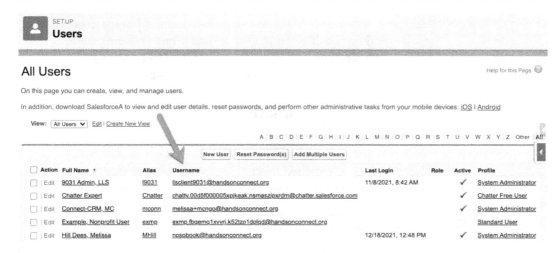

Figure 13.5 – Username in Setup > Users to use in the Trigger Handler record

2. Then, open the **Trigger Handler** record you want to disable for that user. Enter the username in the **Usernames to Exclude** field.

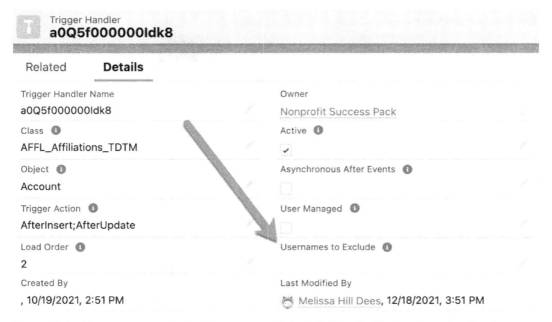

Figure 13.6 – Enter usernames in the Usernames to Exclude field to disable the trigger handler for one or more users

The trigger will not fire for actions taken by the usernames listed in the **Usernames to Exclude** field. Other users will not be affected while the data import is being done. Remember to go back to the **Trigger Handler** record and clear the **Usernames to Exclude** field when the data import is done so that the triggers will operate as expected.

Disabling trigger handlers programmatically

The third way of disabling a trigger handler is programmatically. If you write Apex code, you can temporarily disable the trigger handlers just for the context of that code. By getting the trigger handlers through the cached mechanism and looping through the Contact object, for example, and the Apex class, the code quickly changes the **Active** checkbox to false. Once the code sequence you are performing is complete, the trigger handler records revert.

An example of the code on a Contact object for the ACCT_IndividualAccounts_TDTM TDTM class might look like this:

```
List<npsp__Trigger_Handler__c> handlers =
npsp.TDTM_Config_API.getCachedRecords();
for (npsp__Trigger_Handler__c th: handlers) {
if (th.npsp__Object__c == 'Contact'
&& th.npsp__Class__c == 'ACCT_IndividualAccounts_TDTM')
{
Th.npsp__Active__c = false;
}
}
insert newContact;
```

This method is more advanced and is best used by those who write and are comfortable with Apex code.

Other use cases for disabling trigger handlers

Sometimes, you need to permanently disable trigger handlers. It is possible that custom code is present in the Salesforce instance that mimics a trigger handler in NPSP. You can permanently disable the trigger handler by unchecking the **Active** checkbox on the appropriate **Trigger Handler** record. This is a great help for an older Salesforce instance that has already solved challenges before NPSP was available.

Other cases may include permanently disabling a trigger handler for a specific user when updating contacts via a scheduled **extract, transform, and load** (**ETL**) job that runs as that user. Alternatively, you can temporarily disable a trigger handler to prevent related records, such as **Payment** or **Opportunity Contact Roles**, from being created when opportunities are inserted.

The use cases are many and varied. Regardless of the use case, disabling triggers is simple and easy to do with TDTM. No code is required.

How to create custom code using TDTM

Let's preface this section by saying that creating custom code is an advanced skill. As a Nonprofit Cloud administrator and/or consultant, it is not necessary that you are able to write Apex code. However, it is important to understand how the functionality of NPSP can be extended using custom code created via TDTM.

Steps to create custom code using TDTM

The steps for creating and deploying custom code using TDTM are just a few. If you have a developer who can write the actual code, you as an administrator can install and deploy the customer code using TDTM:

1. Create the `Apex` class.
2. Write the `test` class.
3. Add the `Trigger Handler` record.
4. Deploy to production (remember to add the `Trigger Handler` record).

There is an in-depth technical review available for developers and advanced administrators available in the *Resources and additional reading* section at the end of this chapter.

When to create custom code using TDTM

The use cases for creating custom code using TDTM are as varied as the nonprofits who use Nonprofit Cloud. The following are two examples.

An international nonprofit needs regions assigned to records after the **Opportunity Records** are created in **Gift Entry**. Custom code is written via the TDTM framework so that everything happens in the correct order.

Creating triggers for custom objects is one of the common use cases for TDTM. For one nonprofit, this is done around integrations, specifically where webhooks from an external system come into a custom object in Salesforce. A TDTM trigger is configured to process the external data, convert it, and push it to a queueable job.

Any time a nonprofit needs more granular control over custom code and when it is triggered is also a good time to consider TDTM.

Order of execution

Order of execution is one of the single most important concepts in Salesforce as a whole. From what we have learned about TDTM and how it helps configure the order of execution for triggers, you should have a better understanding of how important the order of execution is. Triggers are only one part of the larger puzzle. You may want to familiarize yourself with the order that things happen and when they happen.

The list is long, and the considerations are many. At a high level, here is what the order of execution looks like when you save a record:

1. Loads the original record from the database or initializes the record for an upsert statement.
2. Loads the new record field values from the request and overwrites the old values.
3. Executes record-triggered flows that are configured to run before the record is saved.
4. Executes all previous triggers.
5. Runs most system validation steps again, such as verifying that all required fields. have a non-null value, and runs any custom validation rules.
6. Executes duplicate rules.
7. Saves the record to the database but doesn't commit yet.
8. Executes all future triggers.
9. Executes assignment rules.
10. Executes auto-response rules.
11. Executes workflow rules.
12. Executes escalation rules.
13. Executes Salesforce Flow automations: processes, flows launched by processes, flows launched by workflow rules, but not in a guaranteed order.
14. Executes entitlement rules.
15. Executes record-triggered flows that are configured to run after the record is saved.

16. If the record contains a roll-up summary field or is part of a cross-object workflow, performs calculations and updates the roll-up summary field in the parent record. Parent record goes through save procedure.

17. If the parent record is updated, and a grandparent record contains a roll-up summary field or is part of a cross-object workflow, performs calculations and updates the roll-up summary field in the grandparent record. Grandparent record goes through save procedure.

18. Executes criteria-based sharing evaluation.

19. Commits all DML operations to the database.

20. After the changes are committed to the database, executes post-commit logic, such as sending an email and executing enqueued asynchronous Apex jobs, including queueable jobs and future methods.

There are myriad caveats around the order of execution that are not included here. For a detailed explanation, check out the *Resources and additional reading* section at the end of this chapter.

Interestingly, the only points of this list that are considered for TDTM are point number *4* and point number *8*. TDTM allows, within the group of triggers, the opportunity to set the order that those triggers fire. It is so important to understand the order of execution of the other 18 executables in Salesforce to put the trigger order in the proper perspective as well as the appropriate sequence.

Summary

In this chapter, we have explored what TDTM is and how it works with Nonprofit Cloud and the larger Salesforce instance to give you more granular control over how triggers fire in NPSP. TDTM allows triggers to be turned off, either permanently or temporarily, for some or all users. TDTM allows triggers to be reordered. TDTM also allows new triggers, or custom code, to be created and placed in the appropriate order within the order of execution.

The order of execution is a critical piece of every Salesforce puzzle. With the added functionality that Nonprofit Cloud brings, the order of execution becomes even more important. Understanding where in the order of execution does the before and after triggers happen helps guide the use of TDTM. There is additional information listed in the *Resources and additional reading* section at the end of the chapter with a variety of ways to learn and remember the order of execution.

We have learned about planning a Nonprofit Cloud implementation and installing and configuring Nonprofit Cloud and delved into some use cases. So, now what is left to learn in the next chapters?

In the next chapter, we will focus on the testing and deployment strategies to ensure that everything we have done up to this point works as expected.

Resources and additional reading

- *Apex class descriptions for NPSP*:

  ```
  https://www.sforgdocs.com/npspdocs/en-gb/product_docs/
  ngo/npsp/install_configure_npsp/advanced_configuration/
  npsp_apex_class_descriptions/topics/npsp-en-gb-apex-class-
  descriptions
  ```

- *NPSP GitHub repository*:

  ```
  https://github.com/SalesforceFoundation/NPSP
  ```

- *Technical overview of TDTM*:

  ```
  https://www.sforgdocs.com/npspdocs/en-gb/product_docs/ngo/
  npsp/install_configure_npsp/advanced_configuration/npsp_
  deploy_custom_apex/topics/npsp-en-gb-deploy-custom-apex-
  tdtm#ariaid-title3
  ```

- *Triggers and order of execution*:

  ```
  https://developer.salesforce.com/docs/atlas.
  en-us.234.0.apexcode.meta/apexcode/apex_triggers_order_of_
  execution.htm
  ```

- *AR WE RUShD*:

  ```
  https://eltoroit.herokuapp.com/Blog.app?page=ArWeRuShD
  ```

- *Order of Execution Salesforce*:

  ```
  https://trailhead.salesforce.com/trailblazer-community/
  files/0694S000001ZNs2QAG?tab=overview
  ```

14
Testing and Deployment Strategies

We have learned so much about what is available from Nonprofit Cloud, how to analyze what is needed, and how to implement the tools available. But wait! There is more. Your testing and deployment strategies are as important as the configuration. Testing and deployment strategies are a part of a larger project. Here, we want to address some specific information (as a reminder) when you get to this step in the process.

Testing is multifunctional in a Salesforce instance. As a Salesforce administrator, you know that code coverage is critical for a successful implementation. **User Acceptance Testing (UAT)** is also important to ensure the adoption of what you have implemented. As testing is done, you may need to iterate and update. Deploying the finished Nonprofit Cloud implementation with its configurations and customizations is the culmination of the entire project.

In this chapter, we will learn how to end the project well by learning these skills:

- How sandboxes work and what is needed for testing

- How to create data for testing purposes using Snowfakery and CumulusCI

- How to complete any post-install customizations

Let's explore the strategy and tools that are available for a successful deployment of Nonprofit Cloud.

Sandboxes and templates

A **sandbox** is a Salesforce tool that, as a Salesforce administrator, you may already know well. It is basically a staging area to do revisions, testing, or updates that will not impact the production instance of Salesforce. Let's review the essentials and some best practices around sandboxes. Then, we will look at specific ways that sandboxes and the templates that are available for Nonprofit Cloud can be used.

Sandbox essentials

Customizing a Salesforce instance should always be done in a sandbox; although Salesforce allows you to make changes directly in production, best practices and vast experience recommend working in a sandbox. This creates a copy of your production environment and allows you to make changes, test functionality, and train others, without affecting the actual production instance that your organization is currently using. Access sandboxes by going to **Setup** > **Environments** > **Sandboxes**. The following figure shows the type and number of sandboxes you have available or in use:

Figure 14.1 – A sandbox page in a standard NPSP Salesforce instance

There are currently four types of sandboxes available for the Enterprise edition (required for NPSP):

1. **Developer** – metadata only
2. **Developer Pro** – metadata only
3. **Partial Copy** – metadata and sample data
4. **Full** – metadata and all data

Sandbox License

Developer	Developer Pro	Partial Copy	Full
Refresh Interval: **1 Day**	Refresh Interval: **1 Day**	Refresh Interval: **5 Days**	Refresh Interval: **29 Days**
Capacity: **200 MB**	Capacity: **1 GB**	Capacity: **5 GB**	Capacity: **Same as Source**
Includes:	Includes:	Includes:	Includes:
• Configuration	• Configuration	• Configuration	• Configuration
• Apex & Metadata	• Apex & Metadata	• Apex & Metadata	• Apex & Metadata
• All Users	• All Users	• All Users	• All Users
		• Records (sample of selected objects)	• Records (all or selected objects)
		• Sandbox Template Support	• Sandbox Template Support
			• **History & Chatter Data (optional)**
Licenses In Use: 0 of 30	Licenses In Use: 1 of 1	Licenses In Use: 0 of 1	Licenses In Use: 0 of 0
Next	Next	No templates exist for this organization.	No licenses are available for your selected sandbox type. Contact your Salesforce representative to purchase additional licenses.

Figure 14.2 – The Sandbox License chart as seen in Salesforce instances

> **Important Note**
>
> The number of licenses available for Sandboxes also varies, depending on the type of Sandbox and whether you have an Enterprise-level instance or Professional. Salesforce instances do not come with full Sandbox licenses available; these must be purchased.

It also makes **Sandbox Templates** available; you can see the tab in *Figure 14.1*. A sandbox template allows you to customize what is created in a new sandbox based on the objects you choose to copy into a sandbox. If you are using a partial-copy sandbox, a template is required. Each object in the partial-copy sandbox will be populated with sample data, if available.

The **Sandbox History** tab shows a log of your sandbox usage. It includes creation, refreshes, and who created the sandbox.

Best practices and use cases for NPSP sandboxes

Because sandboxes do not alter, affect, or change your current production instance of Salesforce, they are a great way to clone what is already in production, and build, test, change, and train in that environment without endangering the ongoing work in production.

New functionality creation and testing

If you've ever updated a workflow rule in Salesforce and suddenly all the donors received an email, you have probably learned your lesson regarding creating or editing functionality in production in Salesforce. Even something as simple as a new upload from a third-party app that captures donor info can cause undesirable consequences. This is the reason behind Salesforce's wide caveat of testing everything in a sandbox and then deploying it to production. No matter how haywire the work may go in the sandbox, neither your production instance nor your production data is affected.

Another advantage of a sandbox is that you, as the system administrator, can create the sandbox and then give access to the sandbox to an external partner or developer to complete the requested new feature. You can provide as much or as little data as you desire for the sandbox user to see. In the interest of privacy, there are options we will discuss in the next section on creating completely anonymous test data.

UAT is also done very well in a sandbox environment without any danger to the production instance itself. The added bonus is the ability to create test data that is randomized and does not contain personally identifiable information.

New Salesforce releases and NPSP bug fixes

Another great use case for a sandbox is as a staging environment where you can test a new functionality that is not produced by you or on your instruction. Salesforce has three releases per year with new functionality and new options. Depending on how your production instance is configured, new functionality may not operate as expected. With the help of **Setup** > **Release Updates**, you can see which release updates need action and how soon Salesforce will enforce the release update, whether you have tested it or not:

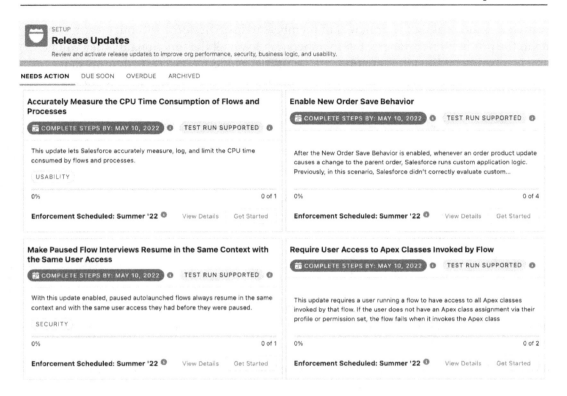

Figure 14.3 – An example of information contained in the Release Updates section of SETUP

As NPSP bug fixes are released, compatibility can be tested in sandboxes as well.

Train new staff

Nonprofit organizations are notorious for staff turnover. New employees are coming in all the time and need to be trained on specific business processes for the organization. Sandboxes are the perfect way to train new staff.

Creating a sandbox allows your new staff members to use Salesforce without creating bad data in the production instance. Staff members can learn all the functionality they will be using in a hands-on learning situation, ask questions, request help, create dummy data, and learn the Salesforce system exactly as it will look when they are released to do work in production:

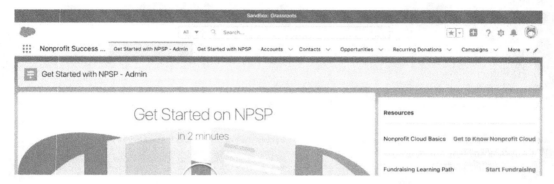

Figure 14.4 – A sandbox looks exactly like production except for the header at the top

Currently, sandboxes do not require multifactor authentication for login, so it is super easy to use for new trainees.

Sandboxes are a very useful tool for testing, training, and deployment once testing is complete. As a Salesforce system administrator, you will remember change sets. **Outbound** change sets are a means of exporting modifications to be imported by **Inbound** change sets:

Understanding Deployments

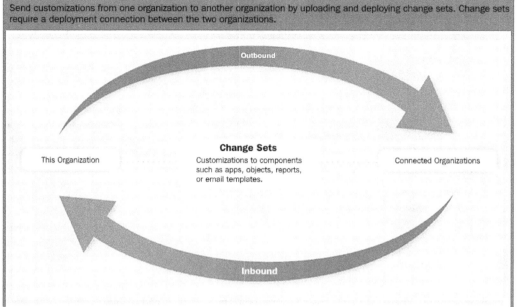

Figure 14.5 – A visual of how change sets work in Salesforce

To move changes from a sandbox to production, an **Outbound** change set is created in the sandbox and sent to production. In production, the **Inbound** change set is found under **Change Sets Awaiting Deployment**. Click **Deploy** to update the production instance with the changes. None of this standard functionality is affected by Nonprofit Cloud.

How to create custom test data

There are several different use cases for custom test data in Nonprofit Cloud. Let's look at three of them and the best ways to create the custom test data to be used:

1. **Test new releases**: NPSP has biweekly bug fixes in addition to Salesforce's three feature releases per year.

2. **New functionality**: Testing for new functionality by developers, QA, and UAT.

3. **Training**: Internal training in Salesforce.

Test data doesn't sound like it should be difficult, right? But it can be. You want to be sure that every worst-case scenario is explored and anything that might befuddle the new functionality, release, or user input is tested. From a trust and security perspective, you don't want to use private information to do this.

When I first began, I laboriously created an entire set of custom data to use in a demo instance. I carefully pulled out all the required fields as well as the preferable ones, specifically for a volunteer management product, and created a spreadsheet. Then, I filled in the spreadsheet with superhero information. It was a long and tiring process, but it worked:

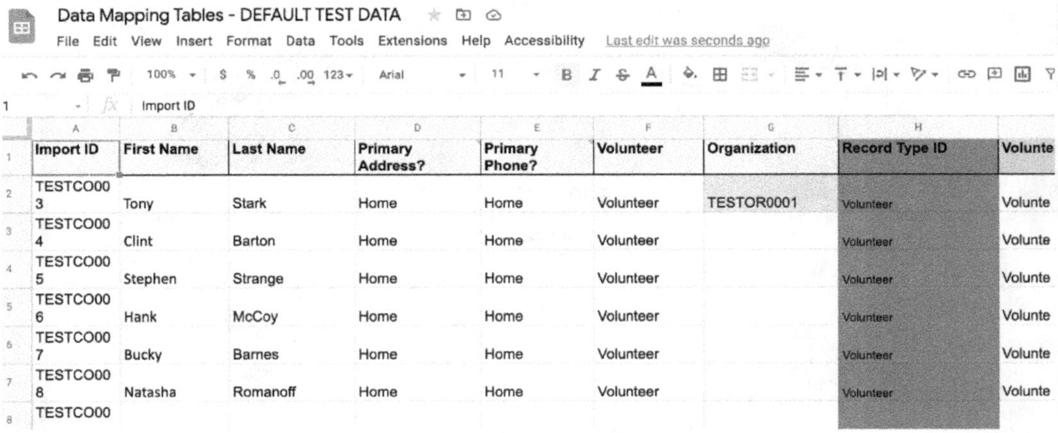

Import ID	First Name	Last Name	Primary Address?	Primary Phone?	Volunteer	Organization	Record Type ID	Volunte
TESTCO003	Tony	Stark	Home	Home	Volunteer	TESTOR0001	Volunteer	Volunte
TESTCO004	Clint	Barton	Home	Home	Volunteer		Volunteer	Volunte
TESTCO005	Stephen	Strange	Home	Home	Volunteer		Volunteer	Volunte
TESTCO006	Hank	McCoy	Home	Home	Volunteer		Volunteer	Volunte
TESTCO007	Bucky	Barnes	Home	Home	Volunteer		Volunteer	Volunte
TESTCO008	Natasha	Romanoff	Home	Home	Volunteer		Volunteer	Volunte
TESTCO00								

Figure 14.6 – An example of test data for contacts

Let's review some of the other options that are available, depending on your goals.

Test new releases with data

The most efficient way to test new releases and have the appropriate data automatically populated is to use either a full-copy sandbox or a partial-copy sandbox. Data from the production instance is automatically copied into the sandbox along with the metadata. This provides a solid test environment. There are pros and cons to both the full-copy sandbox and partial-copy sandbox options for the purpose of testing new releases.

Full-copy sandbox

Let's understand the pros and cons of a full-copy sandbox.

Pros

- The full-copy sandbox is a duplicate of your production instance and includes all data and metadata.
- Only the full-copy sandbox supports performance testing, load testing, and staging.
- There are options to include Chatter activity data and field tracking data.

Cons

- The real challenge with a full-copy sandbox is that there is an expense involved. You must purchase a license(s) from Salesforce to provision this type of sandbox.

- The refresh interval, 29 days, for a full-copy sandbox lends itself to only doing final testing and staging.

- Data is not anonymous.

Partial-copy sandbox

Let's understand the pros and cons of a partial-copy sandbox.

Pros

- The partial-copy sandbox includes a sample of data from the production instance.

- Each Enterprise edition, which is what is required and comes with NPSP, has a partial-copy sandbox already provisioned, so there is no additional expense.

- The refresh interval is only 5 days.

Cons

- Random records are copied from the production instance, and there are no options to choose particular records.

- All the different types of records may not be copied from production. For example, if there are five different Engagement Plan Templates, they may not all be copied into the sandbox.

- Data is not anonymous.

Full-copy and partial-copy sandboxes are quick and relatively easy solutions, depending on the funding and time you have available, and come filled with test data that you do not have to create. Partial-copy sandboxes are the best practice solution for UAT, integration testing, and training.

New functionality test data

You and your developers have created the most wonderful automations and streamlined a process so that it runs incredibly fast and well. Now, you need to test what you have built with actual data. With a new functionality, there is no data in production because the new functionality is not in the production instance. So, how do you create data in a sandbox to test this new functionality?

The volunteer team from Salesforce.org's **Open Source Commons Community Sprints** has the following recommendations.

Create spreadsheets

As a Salesforce administrator, you know that spreadsheets, usually in CSV format, are used to import data. For populating a sandbox, you can do the following:

1. Create a report from the production instance to pull the appropriate data you need, export it to a spreadsheet, and import it into the sandbox.

2. Manually create a spreadsheet and import the data into the sandbox.

Both methods can be time-consuming and error-prone.

Use Mockaroo

If you are working specifically with data around contacts, households, and donations, Mockaroo has a sample NPSP-compatible schema to generate sample data. Plus, it is compatible with the NPSP Data Import tool:

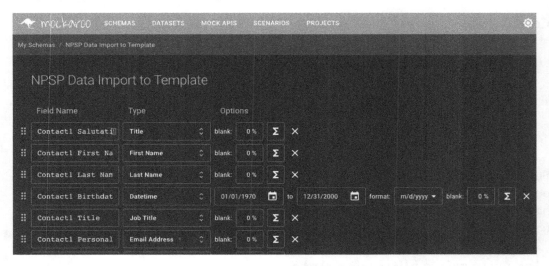

Figure 14.7 – A sample Mockaroo form for generating NPSP data

Mockaroo is cloud-based, and the NPSP-compatible schema can be accessed at `https://mockaroo.com/4392b3f0`. The drawback to using Mockaroo is that the free version has a 1,000-record limit.

What is Snowfakery?

Snowfakery is an open source contribution by Paul Prescod, an engineer on the Salesforce.org team. Snowfakery creates complicated and unique data records for testing purposes. The fake data that is generated comes with the relationships between the records already built in, so you don't have to create multi-tab spreadsheets and perform a multi-step import process.

Snowfakery creates the appropriate data by reading a recipe file you write in the **YAML** programming language. Access to Snowfakery is via the command-line interface, so you need to be comfortable with coding. However, the Open Source Commons team is currently working on recipes and interfaces to expand Snowfakery's use for administrators:

Figure 14.8 – Data Generation Toolkit is a project of the Open Source Commons Community Sprint

One of the most helpful use cases for Snowfakery is to create large volumes of data. For example, if you are doing performance testing, you may need tens of thousands of records. Snowfakery scales easily to accommodate that level of test data.

Because all the data created by Snowfakery is fake, there are no security concerns around personally identifiable data that may have been copied from the production instance.

Data for training purposes

Another use case for creating data is for training purposes. The superhero data spreadsheet mentioned at the beginning of this section was created for training and demoing functionality. It's difficult to show how the system works or train new users without some data being populated, and it's unrealistic that there will be no data unless no one has ever used Salesforce.

> **Note**
> Training should always happen in a sandbox.

If you are using a full-copy sandbox or a partial-copy sandbox, the data that is automatically populated can be used for training. The challenge may be that some of the data is sensitive information. Salesforce offers **Data Mask** to use data obfuscation to modify data and ensure the privacy of any personally identifiable information. There are different levels of masking available, using random characters, replacing data, and deleting data.

For training purposes, your team may want to weigh the benefits and consequences of using test data versus using native data from production. Now, you know that there are options.

Complete post-installation customizations with CumulusCI

If you are just beginning your work with Nonprofit Cloud, your first question may be, what is **CumulusCI**? CumulusCI is a toolset developed by Salesforce.org to collaborate on and share Salesforce-related projects. CumulusCI stands for **Cumulus Continuous Integration**. It basically provides a recipe that can be shared to create a new Salesforce instance. CumulusCI leverages GitHub to store the recipe for sharing and is an advanced tool.

The use cases for CumulusCI vary; however, CumulusCI is a great way to work with the Open Source Commons tools that we have already discussed, such as Outbound Funds Module. With Outbound Funds, the package has already been created using CumulusCI. It has all the basic functionality for tracking most of the work that will be done. But there are customizations that need to be made so that Outbound Funds specifically delivers better information for our test case.

The advantages of post-install customizations using CumulusCI

The post-install customizations can be done manually, but we will use CumulusCI to better understand its functionality and the advantages it provides. What are the advantages?

- We can quickly create a new scratch organization instance so that anyone can test the functionality without endangering the production instance or revealing data.

- We can track the history of changes to the components.

- We can share the metadata and configuration with a third party.

- We can share the finished customizations with other organizations.

CumulusCI may require the assistance of a developer to set up the initial instance; however, once that instance is created, new scratch instances can be generated quickly and easily for the purpose of testing and UAT. Talk to your developer team about using this strategy for testing, training, and deployment.

Summary

In this chapter, we have explored testing and training strategies and the various methods for creating data for testing or training. We also touched on deployment, particularly using CumulusCI, and the standard change set deployment.

Security is always a primary concern for a nonprofit organization's data. Review the ways that are available to maintain the privacy of personally identifiable data, using Salesforce tools such as Data Mask or external tools such as Snowfakery.

We have spent immense amounts of time learning different aspects of data. Data, and the relationships between the different types of data, is critical. In the next chapter, we will learn how to use data to create reports, visualizations, and other tools that make the data actionable for everyone, not just Salesforce users and administrators.

Resources and additional reading

- Mockaroo NPSP schema:

  `https://mockaroo.com/4392b3f0`

- *Snowfakery Documentation*:

  `https://snowfakery.readthedocs.io/en/latest/#snowfakery-documentation`

- *Snowfakery Data Generation with Paul Prescod*: `https://www.youtube.com/watch?v=AopjPcpdcOg`

- *Data Generation Toolkit Resources Trailmix*: `https://trailhead.salesforce.com/users/cassiesupilowski/trailmixes/data-generation-toolkit`

- *Build Applications with CumulusCI*: `https://trailhead.salesforce.com/en/content/learn/trails/build-applications-with-cumulusci`

- *CumulusCI 3.52.0 documentation*: `https://cumulusci.readthedocs.io/en/stable/intro.html`

15
Implementing Analytics Tools for Impact

Everything we have done so far will be wrapped up in this chapter. Let's learn how to use the data that has been collected and tracked by the tools and implementations we have created. The data should show impact and help organizations make better decisions based on the data using the following:

- Reports for detailed data and impact measures
- Dashboards to facilitate executive decision making
- Tableau for visualizing data

Without a clear understanding of how to use these resources, there can be immense amounts of data sitting dormant in a Salesforce instance. Collecting the data in a way that makes it actionable has been our focus all along. Let's look at how we can surface that data to assist nonprofits based on the audience that will be consuming the information and their goals.

Reporting for impact

Reporting is the fundamental piece of any impact measurement for nonprofits. Nonprofit Cloud provides, out of the box, reports that share information on donors, grants, membership, campaign ROI, and more. And, just like with standard Salesforce, you can edit or create new reports with the **Report Builder**.

Options for reports

NPSP also provides reports that will be the basis of **Dashboards**; we'll look at those in the next section when we learn about identifying and utilizing helpful Dashboards.

Most packages that you install, such as the Program Management Module, Outbound Funds Module, or Volunteers for Salesforce, also come with prepackaged reports that are available in Nonprofit Cloud. These reports are contained within folders in your **Reports** tab:

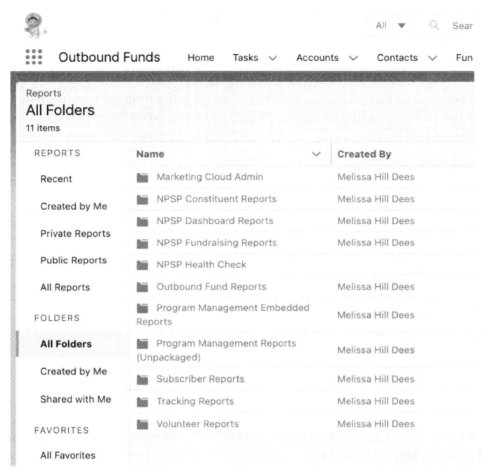

Figure 15.1 – All the folders in Nonprofit Cloud Reports after additional modules have been installed

With all these options available, how do you decide which report to use or whether to build a new one entirely?

Best practices for creating and customizing reports

Reports are a part of the Nonprofit Cloud Analytics section of the Nonprofit Cloud Consultant certification. Although analytics is only 5% of the total weight, reports and dashboards are tools you have already studied to pass the Salesforce Administrator exam.

The best practices for reports in Nonprofit Cloud do not differ from the standard best practices that Salesforce administrators already know. Some examples that are critical are as follows:

- Always start in a sandbox, even when building reports.
- Don't create a new report for every need; be strategic about creating reports.
- Organize reports appropriately so that users have easy access to the reports that they need.

Following these guidelines can help us consider how we leverage reports that already exist and when to create a new report entirely.

Updating and installing new NPSP report packages

Throughout this book, we have been working with a new Nonprofit Cloud instance. However, sometimes, you may be working with an organization that began using Salesforce before NPSP existed or the organization may not have upgraded to the most recent version of NPSP. If you are not certain, the best practice is to check the configuration:

1. Verify that **Reports** and **Dashboards Settings** are enabled in **Setup**.
2. Confirm that the **Grant** record type exists in the Salesforce instance. **Record Type Label** and **Record Type Name** should both be Grant. If you have already created a grant record type with a different name, create a **Grant** record type:

Figure 15.2 – The required Grant record type for installing the new Reports package

3. Now, you are ready to install the NPSP **Reports** and **Dashboards** using the installer; see the link in the *Resources and further reading* section at the end of this chapter.

Once the updated reports and dashboards have been installed, we can update report folder access for the users in Nonprofit Cloud. Click the **Reports** tab and go to **All Folders**. Click the down arrow next to the folder you want to share and click **Share** to define who can access the folder and its contents:

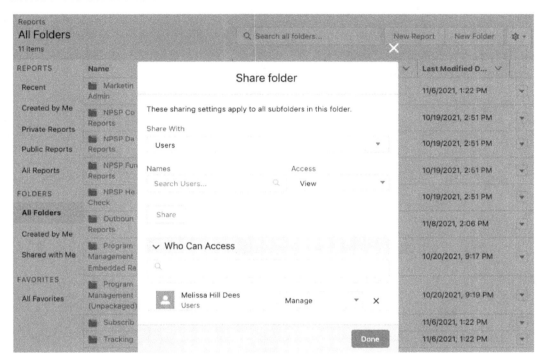

Figure 15.3 – Share folder

Now that the reports are up to date in the Salesforce instance, let's learn how to customize existing reports.

Customizing existing NPSP reports

There are two dozen or more preconfigured reports that are available for NPSP. Some reports come with other packages such as PMM and V4S. With all these reports, you may never have to customize an existing report. However, you need to know how to customize a report if it needs to be done. Beyond the basics, changing the chart type, applying cross filters, and editing a matrix report are customizations you must know about. Let's take a look:

1. One customization that frequently needs to be made involves changing the chart type associated with a report. The **Memberships Over Time** report in the **NPSP Constituent Reports** folder comes preconfigured with a line chart:

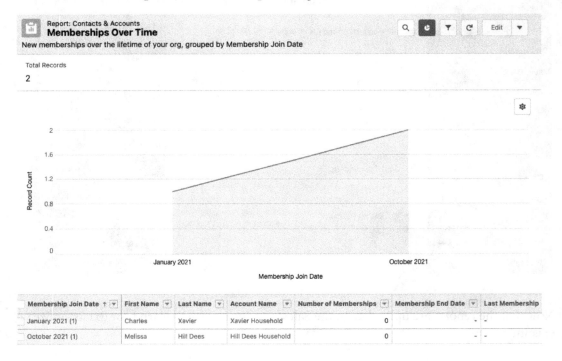

Figure 15.4 – The Memberships Over Time line chart configuration

2. You can also customize the chart to be a funnel chart by clicking the gear icon in the chart area and changing the **Display As** section:

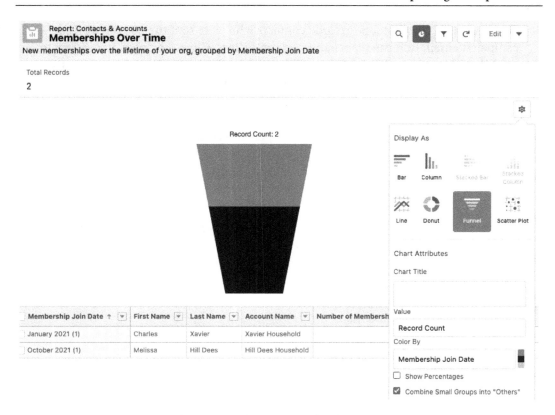

Figure 15.5 – Customizing the chart type

3. You can also customize your **Chart Title**, its **Value**, and the colors for the chart. To preserve the original report, click **Save As** and give the report a unique name.

4. The **Contact LYBUNT** report is a frequently used report for nonprofits, particularly for fundraising teams. It shows which donors gave last year but have not given this year. If it's the middle of January and a large part of your donor base just received your year-end campaign email, how do you filter those donors so that they don't feel inundated with *beg letters* or donation requests from your organization?

5. For this, add a cross filter to exclude contacts who were sent the **2021 Year End** campaign email. Edit the report and click on **Filters**. Click the down arrow next to the **Filters** label and click **Add Cross Filter**. This will show you the cross filters you can apply based on the report type, as shown in the following screenshot:

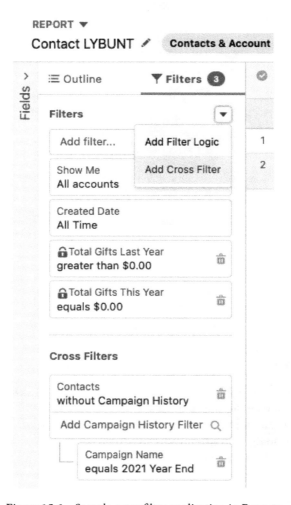

Figure 15.6 – Sample cross filter application in Reports

6. Under **Cross Filters**, add **Contacts** without **Campaign History**. By adding a specific **Campaign Name**, we can filter out any contacts who were sent the **2021 Year End** campaign email.

7. Save the report with a unique name to maintain the standard **Contact LYBUNT** report.

Another useful tool is the matrix report; one example is the **Closed/Won Opps by Type and Fiscal Year** report under **NPSP Fundraising Reports**. In this scenario, let's change **Fiscal Year** to **Calendar Year**. In the standard report, **Fiscal Year** is the column grouping. To change it to group by **Calendar Year** instead, add **Close Date** to **Group Columns** and remove **Fiscal Year** from **Group Columns**:

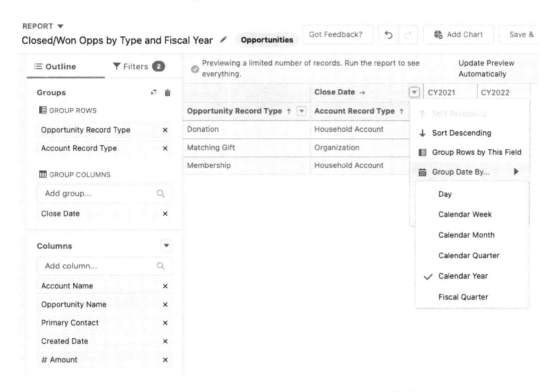

Figure 15.7 – Customizing a matrix report in Nonprofit Cloud

Click the down arrow next to the close date and choose **Calendar Year** under **Group Date by**. Save the report with a unique name that reflects its functionality.

Creating new report types

As many reports as you have and as customizable as they are, not every report type is available out of the box. A good use case is **Contacts** and their affiliations to **Accounts**. Let's do a quick Salesforce admin review of how to create a new report type:

1. Go to **Setup** > **Feature Settings** > **Analytics** > **Reports & Dashboards** > **Report Types**. Click **New Custom Report Type**:

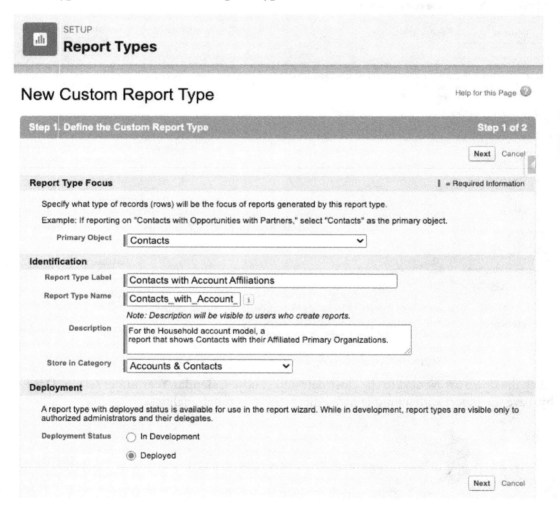

Figure 15.8 – Creating a new custom report type

2. Provide a **Primary Object**, **Report Type Label**, **Description,** and an appropriate **Store in Category** values.

3. Confirm that **Deployed** is selected and click **Next**. No secondary object is required for this report type, so click **Save**.

4. Next, we need to confirm that our new report type includes the fields we need in the report. Click **Edit Layout** under **Fields Available** in the **Report** section. Then, click **Add Fields related via lookup**. The objects that are related to **Contacts** will be shown.

5. Click **Primary Affiliation** to surface the fields from the related account:

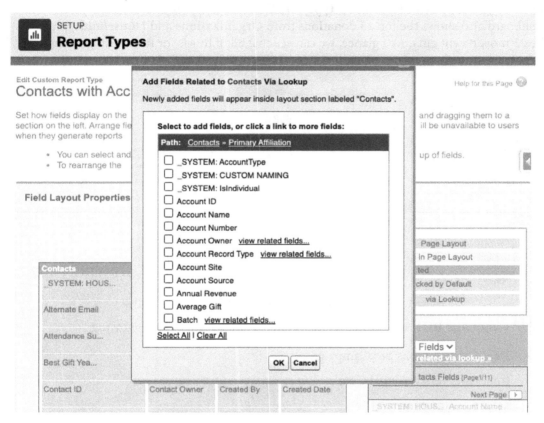

Figure 15.9 – Adding fields from related objects to the report type

6. Select the required fields by checking the boxes next to them. For this report type, we recommend using **Account Name, Billing City, Billing State, Billing Zip/Postal Code**, and **Employees**. Click **OK** and then **Save**. Now, you can create reports on constituents based on their employer affiliation.

Now that you've refreshed your reporting skills, let's refresh your **dashboard** skills.

What dashboards do the decision-makers need?

NPSP provides four dashboards *out of the box*; three are specifically analysis-based, while the fourth is for forecasting.

The **Development Analysis** dashboard provides information on giving by **Account Record Type**, **Opportunity Record Type**, and **GAU** for this year and the last 3 years. This dashboard also shows the top 25 donations from **Organizations** and **Households**, plus the 25 most recent gifts. At a glance, we can see that all of this is for fundraising teams and executives to see, weigh, and pivot, if needed, based on the data:

Figure 15.10 – The Development Analysis dashboard from NPSP

NPSP Campaign ROI Analysis surfaces important data, such as the following:

- Total Contributions per Campaign

- Total Gifts versus Actual Cost

- Return on Investment (ROI)

- Cost Per Donor (CPD)

- Cost Per Dollar Donated

- Return on Initial Investment (ROII)

- Average Gift

- Number of Gifts

This dashboard shows which campaigns are contributing the most fundraising dollars to the organization so that fundraisers and executives can tweak spending to maximize the most effective campaigns.

The **Giving Range Analysis** dashboard shows how the donated amount ranges for this year, last year, and 2 years ago. This is a great benchmark for executives and fundraisers to measure current success.

The **Development Forecasting** dashboard is the most familiar dashboard and very similar to dashboards that are used in standard Salesforce to show **Open Opportunities by Stage**, Record Type, and Campaign. This dashboard also reveals any **Overdue Payments, Upcoming Payments, Delinquent Accounts**, and **Top 25 LYBUNT and SYBUNT Households and Organizations**.

V4S and PMM also come with standard dashboards. These tools are only as good as the data behind them. Any errors become exacerbated during the rollup process and when formulas are applied. Fundraisers and executives rely on the Nonprofit Cloud administrator to provide good data in the dashboards that have been created to show critical trends and information immediately. Do you remember the work we did in *Chapter 7, Is Change Difficult for Your Organization?*, and *Chapter 8, Requirements – User Stories – Business Processes – What Is Your Organization Trying to Achieve?* **Specific, Measurable, Achievable, Relevant, and Timely (SMART)** metrics define the reports and dashboards that are implemented.

Visualizing data

As we mentioned previously regarding reports and dashboards, all the work we've done so far in Nonprofit Cloud has been to ensure that we have accurate data and are collecting the appropriate data. We have used Nonprofit Cloud to connect to, organize, and scale nonprofit programs and services.

In August 2019, Salesforce acquired Tableau, which is considered the number one analytics platform available. The Tableau Foundation, like the Salesforce Foundation before it, donates Tableau Desktop to small nonprofits and NGOs. Simply apply for the licensing at `https://www.tableau.com/foundation/license-donations`.

Tableau allows nonprofits to see, or visualize, data that can help nonprofit users see trends or outliers, highlighting what the data is saying. Depending on your data, you can learn more about the behavior of donors and program recipients. Or perhaps your focus is on tracking and reporting on impact. Let's learn how to leverage Tableau to visualize Nonprofit Cloud data.

Tableau Accelerators are available for both nonprofit fundraising in NPSP and PMM in NPSP. The accelerators speed up the process of visualizing data as much as the pre-built reports and dashboards do. You can edit and change them as necessary to reflect the goals of your organization:

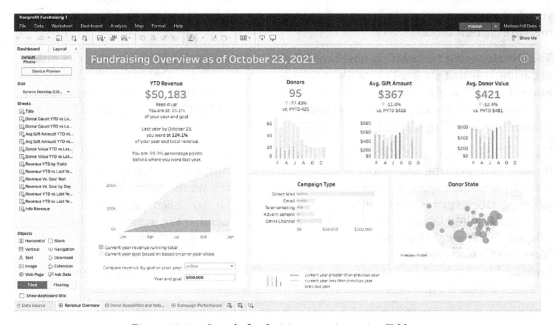

Figure 15.11 – Sample fundraising overview using Tableau

The preceding screenshot shows how easy it is to see the important statistics around fundraising for this organization. Take a look at **YTD Revenue**; here, we can see that the organization is only at 25.1% of the year-end goal.

Similarly, the accelerator for PMM helps us see the trends associated with client enrollment and participation:

> **Note**
>
> The maps show where clients are located geographically. The bar charts on either side of the map show the clients (by stage) and delineate clients by age. As with the fundraising overview, the dashboard can be edited.

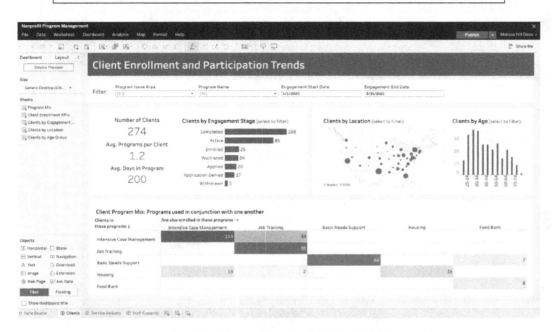

Figure 15.12 – Sample PMM trends using Salesforce's Tableau accelerator

Another advantage of using Tableau is the ability to easily connect the organization's Salesforce instance. Not only does Tableau connect to Salesforce, but it also connects to a long list of data sources:

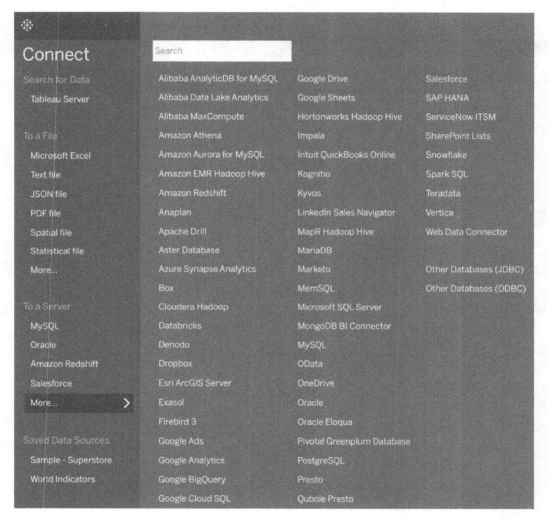

Figure 15.13 – List of files, servers, and saved data sources for connecting to Tableau

Visualizing data is critical for nonprofit executives to leverage data to make the best mission-driven decisions for their organization. As a Nonprofit Cloud practitioner, providing the most useful way, whether it is a Dashboard or a Tableau Overview, is critical.

Summary

In this chapter, we learned how to bring all the data that has been collected together and relate it in ways that help a nonprofit increase its impact. Reports are the primary building blocks for this. Dashboards enhance the user interface with data to make it easy to see, read, and recognize trends, data skews, and other decision-making points that executives may need. We also learned that Tableau is the premier data visualization tool for doing this.

At this point, you should be familiar with the standard reports and dashboards that are part of NPSP. As a Salesforce administrator, you learned how to customize existing reports and create new report types. Understanding the data schema of NPSP itself gives you the knowledge to customize and create reports and dashboards for NPSP and its related modules, such as V4S and PMM.

Tableau is an immense and robust product and in this chapter, we saw a very high-level overview of how it might be leveraged for nonprofits and in conjunction with Nonprofit Cloud. For the Nonprofit Cloud Consultant certification, the awareness here is sufficient. Tableau has certification programs outside the Nonprofit Cloud arena.

The next chapter will conclude this book by discussing what you need to maintain the grand platform that we have built using Nonprofit Cloud and all the tools at your disposal. Maintaining data integrity and the best practices for maintaining the Salesforce instance are critical to automating what can be automated to increase the nonprofit's impact on their mission with Nonprofit Cloud.

Resources and additional reading

For more information regarding the topics that were covered in this chapter, take a look at the following resources:

- *Reports & Dashboards for Lightning Experience*: `https://trailhead.salesforce.com/content/learn/modules/lex_implementation_reports_dashboards`

- *Nonprofit Success Pack Reports Workbook*: `https://s3-us-west-2.amazonaws.com/sfdo-docs/npsp_reports.pdf`

- *NPSP Reports & Dashboards Installer*: `https://install.salesforce.org/products/npsp/reports`

- *Chart Types*: `https://help.salesforce.com/s/articleView?id=sf.chart_types.htm&type=5`

- *Achieving Agenda 2030*: https://www.salesforce.org/wp-content/uploads/2020/10/SFDO-Achieving-Agenda-2030-Impact-Management-Imperative.pdf

- *Tableau Basics for Nonprofits*: https://trailhead.salesforce.com/en/content/learn/modules/tableau-basics-for-nonprofits

- *Get Started with Data Visualization in Tableau Desktop*: https://trailhead.salesforce.com/en/content/learn/trails/get-started-with-data-visualization-in-tableau-desktop

- *Get Tableau Certified*: https://www.tableau.com/learn/certification

- *Nonprofit Success Pack Reports Workbook*: https://sfdo-docs.s3-us-west-2.amazonaws.com/npsp_reports.pdf

16
Ongoing Data Management and Best Practices

We have covered the basic functionality of Nonprofit Cloud and addressed correlating an organization's needs with the Nonprofit Cloud tools. We practiced implementing those tools and looked at the configurations and customizations needed for some use cases. We've discovered, strategized, tested, and deployed. So now, what's next?

Although this is the last chapter, it is not the least. Managing vast amounts of data coming into a Salesforce instance will be an ongoing process. As with any work, maintenance is an important task that continues after the initial excitement of the project is long gone. We will cover three areas:

- How to prevent, mitigate, and resolve duplicate data
- Importing data
- General best practices, tips, and tricks

In *Chapter 2, What Is NPSP?*, we studied the architecture of NPSP; in this chapter, we'll use that knowledge to prevent corrupt and duplicate data. Leveraging that knowledge, we will learn how to use the Nonprofit Cloud Data Import tool. And, finally, we will look at best practices to share with users to maintain data integrity.

Why is there so much duplicate data?

If you have a Salesforce instance, the chances that you have duplicate data in that system are almost certain. Duplicate data diminishes the impact of having Salesforce as a single source of truth. And that is only one challenge with duplicate data. Storage becomes an issue as well. Reports are not accurate. AI can be skewed. Data can even become corrupted.

An ounce of prevention is worth a pound of cure.

Let's first look at how we can prevent duplicates.

Preventing duplication

As a certified Salesforce administrator, you are aware of the **Matching** and **Duplicate** rules available in Salesforce, which can be found by navigating to **Setup** > **Data** > **Duplicate Management**. NPSP adds a **matching rule** named NPSP Contact Personal Email Match.

This matching rule sets the **HomeEmail** field and the **LastName** field as the unique identifiers, along with a fuzzy match of the first name:

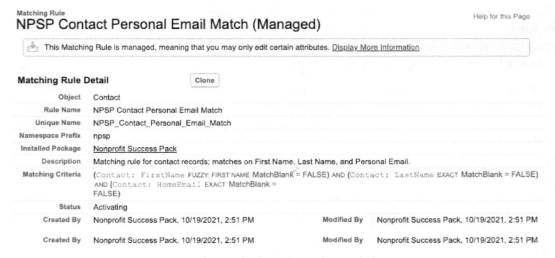

Figure 16.1 – The standard NPSP matching rule for contacts

If the nonprofit needs more stringent or less restrictive matching rules for contacts, this rule can be cloned and reconfigured.

> **Note**
> When the standard **NPSP Contact Personal Email Match** rule is activated, the standard account, contact, and lead matching rules are deactivated. Therefore, there is no standard NPSP matching rule for accounts.

Once you have the matching rules configured as you need them, it's time to add the matching rule to the appropriate **duplicate rule** or, if it has not already been done, activate the duplicate rule. Go to **Setup** > **Data** > **Duplicate Management** > **Duplicate Rules**:

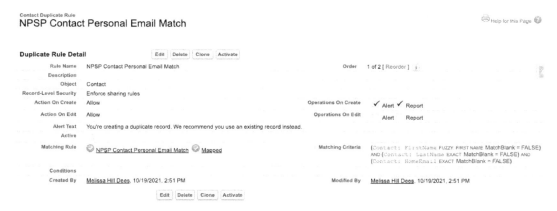

Figure 16.2 – The preconfigured NPSP Duplicate Rule for NPSP Contact Personal Email Match

When NPSP is installed, the standard NPSP matching rule and the standard NPSP duplicate rule are added to the Salesforce instance. However, you do need to check that it is activated if you intend to use the standard rules instead of creating custom matching and duplicate rules.

Depending on the actions and operations you have set, the duplicate rule can prevent what it thinks is a duplicate from being created at all, or (and best practices recommend it) the rule can allow the creation of the duplicate but not before a warning is generated that it may be a duplicate.

Great work! Now, how are the matching and duplicate rules leveraged?

Mitigating duplication

For a user in the Salesforce system, there are two options when what is suspected to be a duplicate contact is created, depending on how you configured the duplicate rule. If the duplicate rule is set to **Block** in the **Action On Create** field, the user will receive an error message:

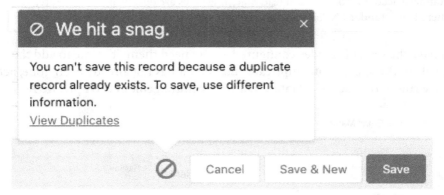

Figure 16.3 – The duplicate contact creation error message for the user

Although the **Save & New** and **Save** buttons appear, the only options the user has are **Cancel** or **View Duplicates**.

Clicking the **View Duplicates** link will open a page with the suspected duplicated contact records, based on the matching rule being used:

Figure 16.4 – Suspected duplicate contact records related to the information being used to create a new contact record

This view is meant to give the user enough information to assess whether the contact record truly is a duplicate. However, the user will not be able to create a new record with the same information, even if the record is not a duplicate.

> **Note**
> Not only are you creating a duplicate contact record; you are also creating a duplicate household account.

The second option is to set the action in the duplicate rule to allow for creation and to alert the user. The process is very similar to what we have already seen:

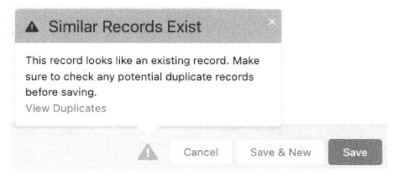

Figure 16.5 – When the action in the duplicate rule is set to allow for creation, this is the error message that appears

The difference here is that the user can choose to **View Duplicates**, which directs the user to a page such as the one seen in *Figure 16.4* to identify whether the contact record is a duplicate. Alternatively, the user can choose to save this contact record and possibly create a duplicate.

If the user immediately realizes the mistake and deletes the contact record, remember that a duplicate household account record has been created, too. If the appropriate NPSP configurations have been done correctly, the user should receive a warning to alert them to this possibility:

Figure 16.6 – The household account management warning prompted by deleting a contact record

The options for the user are as follows:

- Delete the contact and leave an empty account.
- View the contact record.
- Delete the account.

For the use case of accidentally creating a duplicate contact record, the third option is the choice. If the household account record is not empty, deleting only the contact will be appropriate.

The most common use cases for mitigating duplication of data for end users occur around contacts, accounts, leads, and opportunities. They all follow the same pattern as the examples here for contacts.

You have all your internal users trained on using the alerts and are still getting duplicate data. What do you do next?

Resolving duplicate data

Duplicate data is with us always, no matter how diligent users are. It's a fact of life. For example, Salesforce does not alert users to duplicates on the mobile app. What are the best practices for resolving duplicate data?

Creating a data maintenance schedule is an excellent way to prevent and resolve duplicate issues. Most objects have a list view entitled **New this Week**. Reviewing those records for completeness, accuracy, and duplication helps resolve challenges early. Additionally, creating reports for users that uncover missing or inaccurate data can improve overall results as well:

Figure 16.7 – A report showing the contact records that are missing phone data

Reviewing this information on a regular basis maintains data integrity.

Another tool native to Salesforce is **Adoption Dashboard**. It is a great review of what has happened in the organization:

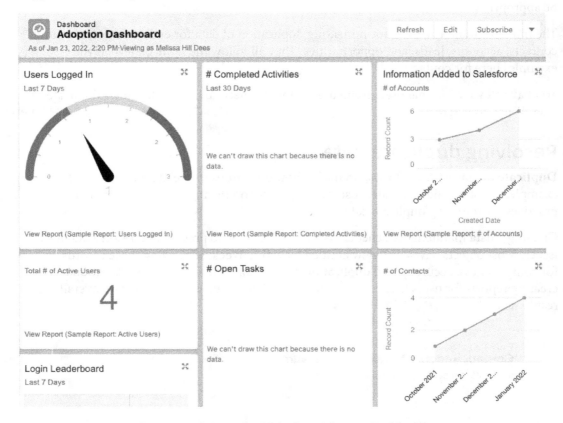

Figure 16.8 – A standard Salesforce Adoption Dashboard

These tools work well with new or well-maintained organizations.

The **NPSP Health Check** identifies NPSP-related data issues. It can be accessed via **NPSP Settings** > **System Tools**. The results identify where data inconsistencies may be:

✓ All Health Check tests have successfully passed.

☑ Show Passed Tests   Last run: 1/23/2022, 2:34 PM   Detection time in seconds: 6.459

✓ Passed   Opportunity Payments

All Opportunities with Payments have expected Payments.

✓ Passed   Opportunity Contact Roles

No Opportunities were found with multiple Primary Opportunity Contact Roles.

✓ Passed   Account Data

✓ Passed   Household Data

✓ Passed   Contact Data

✓ Passed   Account Model Data

Account system fields for any Household Accounts and One-to-One Accounts are set correctly.

✓ Passed   Account Model Data

Bucket Individual: 0
One-to-One Individual: 0
Household Account: 3

Figure 16.9 – Sample health check results from the NPSP Health Check

Using these tools on a regular basis to maintain the integrity of your data will improve NPSP functionality. If you are working in an older instance or one that has not been well maintained, you should explore third-party tools on AppExchange to do the initial duplicate cleanup.

Responsible ways to import data

One of the reasons that data gets duplicated is that there are many ways for data to enter a Salesforce system. Data can be instantiated by an Experience Cloud user or a Salesforce user. It can be arriving via an API. It can be manually imported using *dataloader.io* or other tools you learned about as a Salesforce administrator. Some of those ways may not respect the duplicate and matching rules an administrator has created. And, as we reviewed, the NPSP data architecture is different from the standard Salesforce architecture.

The Nonprofit Cloud Data Import tool

NPSP Data Importer is designed specifically for the task of importing data into NPSP. The standard data import requires several passes. For example, if you're importing new donors and their donations, it can take a minimum of three imports:

- Accounts (or households)
- Contacts (or donors)
- Opportunities (or donations)

All these require the appropriate .csv files and the appropriate way to relate each object to another. It can be incredibly time-consuming and arduous, and it's prone to human error. NPSP Data Importer streamlines the import by creating accounts, contact records, opportunities, and other related records in one shot. NPSP Data Importer also has built-in matching rules to help prevent duplicates. Sounds too good to be true? Let's examine a use case.

Although you can use NPSP Data Importer to update current data or add new members to campaigns collected at an event, in this use case, we are going to continue the premise that we are setting up by configuring a new Nonprofit Cloud instance. The nonprofit has data from their legacy system that they want to import into Salesforce.

> **NOTE**
> Any time that data is imported, it is always best practice to do a test load into a sandbox first before importing it into production.

Using Data Import Templates

There are four **Data Import Templates** available in the form of Excel spreadsheets:

- Accounts and Contact Import
- Donation Import (Individuals)
- Donation Import (Organizations)
- Recurring Donations Import

Most of the work to import data is done in spreadsheets and `.csv` files; you want the data to be as error-free as possible before importing it. A best practice is to start with a set of sample data. The nonprofit we are working with here has individual donors and the amounts they have given over the past 5 years that need to be imported into Salesforce. So, we will start with the **Donation Import (Individuals)** spreadsheet. Here is where we will stage the data from the nonprofit. We have ten sample donors in the following screenshot of our spreadsheet:

	A	B	C	D	E	F	G	H	I	J	K	L	M	N	O	P
	Contact1 Sal	Contact1 Fir	Contact1 Las	Contact1 Bir	Contact1 Titl	Contact1 Pe	Contact1 W	Contact1 Alt	Contact1 Pre	Contact1 Ho	Contact1 W	Contact1 Mo	Contact1 Ot	Contact1 Pre	Contact1 Im	Contact2 Sal
	Ms.	Haley	Brown			haleybrown@mailinator.com			Personal			5559871423		Mobile		Mr.
	Ms.	Haley	Brown			haleybrown@mailinator.com			Personal	5556005017	5554195740	5554211037		Home		Ms.
	Ms.	Haley	Brown			haleybrown@mailinator.com			Personal	5558608460		5559289783		Mobile		Mr.
	Mr.	Justin	Chiu			justinchiu@mailinator.com			Personal	5556167371	5552525918	5559785590		Mobile		
	Dr.	Yasin	Callahan			YasinCallahan@mailinator.com			Personal			5552978779		Mobile		Mr.
	Dr.	Yasin	Callahan			YasinCallahan@mailinator.com			Personal			5558195832		Mobile		
	Ms.	Tabitha	Maldonado		Marketing manager	tabitha@elsmail.com		Work		5559762897	5554309947			Home		
														Home		
	Mr.	Daanish	Woodcock			DaanishWoodcock@mailinator.com			Personal	5553145204	5558044390	5554532950		Work		
	Prof.	Amer	Shakil			ashakil@ma amershakil@cloudyu.edu				5555443713		5557433187		Home		

Figure 16.10 – A sample Donation Import (Individuals) spreadsheet for NPSP Data Importer

Note that the spreadsheet has **Contact1** and **Contact2** headers. Contacts in these fields are grouped into the same household account.

> **Note**
> You can add multiple donations by using the same **Contact1** fields on as many rows as there are donations.

You can also designate the donations as grants or membership by changing the record type in the **Donation Record Type Name** field. Once you have the data in the spreadsheet ready, it's time to configure the **Data Import Wizard**.

Configure the Data Import Wizard

There are several steps to configure the Data Import Wizard based on the use case:

1. Access the Data Import Wizard via the app launcher (or waffle menu) and select **NPSP Data Imports**; then click **Import**.

2. The following wizard opens:

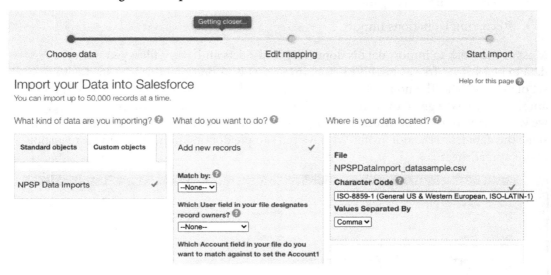

Figure 16.11 – The NPSP Data Import Wizard page

3. Confirm that the custom object that shows in the left-hand column is **NPSP Data Imports** and click it. For NPSP Data Importer, you always want to select **Add new records**, but you can leave all the additional settings in the center column. Then, connect the appropriate `.csv` file with your data in the right-hand column.

4. Click **Next**.

5. This will open the **Edit Field Mapping** page. Confirm that the fields in the spreadsheet are accurately mapped to the fields in Salesforce:

Figure 16.12 – A sample Edit Field Mapping page for NPSP Data Imports

6. Click **Next** to review the information. Then, click **Start Import**.

7. Click **OK**, and the system will take you to the **Bulk Data Load Jobs** page to verify the success of your import.

8. Return to the **NPSP Data Imports** tab and access the **To Be Imported** list view to confirm the records.

> **Note**
> This import is a staging area; it is not the actual instantiation of data into production.

9.   We're almost done. But, first, on the list view page, click **Start Data Import**. The
     system will open a page like the following example, where you can more granularly
     configure the import options:

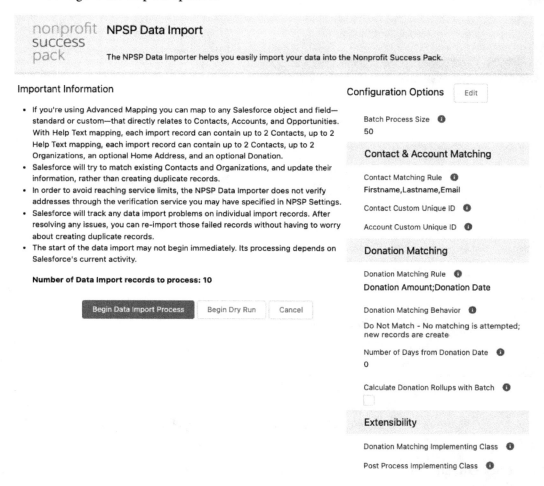

Figure 16.13 – A sample NPSP Data Import Configuration Options page

Take a look at the default configuration options. Depending on the data you are
importing and the business rules of the nonprofit, these may need to be adjusted
for the best results. The batch process size is often a challenge and may need to be
configured to 10 or lower. Doing a test run or dry run is helpful to work out these
challenges before the actual data is imported.

10. Do this by clicking **Begin Dry Run**. If the dry run returns errors, these can be addressed in the **Dry Run:Errors** list view. If the dry run does not return errors, or once the errors have been corrected, we are ready to import the data.

11. Follow the same steps for the dry run, but click **Begin Data Import Process** on the **Configuration Options** page. NPSP Data Importer shows the progress, just as it did on the dry run:

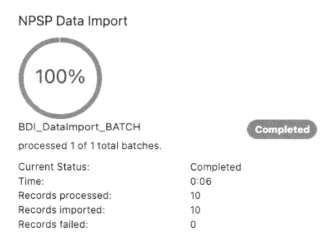

Figure 16.14 – An example of a successfully completed NPSP Data Importer sample import

A quick search for Haley Brown, one of the contacts in the sample data, shows that her contact record was created along with her household and her donation:

Figure 16.15 – A sample search for Haley Brown reveals her contact, household, and donation details

Haley Brown's family members, affiliated place of employment, and address have been created in related records as well. Voila! All the data in a single import. This is the simplicity of NPSP Data Importer.

> **Note**
> Once you have completed the preceding steps, validate that the data has been imported correctly. This is always a best practice for data imports of any kind.

Extending the Data Import tool functionality

Have more complex data imports to do? You can extend NPSP Data Importer with advanced mapping. An example of a use case would be importing a custom field on the contact record, such as a checkbox to confirm that a volunteer has been vaccinated, or a standard field, such as an email opt-out, that is not currently a part of the NPSP Data Import object. Advanced mapping is not a complex process:

1. Create the custom field(s) on the object, if needed.
2. Create the custom field(s) on the NPSP Data Import object.
3. Map the new custom field(s) on the NPSP Data Import object to the custom field(s) or standard field(s) of the object itself.

Step 1 and *Step 2* are familiar to Salesforce administrators. To accomplish *Step 3*, go to **NPSP Settings** > **System Tools** > **Advanced Mapping for Data Import & Gift Entry**. Toggle the button to enable **Advanced Mapping**. It may take a few minutes to configure before you see the success screen:

System Tools - Advanced Mapping for Data Import & Gift Entry

When you enable Advanced Mapping, we convert your existing Help Text field mappings to Advanced Mapping. Once enabled, you'll edit mappings and create new ones on this page.

You can disable Advanced Mapping and go back to Help Text mapping, but any changes you made with Advanced Mapping will be lost.

Find complete Advanced Mapping setup documentation here.

Advanced Mapping

Figure 16.16 – A sample Advanced Mapping for Data Import & Gift Entry settings page

Now, we are ready to click **Configure Advanced Mapping** and tell NPSP Data Importer where to write the standard or custom field(s) being added.

Best practices, tips, and tricks

Helping your users understand how important it is to maintain the integrity of your data is critical. It really is a team effort to leverage Nonprofit Cloud to get the highest return on your investment. Good data hygiene will protect an organization's investment and return information via reports and dashboards or tableau for more impact on the social issues that the nonprofit is tackling.

Get your users on board

For all the work that you do in Salesforce, your users probably do much more. They are constantly creating new data and updating existing data. Make it easy for them.

Set the matching rules and duplicate rules so that users are easily alerted when they start to create a record that may be a duplicate. Configuring the settings to alert users to duplicates when they edit records can also help with ongoing maintenance and data hygiene. Merging a duplicate record as it is discovered allows distribution of the hygiene duties.

> **Note**
> Merging requires **Delete** permissions.

Providing your users with access to the appropriate data, reports, and dashboards also encourages them to be good housekeepers. Training is an integral part of understanding. Trailhead (`https://trailhead.salesforce.com/`) is a free training tool that is gamified to encourage users to better understand the system.

Document, document, document

One of the single best practices that you can adopt when using Nonprofit Cloud, internally or as a consultant, is to document. Document each change, each process, and each discussion. You may not always be the one who is the system administrator. And, putting the thought process together after the fact is difficult when you are trying to troubleshoot something that was created before you began.

There are as many ways to document as there are to configure. So, choose one that all of the stakeholders on the team can access. It may be a Google document, it may be GitHub, or it may be a third-party project management app. Start documenting from day one; you will never regret it.

Summary

In this chapter, we looked at the next steps once Nonprofit Cloud has been implemented, configured, and customized. Data maintenance is an ongoing task that must be done to fully leverage all the functionality of Nonprofit Cloud and NPSP.

Data imports are also a regular task, so we have explored how to make this task simple and accurate with NPSP Data Importer and advanced mapping. Managing technology is an important role for a Nonprofit Cloud consultant; however, managing human expectations is equally important. Knowing how to get users interested, excited, and motivated to use the functionality is a valuable tool for your career.

Nonprofit Cloud is a flexible and robust tool, and now you are well trained in how to use it to do more good. I wish you the best in passing your Nonprofit Cloud Consultant certification and look forward to meeting you in the Trailblazer Community, `https://trailhead.salesforce.com/en/trailblazercommunity`. And remember:

Automate what can be automated so
humans have more time to do what can't be automated.

Resources and additional reading

- *Standard Matching Rules*: `https://help.salesforce.com/s/articleView?id=sf.matching_rules_standard_rules.htm&type=5`

- *Find and Merge Duplicate Contacts*: `https://powerofus.force.com/s/article/NPSP-Merging-Contacts`

- *Constituent Data Management with Nonprofit Success Pack*: `https://trailhead.salesforce.com/content/learn/modules/constituent-data-management-with-nonprofit-success-pack`

- *The Data Are Alright*: `https://thedataarealright.blog/salesforce/`

- *Import Data With Nonprofit Success Pack (NPSP)*: `https://trailhead.salesforce.com/en/content/learn/trails/import-data-with-nonprofit-success-pack-npsp`

- *NPSP Data Importer Templates*: `https://powerofus.force.com/s/article/NPSP-Data-Importer-Documentation`

Index

O

Packt.com

Subscribe to our online digital library for full access to over 7,000 books and videos, as well as industry leading tools to help you plan your personal development and advance your career. For more information, please visit our website.

Why subscribe?

- Spend less time learning and more time coding with practical eBooks and Videos from over 4,000 industry professionals

- Improve your learning with Skill Plans built especially for you

- Get a free eBook or video every month

- Fully searchable for easy access to vital information

- Copy and paste, print, and bookmark content

Did you know that Packt offers eBook versions of every book published, with PDF and ePub files available? You can upgrade to the eBook version at packt.com and as a print book customer, you are entitled to a discount on the eBook copy. Get in touch with us at customercare@packtpub.com for more details.

At www.packt.com, you can also read a collection of free technical articles, sign up for a range of free newsletters, and receive exclusive discounts and offers on Packt books and eBooks.

Other Books You May Enjoy

If you enjoyed this book, you may be interested in these other books by Packt:

Salesforce CPQ Implementation Handbook

Madhu Ramanujan

ISBN: 9781801077422

- Understand Quote-2-Cash business processes and configure opportunities and quotes
- Create custom CPQ actions and use custom filters for automating business needs
- Discover how to configure products and product rules
- Understand the CPQ pricing structure and methods, rules, multidimensional quoting, and quote automation
- Explore the CPQ data model and use the Salesforce Schema Builder to view and configure object relationships
- Configure contracts, amendments, and renewals in Salesforce
  Focus on CPQ billing and its advantages
- Gain comprehensive insights into Industries CPQ

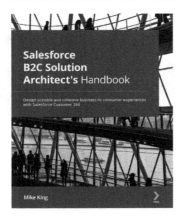

Salesforce B2C Solution Architect's Handbook

Mike King

ISBN: 9781801817035

- Explore key Customer 360 products and their integration options
- Choose the optimum integration architecture to unify data and experiences
  Architect a single view of the customer to support service, marketing, and commerce
- Plan for critical requirements, design decisions, and implementation sequences to avoid sub-optimal solutions
- Integrate Customer 360 solutions into a single-source-of-truth solution such as a master data model
- Support business needs that require functionality from more than one component by orchestrating data and user flows

Becoming a Salesforce Certified Technical Architect

Tameem Bahri

ISBN: 9781800568754

- Explore data lifecycle management and apply it effectively in the Salesforce ecosystem
- Design appropriate enterprise integration interfaces to build your connected solution
- Understand the essential concepts of identity and access management
- Develop scalable Salesforce data and system architecture
- Design the project environment and release strategy for your solution
- Articulate the benefits, limitations, and design considerations relating to your solution
- Discover tips, tricks, and strategies to prepare for the Salesforce CTA review board exam

Packt is searching for authors like you

If you're interested in becoming an author for Packt, please visit `authors.packtpub.com` and apply today. We have worked with thousands of developers and tech professionals, just like you, to help them share their insight with the global tech community. You can make a general application, apply for a specific hot topic that we are recruiting an author for, or submit your own idea.

Share your thoughts

Now you've finished *Accelerating Nonprofit Impact with Salesforce*, we'd love to hear your thoughts! Scan the QR code below to go straight to the Amazon review page for this book and share your feedback or leave a review on the site that you purchased it from.

https://packt.link/r/1-801-07091-1

Your review is important to us and the tech community and will help us make sure we're delivering excellent quality content.

www.ingramcontent.com/pod-product-compliance
Lightning Source LLC
Chambersburg PA
CBHW062105050326
40690CB00016B/3215